Standard of the West

STANDARD of the WEST
THE JUSTIN STORY

BY IRVIN FARMAN

TCU TEXAS BIOGRAPHY SERIES:
NUMBER TWO

TEXAS CHRISTIAN
UNIVERSITY
PRESS
FORT WORTH

TCU *Texas Biography Series: Number Two*
Max Lale, Series Editor

All photographs are used at the courtesy of John S. Justin, Jr.

Library of Congress Cataloging-in-Publication

Farman, Irvin
      Standard of the West : the Justin story / by Irvin Farman.
          p. cm.—(Texas biography series ; 2)
      ISBN 0-87565-167-4
      1. Justin, H. J., 1859-1918 2. Industrialists—Texas—Biography.
3. Justin Industries—History. 4. Justin Boot Company—History.
5. Cowboy boots. 6. Footwear industry—Texas—History. 7. Spanish Fort
(Tex.)—History. I. Title. II. Series.
HD9787.U6J874 1996
338.7'67'09764—dc20   96-14897
                                                                        CIP

Design by Shadetree Studio

To the memory of H. J. Justin, who said before his death in 1918 that he hoped to leave behind him "an institution that would uphold the standards and spirit of the true West," and to John S. Justin, Jr., chairman of the board of Justin Industries, who brought that hope to a fulfillment far beyond his grandfather's wildest dreams.

contents

acknowledgments

This book could not have been possible without the assistance of a great many people. I would especially like to acknowledge the many contributions of John Justin, Jr., who opened the Justin Industries archives to my research and who provided a storehouse of knowledge and reminiscenses about the company.

I also would like to express my gratitude to Jane Justin for her whole-hearted cooperation during several interviews and for her insights into her husband as a businessman, civic leader and long-time companion in marriage.

I would like to give special thanks to Dorothy Morell and Eddie Kelly, whose documentation of the archives—old photographs, correspondence, newspaper and magazine clippings—contributed mightily to the effort.

A number of Justin executives also contributed greatly with their own recollections and reminiscences, including Jon Bennett, Jack Carey, J. T. Dickenson and Ed Stout. My thanks go to them.

Others from outside the company, notably Perry R. Bass, Bayard H. Friedman, Ben J. Fortson, Dee J. Kelly and Bob Watt, provided notable insights and incomparable recollections, for which I am everlastingly grateful.

My special gratitude goes to my wife, Kay Dickson Farman, who contributed encouragement, support and a critical eye for style and syntax.

Special Note: In all instances, where newspaper or magazine articles were cited, they were accompanied by name and date of the publication and the author.

prologue

There's not much reason to go to Spanish Fort nowadays, unless you're drawn there by its past. Today, it's little more than a ghost town with a handful of residents, a half dozen or so ramshackle, weather-beaten frame houses, an abandoned schoolhouse and a padlocked general store with a sign proclaiming that the Spanish Fort Coon Hunters Association used to gather there for weekly hunts every Saturday. An out-of-use gas pump keeps a lonely vigil in front of the store.

But in 1759, it was the site of a historic battle that ended Spanish efforts to secure hegemony over North Texas and the territories beyond the Red River. Then, after the Civil War, during the era of the great cattle drives, Spanish Fort enjoyed another brief flirtation with history as a ripsnorting, wide-open Chisholm Trail town on a bend of the Red River, a final stopping -off place for cowboys seeking a little rest and recreation before pushing their herds of Longhorns north across the river into the Indian Territory.

To get to Spanish Fort, you take State Farm Road 103 northeast from Nocona for seventeen miles, and where the road ends Spanish Fort begins. Close by, in a field covered with Johnson grass, a bronze historical marker erected by the state of Texas recaptures the story of the battle that gave Spanish Fort its name, even though it never really was a fort and no Spaniards were ever stationed there.

The marker retells the story of the 1759 victory of Taovaya and the Comanches over a Spanish attacking force. Historians agree that the triumph of the Indians seriously damaged the reputation of Spanish arms in

North Texas and deterred Spain from exploring and claiming lands beyond the Red River.

Permanent occupation of the battle site by white settlers was prevented by Indian raids until the early 1870s. The opening of the Chisholm Trail in the aftermath of the Civil War transformed Spanish Fort from a sleepy settlement into a squalling, brawling trail-drive town. During the war, cattle in the heavily populated areas of the North and East had been slaughtered to feed the Union armies. With the end of hostilities, the nation was hungry for beef. In Texas, beef was the only major asset. Broad prairies that seemed to stretch endlessly across the western half of the state were covered with a thick growth of what was known as "free grass," upon which nomadic cattle herds, untamed and unbranded, roamed at will. Because of their wide horn spread, they became known as Longhorns, or Texas Longhorns. They were poor eating, tough and stringy, but they were the only available source of beef. Texans began driving herds of Longhorns north to market.

The seas of cattle flowing northward along the Chisholm Trail represented gold on the hoof since the economics of the cattle drives were staggeringly favorable for the men who owned the herds. The cattle multiplied in value by as much as 1,000 percent by the time they reached the pens in Abilene or Dodge City. Between 1866 and 1880, more than five million head made the journey.

The first drives in the early 1860s were by way of the thousand-mile Chisholm Trail, first to Kansas and then as far north as Illinois and Iowa, where the cattle were sold, then shipped to the slaughterhouses. The cattle drives ushered in the era most people associate with the storied days of the Old West, when for a period of some twenty years, between 1865 and 1885, cattle and cowboys dominated life in the region. Time and nostalgia have obscured much of the harshness of the trail drives. The heat, the dust and the sweat, work from dawn to dark, night herding, days on end without seeing a town—all are lost in more romantic memories of trail towns, saloons, gambling halls, outlaws, gunfighters and town tamers. Today, the mystique remains, stronger than ever, as evidenced by the ever-increasing popularity of cowboy boots, western clothing and country-western music.

Spanish Fort's ability to cash in on the cattle boom was due to its proximity to the busy Yellow Bank crossing of the Red River on the Chisholm Trail. It soon became home to some two hundred residents catering to the needs of trail hands, cowboys, drifters and desperadoes. Of its twenty or so buildings, four were saloons. The most notorious was the Cowboy

Saloon, which quickly developed a reputation for fights, both gun and fist. Spanish Fort also was a favorite haven for outlaws, who had only to "run for the river" to evade the long arm of the law.

This was the setting that greeted a twenty-year-old transplanted Hoosier named H. J. Justin when he stepped off a wagon into Spanish Fort in September 1879. Two years earlier, he had left his home in Lafayette, Indiana, and ridden the train to Gainesville, Texas, where he had apprenticed himself to a cobbler. Now, having heard tales of the new boomtown on the Red River called Spanish Fort, he had decided to head there to begin a new life for himself on the edge of the last frontier.

He set up shop in a little one-room frame building that held a workbench on the inside. On the outside of the tiny structure he painted a sign that read, "H. J. Justin, Boot Maker." The opening of his crude, one-man shop marked Spanish Fort's final brush with history. The trail town would fade into oblivion, but it would be remembered as the original home of the company whose name became synonymous with cowboy boots and a part of western lore.

The Justin name is still synonymous with cowboy boots, not only in cow country but around the world. Justin boots are as routinely seen on Fifth Avenue in New York, Rodeo Drive in Beverly Hills, the Via Veneto in Rome or the Champs Elysees in Paris as they are in Fort Worth, the company's headquarters. But the Justin brand now means much more than cowboy boots.

Today, the name belongs to Justin Industries, a diversified company that encompasses a building materials operation that includes Acme Brick Company, Featherlite Building Products Corporation and Tradewinds Technologies; a footwear operation that consists of the Justin Boot Company, Nocona Boot Company and Tony Lama Company; and a publisher of western and southwestern Americana, art and American Indian culture, Northland Press. Under the leadership of John Justin, Jr., a grandson of H. J. Justin, Justin Industries today is a far cry from the one-man boot shop that opened in Spanish Fort more than a century ago. It wasn't always an easy trail. At one point, shortly after World War II, the company, then in the hands of H. J. Justin's three sons, experienced serious difficulties, and John Justin, Jr., rode to its rescue. Later, he would assume the helm of Justin Industries under adverse conditions and build it into a $500 million enterprise, surviving an unfriendly takeover effort along the way.

The Justin brand has come a long way from Spanish Fort.

This is the story of the journey.

one

A date with destiny

On a hot and windy September afternoon in 1879, a tall, ruggedly handsome, brown-haired young man carrying a small bag approached a wagon-train driver on the dusty main street of Gainesville, Texas. He was looking for a ride to Spanish Fort, the broad-shouldered youth told the driver in an accent that would have sounded more at home along the banks of the Wabash than the nearby Red River.

Spanish Fort was where he was headed, the driver replied. The young man asked how much the fare was. The driver's response was to ask how much money he had. His answer was $5.25. The driver now dispensed the news that the fare was $5. The young man hesitated. Parting with the $5 fare would leave him virtually penniless when he arrived at his destination. But he'd found himself in the same financial straits when he had stepped off the train in Gainesville after a lengthy ride from Indiana and had found a job right off the bat as a cobbler's apprentice. Now he was ready to venture out on his own once more. Spanish Fort, a booming Chisholm Trail town on the Red River some forty miles northwest of Gainesville, was beckoning him. So he told the wagon driver it was a deal.

He dug into his pocket, pulled out a $5 shinplaster, a form of paper currency of the era, and handed over the fare. Slinging over his shoulder the rucksack that held his worldly possessions, a hammer and an awl, the tools of his new trade, he climbed aboard.

The young man, whose name was H. J. Justin, was then some five months past his twentieth birthday. Justin was born in Lafayette, Indiana, on April

7, 1859, to Nicholas and Katherine Hubertz Justin, both natives of Prussia. They had migrated to Lafayette in the early 1850s, after brief stopovers in London and New York. The family name was originally spelled "Justan" or "Justen" (it was spelled "Justan" on Nicholas' naturalization papers and "Justen" on his death certificate and grave marker). But after H. J. Justin departed for Texas in 1877, the spelling was changed to "Justin."

H. J., who was called Joe, was the oldest of seven children, six sons and a daughter. Nicholas, who became a naturalized citizen of the United States in Tippecanoe County, Indiana, in 1865, was a cigar maker by trade. His oldest son, however, contrary to the custom of the time, had no desire to follow in his father's footsteps. Joe had become fascinated by working with leather while in his early teens and had decided he would rather make boots for a living than roll tobacco leaves. On his eighteenth birthday in 1877, he informed his father he was going to Texas to become a bootmaker.

The youthful adventurer bid his family farewell and boarded a train headed southwest. It was an arduous journey that finally ended with Justin's arrival in Gainesville, a small North Texas town at the end of the railroad line. There he quickly found a job as an apprentice cobbler in the Norton Shoe Shop, owned by two sisters who had inherited the business from their father. Justin worked there for two years, learning the trade and honing the skills in which he would make his mark.

Why did Justin elect to leave home and family in Indiana and head for Texas? "I never heard my father or any of my uncles say for certain," John Justin, Jr., said, "but I think it just got to where there were more mouths than his father could feed. After all, there were six younger children and it wasn't easy to make ends meet. And, of course, in those days the slogan was, 'Go west, young man,' and he decided to come west."

This was an era when there were many adventurous souls following Horace Greeley's advice. Some of them, especially those seeking to resettle in the Indian Territory, didn't mind breaking the law to stake out their claims on the broad, fertile ranges north of the Red River. In 1879, a well-funded movement known as "booming" was launched to promote the opening of the Indian Territory to white settlement. This caused President Rutherford B. Hayes to issue a warning that people moving into the territory without the permission of the proper agent of the Indian Department "would be speedily and immediately removed."

President Hayes was occupying the White House under a cloud. He had won a wildly contested and heatedly disputed election in November

1878 over his Democratic opponent, Samuel B. Tilden. Tilden had out-polled him by some 250,000 votes out of 8,300,000 cast, and Congress had to decide between two sets of returns from South Carolina, Louisiana and Florida before Hayes was finally named the winner.

Texas, however, was enjoying an influx of legal settlers, causing the *Fort Worth Democrat* to observe on April 24, 1879: "Immigration to Texas may be greatly increased, but the character is greatly improved of late. Instead of covered wagons, filled with tow-headed children and followed by yellow dogs, they are coming in Pullman cars, with pocketbooks filled with bills of exchange."

Back east, far from the western frontier, several other noteworthy events marked the year in which Joe Justin arrived in Spanish Fort and began making boots. In Menlo Park, New Jersey, a talented tinkerer named Thomas A. Edison unveiled the first electric light. In Boston, Mary Baker Eddy founded a new church called the Church of Christ, Scientist. In Washington, D. C., female attorneys won the right to practice before the Supreme Court. In Norway, Henrik Ibsen's play, *A Doll's House*, contained a line that read, "There can be no freedom or beauty about a home life that depends on borrowing and debt."

Apparently the members of the United States Congress even then were not averse to spending borrowed money, causing the *Philadelphia Times* to editorialize, "Enough bills were introduced in Congress yesterday to supply all the demand of this country for the next two or three hundred years. What we need is a smaller Congress or a bigger country." Both Congress and the country were destined to grow much larger.

In 1879, the nation boasted thirty-eight states, with the Mississippi as the demarcation point between civilization and the frontier. In the vast territories beyond, the West remained wild, woolly and untamed. The bloody undeclared war between the United States Cavalry and the American Indians was still being waged with relentless ferocity by both sides. Sitting Bull, the leader of the Sioux war party that had massacred Lieutenant Colonel George A. Custer and his entire command on the Little Big Horn River in Montana on June 25, 1876, was still a fugitive in Canada in 1879. The same year, Ute Indians staged an uprising that was put down by the United States Cavalry, and the fierce Kiowa war chief, Lone Wolf, whose forays had terrorized settlers in Texas, died on a government reservation in the Indian Territory. In captivity on the same reservation, Chief Joseph of the Nez Perce tribe, who had surrendered to federal troops following a bitter winter battle, issued a statement echoing with poignancy: "I am tired of fighting. Our chiefs are killed, the old men are dead. He who leads the young men is dead. It is cold and we have no blankets. The little children are freezing to death. Hear me, my chiefs, my heart is sick and sad. I am tired."

But on the sunbaked sands of southwestern Arizona, another celebrated chief, Geronimo, was still on the warpath. Billy the Kid and his six-shooter were still the scourge of Lincoln County, New Mexico, and it would be two years before the famed gunfighter would be killed by Sheriff Pat Garrett. And all across the Old West, the cowboy still sat tall in the saddle, riding the dusty trail into legend.

During the two years H. J. Justin spent in Gainesville, he heard a great deal of talk about the trail drives and about a place called Spanish Fort. A town of two hundred, it was a favorite stopping-off place for cowpunchers driving herds of Longhorns to market. Besides four saloons and an ample assortment of bartenders and dance-hall girls, it had five doctors who ministered to everything from black eyes and bloody noses to a deadlier variety of wounds inflicted by Colts and Remingtons. It had an undertaker to take care of those unfortunates who suffered traumas beyond the doctors' expertise. Spanish Fort also boasted three hotels, a barbershop and a general store, all concentrated on three sides of the town square.

But, unusual for a town that catered to men who made their living in the saddle, Spanish Fort had no bootmakers. Justin decided to rectify that lack. The fortuitous arrival in Gainesville of a wagon train to pick up a shipment of whiskey bound for the notorious Cowboy Saloon in Spanish Fort provided him with the opportunity to make his move.

Disembarking after the dust-eating, spine-jolting wagon ride from Gainesville, young Justin found himself in front of the barbershop. The barbershop, in the frontier towns in those days, was the place where the trail hands who hadn't had a bath in a month or more came to take a leisurely soak. The barber would heat water over a fire and fill the bathtub with the steamy liquid into which the cowboys immersed their aching backsides. After luxuriating in the tub, they would take a seat in the barber's chair for a shave and a haircut. Only then would they be ready to hit the saloons.

Justin was badly in need of a bath and something to eat. He decided to try his luck at getting a job that would satisfy both needs. Squaring his shoulders, he opened the door to the tonsorial emporium and walked up to the proprietor, Frank P. See, who was scraping stubble from the jaw of a lanky cowboy sprawled out in the shop's single chair.

Coming directly to the point, Justin told See he was looking for a job to pay for a bath and to get himself something to eat. See pointed to a broom and told Justin he could begin by sweeping the floor. Before the day was out, Justin had proven himself adept at a variety of chores from heating water for the bathtub to emptying the spittoons. By quitting time, he had a steady job.

For the first few weeks after his arrival in Spanish Fort, Justin was content to bide his time in the barbershop. But inwardly he chafed over his inability to make any progress toward his ambition to become a bootmaker. Fate then intervened in the form of a cowboy who sauntered into the barbershop one morning, spurs jingling from a pair of boots badly in need of repair. While the cowboy waited his turn in the barber's chair, Joe Justin, noting the dilapidated condition of his boots, saw opportunity beckoning. He informed the cowboy that he could patch up his boots as good as new. Figuring he had nothing to lose, the cowboy acquiesced.

With the few coins he had in his pocket, Justin had bought some scraps of leather, thread and other materials. For a workplace, he appropriated a rickety two-by-two lean-to that stood in back of the barbershop. He had built a workbench out of some spare pieces of lumber and dug out the hammer and awl that had been gathering dust in his rucksack.

"He tried to do anything he could to earn a little money," John Justin, Jr., said, "so he patched up the cowboy's boots." Apparently, he did a good job because the next day another customer with boots needing repair appeared on the scene, having heard in one of the bars about the young man who did odd jobs in the barbershop and who claimed to be an experienced cobbler. In Spanish Fort, there was no better grapevine for the dissemination of news than the bars in the town's four saloons. And as the word got out about Justin's skill at patching boots, more business followed.

But patching boots was not Justin's goal in life. Yearning for the opportunity to demonstrate his artistry with his hammer and awl, he was forced to content himself for a time with patching boots instead of making them. The reason was a matter of simple economics. To make boots he needed to lay in a variety of leathers, but with his limited income he couldn't afford to buy even a single hide. As time passed, his frustration mounted and he began contemplating throwing in the sponge and going back to Indiana. He was on the verge of leaving Spanish Fort without producing a single pair of the cowboy boots that would make him famous. Disconsolately, he shared his woes with Frank See, with whom he had become close friends.

See had arrived in Spanish Fort shortly before Justin. In an interview published in the *McAllen Monitor*, in Hidalgo County, Texas, on January 22, 1932, See told a reporter:

Joe Justin came to old Spanish Fort in 1879 with a hammer, an awl and 25 cents in cash. I am an eye witness to the fact, and I came the same year with an old pony and 65 cents in cash. I went to picking cotton at 50 cents per hundred, paid 50 cents a day for board, and did well. At the end of two weeks I came out even to the cent. That was first time I had ever picked cotton and I saw that wouldn't do, so I went to town. I bought a little old home-made chair from a fellow on credit and for the next year I ran this barber shop while Joe ran his hammer and awl.

Then, one evening after supper, Joe came in and said, 'Frank, I am going to have to leave. I can't get by at this unless I can get hold of some money. Have you any money?'

I said, 'Mighty little, Joe.'

Well, he said, 'if I can get enough to buy a little stock, just two or three hides, I'll make the world sit up and take notice that H. J. Justin can make the best boots in the world. How much have you got?'

I said that I had just an even $35, not a cent more, but I told him he could have it and counted it out to him and said, 'Now, Joe, go do your best.'

In a week, he was hammering out a pair of boots for me and soon I was wearing the first pair of boots made by H. J. Justin. They cost me $9. Sandy Horton got the second pair and Meel Morris got the third pair.

As he was finishing Meel's pair, a big cowboy named Joe, who worked on Meel's ranch, came in and said, 'Mister Justin, please take my measure. I wants a pair of boots pizactly [sic] like Mister Meel's, red tops, pretty work, and everything.' That cowboy's foot was as long as my arm and as big as a ham. I said to Joe, 'How are you going to work on his boots in this little place?' Joe said, 'Oh, we'll work when it's not raining, so we can go outside to turn them around.'

Now his business began to grow, so he had to have more room. He moved into a larger place, about eight-by-eight feet, and that gave him room for a helper. He got an old man to help him and he was a good work-man, but he later became insane and had to be taken to the asylum.

See left Spanish Fort in 1886 and went into the cattle business. He never saw Joe Justin again. But he wore the boots Justin made for him until 1905, when, as he put it, he quit riding herd on cattle.

The larger quarters that Joe Justin found for his fledgling business was a vacant board-and-batten one-story building located just off the town square. It could be rented inexpensively, and there was room for a workbench and for the storage of leather, thread, wax and tools. That was all Justin needed in the way of facilities. The budding business now lacked only one thing—a sign—and Justin rectified that. In front of the building, on two long spikes, he affixed a cowboy boot. And over the front door, he painted the words, "H. J. Justin, Boot Maker."

The new shop couldn't have been better located. Only a few doors away was Spanish Fort's most popular attraction, John Schrock's Cowboy Saloon, to which a steady stream of customers, mostly cattle drivers, flowed around the clock. After imbibing a few drinks and letting off a little steam, they would stop by Justin's shop to have their feet measured for a new pair of boots that they would pick up some weeks later on their way back to Texas.

The boots that Joe Justin began producing in his little shop were made to last, to withstand the rigors to which they would be subjected in the saddle, on the trail and on the ranch. They were made to fit comfortably, but above all, they were crafted to meet the needs of the men who would literally live in them and depend on them. They were tight-fitting to provide sure footing on the ground. They had high leather tops that protected the wearer's legs against rattlesnakes, brush, and the elements. And they, of course, had the traditional high heels that set cowboy boots apart from more pedestrian footwear.

"That high heel was the most important part of it," Ramon F. Adams wrote in his classic *The Old-Time Cowhand*:

> It kept his foot from slippin' through the stirrup and hangin'; it let 'im dig in when he was ropin' on foot and gave 'im a shore footin' in all other work on the ground, and there was a lot of times he shore couldn't afford to slip when he was handlin' a hoss with flyin' hoofs. He never knowed when he'd need the shore, quick footin' them high heels gave 'im. A narrow heel with a decided underslope was made to prevent bein' hung up in case the rider was throwed and brought a stirrup up over the seat of the saddle with his foot . . . . There was nothin' that made chills run up and down a cowboy's spine more'n hearin' 'about a man gettin' hung up, or thinkin' of it happen' to 'imself. Maybe high heels wasn't made for walkin',' but a cowboy took mighty little exercise on foot. When he walked in town he liked to hear the poppity-pop of them high heels on the board sidewalk.

Another opinion about high heels was offered by Foster Harris in *The Look of the Old West:*

> Don't let them kid you about the reason for heels, either. So your foot wouldn't slide through the stirrup? Or to dig in the ground for leverage, to hold a wild one after you'd roped him? Maybe. But the Army in flat heels, the Injuns in moccasins and the gauchos of South America all managed, right along with the gents on stilts, when it came to handling the rough ones. The truth is, those cowboy heels were and are a mark of position, an insignia, like a colonel's eagles or a policeman's badge. When you get a good pair on, they shove you up into another world altogether, a world that's not as mean and petty as the flatfoot pedestrian landscape most of us have to hoof it through, day after day. They're wings to the spirit, those cowboy boots—and who doesn't want wings?

Nearly all of the boots of that era were made of black leather. Ornamentation, if any, was limited to a little fancy stitching on the boot tops. Joe Justin was one of the early innovators in the use of decorative stitching and is generally credited with being the first to sew rows of stitching across the boot tops as a means of stiffening the leather. This made the boots last longer and prevented them from folding down towards the ankle as they became worn. Later, Justin began decorating his products with more elaborate stitching, hand-tooling, colorful leather inlays, silver conchos and pictorial designs, and using quilted tops embellished with seams of colored thread.

"My grandfather's first boots were pretty rough," John Justin, Jr., noted. "He made a retan boot, a boot that was made to wear out on the range and in the stirrup. If you were to go and round up cattle for a week or something, you'd want a heavy boot. The boot I'm wearing would be all right, but you'd really want a heavier boot. In the old days they used a lot of French wax calf to make a dressy boot and then they used a lot of retan. Retan is a leather that's been tanned twice. It's tanned once in vegetable tan and once in chrome tan. It makes a tough boot. It has a lot of oil and grease in it. It's not made to look good. It's made to take a lot of wear and tear and briar cuts. You can ride through a lot of brush and it won't bother you. If you were going out on the trail and be gone a long time, that's what you'd want on your feet."

The first three pairs of boots that Joe Justin turned out for Frank See, Sandy Horton and Meel Morris were walking advertisements for the aspiring young bootmaker. The fourth pair were made to order for a

Chisholm Trail cowhand who lost no time showing them off as he went north with his herd of Longhorns. Word now began to spread up and down the trail and in the watering holes in Fort Worth, south of the Red River, and in Dodge City and Abilene to the north that what you really wanted on your feet was a pair of boots made by H. J. Justin in Spanish Fort. As the business grew, Justin hired his first employee, an elderly itinerant bootmaker named Bill Grace who showed up at the front door one morning looking for a job. By the end of his first year in business, Justin had sold $1,000 worth of boots at a price of $8.50 a pair. To many a cowboy that price represented an investment equal to a week's wages, but to a man who made his living in the saddle, a pair of good made-to-measure boots like the ones Joe Justin crafted were more than mere coverings in which he encased his feet. They were his pride and joy.

One of Joe Justin's early sales pieces took note of the love affair between the cowboy and his boots: "Next to his gun," the preface to the folder declared, "a man's boots are his most prized possession, often spelling the difference between life or death. It is only natural that he should choose his boots with the greatest of care and go to great lengths to acquire them."

Spanish Fort was still a rough and tough place when Joe Justin hung out his sign. The forty-three graves in its boot hill cemetery bore mute testimony to that fact. Gunplay was still the preferred way to settle a saloon dispute, and the favorite pastime of patrons of the Cowboy Saloon was still blasting away with a six-shooter at a large painting of a bull that hung on the wall near the bar. The town marshal was still busy trying to maintain a semblance of law and order. Old court dockets of the era chronicle that one J. M. Tucker was charged with the murder of James Hill, that a Frank Morgan was charged with rape, and that G. E. Howard and James Hogue were cited for racing horses through the middle of town. There were also entries for the more mundane peccadilloes of drunkenness, disorderly conduct and brawling.

But there was another side to life in Spanish Fort that the patrons of the saloons and bawdy houses never glimpsed, never even knew existed. Beyond the environs of the town square there were people living lives of quiet decorum in houses with picket fences, chintz curtains, rose bushes, vegetable gardens and barking dogs, an enclave of civilization within a stone's throw of the last vestiges of the Old West. These were honest, hard-working, churchgoing people trying to bring a semblance of gentility to the rough frontier for themselves and, especially, their children. They were the merchants, businessmen, artisans, and craftsmen who provided the goods and services for the ranchers and farmers who lived around Spanish Fort and who came to town regularly to buy supplies, get a haircut, go to the bank, transact business or to see one of the five physicians who served the community.

Among this group was Dr. S. A. Allen, who had moved to Spanish Fort from Lipan, southwest of Fort Worth, in 1876 with his wife, Elijah Jane, and their daughter, Louanna, who was then thirteen and who later would become Joe Justin's bride. Louanna, who was called Annie, had been born in Lipan in 1864 at a time when Comanche raids were still common in Hood County. While growing up and attending school in Spanish Fort, she often accompanied her father on his medical rounds and was often at his side when he treated patients for bullet wounds. She was an eyewitness to a number of gunfights, including one shootout on a Christmas morning that claimed the lives of three gunmen before breakfast. In later years, she enjoyed regaling her children and grandchildren with tales of the old days, of seeing outlaws riding into Spanish Fort, shooting up the town and then heading back across the Red River beyond the reach of the law. She also recalled the time two outlaws were hanged. Joe Justin witnessed the hanging and noted that both men were wearing Justin boots. He told her he admired their taste in footwear.

Annie never tired of talking about the weather, of sandstorms that lasted three days and piled mounds of sand as high as the stake fences, and of "blue northers" that turned the Red River into a solid sheet of ice over which wagons could cross into Indian Territory. And there was always talk of buried treasure dating back to the days of the Spanish and the French, but none was ever found.

Annie was a pretty young woman with a temper that earned her a mention in the Spanish Fort court ledger on May 30, 1884, when she drew a $5 fine for engaging in a public altercation with a woman named Sarah Truman. It seems that Annie had bought a new hat in Gainesville and had worn it to church the following Sunday. A week later, she had encountered Miss Truman, a woman of dubious respectability, who was wearing a hat that was an exact replica of Annie's. That was more than Annie could abide. Accusing the other woman of copying her hat, Annie proceeded to remove it from her head. A fight ensued which Annie reportedly won handily. She always maintained afterwards that the $5 fine she paid was worth every penny it cost her.

It was inevitable that Annie's and Joe's paths would cross in a place as small as Spanish Fort. She caught his eye at one of the weekly square dances that were the town's main social events. Soon after that he began courting her. The fact that they both were avid and accomplished dancers was no deterrent to the progress of the courtship. They were married in Spanish Fort on January 12, 1887.

By then Justin was working night and day trying to keep up with growing boot orders. The situation had been exacerbated by the loss of his elderly helper due to ill health, and Annie plunged in to offer a helping hand, working long hours at her husband's side. Annie measured many a cowboy's foot during the day and at night joined her husband cutting out patterns in the dim light of a kerosene lamp. She also helped her husband design a revolutionary self-measuring kit that made it possible for customers throughout the nation to order Justin boots by mail.

The development of the innovative marketing tool resulted from a letter Justin received from a wealthy Montana rancher named O. C. Cato, who said he was writing on behalf of cowboys in Montana who wanted made-to-order Justin boots but couldn't travel all the way to Texas to be measured. The package which Joe and Annie devised included a tape measure and foot chart that enabled customers to measure their feet and legs at the ball, instep, heel, ankle, and calf, and mail in the order in a pre-addressed envelope. The self-measuring kit was an instant success, not only for Justin but for other bootmakers around the country. Justin, however, refused to patent the kit, declaring: "If it will help me, let it help others."

The new business resulting from the mail orders that began to pour in caused Justin to seek additional help. He wrote to his younger brother, William, back home in Indiana, offering him a job. William readily accepted. Years later, William's son, Vane Justin, recalled the incident. "Uncle Joe wrote my daddy, Willie, in Lafayette and told him he needed some help. Uncle Joe said it was a new, exciting country, and he loved challenge. It didn't take my daddy long to make up his mind to come to Spanish Fort."

Vane Justin followed his father into the company's employ and became an expert fancy top stitcher. Vane's brother, Bill Justin, also worked for the company and became one of its outstanding salesmen. Both are now deceased. Their father, William, died in 1907 in Nocona at the age of thirty-six, after contracting tuberculosis.

Annie and Joe had occasion to rejoice at another first for them, the birth of a baby boy on January 31, 1888. He was named John Sullivan

Justin in honor of John L. Sullivan, the then-reigning world's heavyweight boxing champion.

"My grandfather was a big fight fan," John Justin, Jr., explained. "He thought John L. Sullivan was the greatest fighter ever to step into the ring. He once made a trip all the way to New York to see him fight and got his picture in the rotogravure section of one of the New York newspapers under the caption, 'Joe Justin, famous bootmaker from Nocona, Texas, was in town to see the Sullivan fight.' This was after my grandfather moved the business from Spanish Fort to Nocona in 1889."

The move to Nocona took place a little more than a year after John Sullivan Justin observed his first birthday. It came as the result of a decision by the Missouri, Kansas & Texas Railway to bypass Spanish Fort in favor of a route farther south when it extended its line from Denison to Henrietta in 1887. The decision shocked the residents of Spanish Fort who had counted on the railroad coming through. But the new route, which created the town of Nocona, had one distinct advantage: it ran on a straight line south of the Red River and, therefore, would require no bridges to be built along the right-of-way, as would have been the case with the route through Spanish Fort.

The railroad's decision to bypass Spanish Fort made Justin's move inevitable. He was well aware of the importance of the railroad to his growing business. The cattle drives were beginning to slow and he knew his future lay in shipping his products by rail to a broadening array of customers. Much as he and Annie hated leaving Spanish Fort, there was no alternative but to follow the railroad.

Most of the other residents of Spanish Fort felt the same way. Soon the exodus began, as Spanish Fort literally moved lock, stock and homestead to Nocona. The favored mode of transportation was a skid upon which an entire building was placed. The skids were made by cutting down six to eight trees and lashing the logs together. Teams of horses were then attached to the loaded skids.

For Spanish Fort, it was the beginning of the end. In a few years, with the demise of the cattle drives, the once-prosperous trail town faded away into the twilight of history. For Joe Justin, the move to Nocona marked the end of an era. A new one, full of promise, he hoped, was about to begin.

two

"The best boots in the world"

Nocona was born in 1887 as a tent city, a temporary home for the workmen laying the track for the extension of the rail line from Denison to Henrietta. It owed its existence to a railroad surveyor named B. S. Walten, who decided the new line should bypass Spanish Fort. Walten also gave Nocona its name, in honor of a Peta Nocona, a legendary Comanche war chief who was killed in 1860 in the bloody battle against a company of Texas Rangers led by the famous Captain Sul Ross. The suggestion to name Nocona after the Comanche chieftain was made to Walten by a close friend, John L. Davis, who had fought alongside Sul Ross in the bitterly contested engagement which had followed a series of raids by Chief Nocona and a large band of Comanche warriors in Parker County, west of Fort Worth.

In the confrontation that took place along the Pease River in northwest Texas on December 18, 1860, Ross and his outnumbered Rangers soundly defeated the Comanches who fled in disarray for sanctuary across the Red River. They left behind them their fallen chief, who had been mortally wounded by two bullets fired by Captain Ross.

The city of Nocona enjoyed rapid growth after its birth in 1887. Permanent buildings were erected there, even as the tents that housed the railroad workers were being dismantled. By the time H. J. Justin moved his family and boot business there in 1889, Nocona already boasted a thriving business area that included a general merchandise store, a hardware store, a restaurant, a lumberyard, a bank, a livery stable, and a hotel. Later on, daily train service would bring in additional newcomers, and cattle-men would begin using the town as their base for supplies. Nocona was incorporated in 1891.

H. J. Justin's first shop in Nocona was located in a small, one-story rock building with a wooden front, near the new railroad depot. The building would later be taken over by a barbershop when Justin moved his growing business into larger quarters across the street.

The Justins' first home in Nocona consisted of two tiny rooms in the rear of the boot shop, but they abandoned the cramped quarters and moved into the nearby hotel when Annie became pregnant. By this time, her husband had already begun building a modest frame house behind the shop. The house would undergo numerous expansions over the years, including the addition of a second story to accommodate the six offspring who would join the family.

The new house was still under construction when Annie gave birth to a second son, William Earl, on January 26, 1890. The birth took place in the hotel room in which the family was living, with the delivery made by Dr. S. A. Allen, Annie's father. Four girls and a third boy would be born to the Justins in Nocona: Fern, in 1882; Enid, in 1894; Samuel Avis, in 1896; Anis, in 1898 and Doris Myrl, in 1907.

"My grandfather was a hard working man," John Justin, Jr., recounted. "He thought everybody ought to get up early and work late. He was a good man and a good provider for his family, but he was stern, the kind of man that we need more of today. He believed in working, and he brought his family into the business, beginning with my dad and my Uncle Earl. My dad worked from early childhood. He never finished school. Neither did my uncles. They worked from six till six, five days a week. On Saturdays, they got off at four sometimes. They worked hard. That's all they knew to do. That's how they made their living."

John Justin, Sr., enjoyed recounting the thrill of receiving his first pay-check in 1901. He had just turned thirteen and had worked all week in his father's boot plant. Not eight-hour days, either, he emphasized. On Saturday, at the end of the six-day work week, he received the grand sum of $1.50.

"I was paid at the rate of twenty-five cents a day," he reported. "That wasn't really as bad it sounds. Twenty-five cents was all the capital my father had when he started this business."

Earl Justin's first job in the boot plant was as a lace maker. When he advanced to cutting uppers, he decided it was time he was put on the payroll. His father agreed to pay him $2 a week, Earl later recalled, but informed him he would have to "knuckle down" and prove he was worth every penny.

Enid Justin began going down to the shop after school from the time she was ten. Her first job was making up catalogs, folding the order blanks and inserting them into the catalogs along with the little tape measure and the price list. She recounted in her biography, *Miss Enid, The Lady Bootmaker*:

> I'd put all this into an envelope, so when Daddy Joe would get a request, all he had to do was to address it and send it out. I also did little odds and ends around the shop. I started stitching boots when I was about twelve. I'd stitch those tops on an old foot-pedal type Singer sewing machine. When I was thirteen, I quit school and went to work for my father full-time. Daddy Joe was a stern boss. He demanded quality in everything we did, our living, our work and our play. A lot of times, relatives get along just fine until they start working together. Well, nothing ever changed. We realized that Daddy Joe was the boss and we did what we were told to do.

H. J. Justin never benefitted from attending motivational seminars, but he apparently knew how to go about increasing employee morale. In the summertime, when it was hot in the shop, Joe would buy up a load of watermelons and shut down production so that everyone could go outside and cool off with a slice of watermelon. Once, he got the employees together and promised if they got production up to twenty-six pairs of boots a day and kept it up for several weeks, he would give everyone a two-week paid vacation. There had never been any paid vacations before. The quota was met, Justin shut down the plant for a couple of weeks and every-one went fishing. The story goes that the employees laughed among them-selves that they could have made thirty-six pairs a day if he'd set that goal.

Despite his reputation as a stern taskmaster, Daddy Joe doted on his children. The backyard of the Justin home resembled a playground, com-plete with swings, slides and a trapeze, among other equipment. It attract-ed children from all over town. But Justin could be a strict disciplinarian when the occasion arose. His favorite saying was, "You're either right or you're wrong. There's no in-between." He enforced that principle with the aid of a razor strop that hung in the dining room as a constant reminder.

When the children started attending school, they were given to under-stand that any paddling they received from their teacher for some infrac-tion in the classroom would be repeated at home. On one occasion, John, the oldest child, showed his gumption and creativity by attempting to put one over on his father and take the sting of the razor strop. He placed a roofing shingle in the seat of his pants. The ruse, of course, backfired when Daddy Joe began applying the leather to John's rear end. He then proceeded to mete out the prescribed punishment with no interference between seat and strop.

As the children grew into teenagers, Justin converted a boot shop behind the house into a large family recreation and entertainment center that became known as the Justin Clubhouse. The clubhouse soon became the heart of Nocona's social life, the scene of dances and parties. On many a night, the sound of music from the Victrola or from live musicians emanated from the Justin Clubhouse, as the parents or children entertained guests.

Joe loved to dance and was quite a waltzer. His sons often watched him gliding across the dance floor with Annie in his arms. Although alcoholic beverages were served at adult parties, Joe generally refrained from partaking while acting as host. He had another rule, refusing to discuss politics, but he did permit himself the luxury of smoking cigars. Annie, however, quaffed four bottles of beer daily under her doctor's orders, one with each meal and one just before retiring.

"Grandmother Justin was very petite," John Justin, Jr., said. "I don't think she weighed over eighty-five or ninety pounds. So the doctor had her drink beer as a supplement to her diet to help her gain weight."

John, Jr., recalled how he helped make home brew for his grandmother as a small boy. "I usually spent weekends at her house," he related. "My parents would drop me off after school on Friday and I would spend Friday and Saturday night there. Then they would pick me up on Sunday. Grandmother Justin originally bought beer from Canada by prescription, but that got too expensive. So she began making it at home. She had a ten-gallon crock in which the beer was made. We would measure in Pabst Blue Ribbon malt and add water and sugar. Each batch made about eighty bottles of beer. We spent a lot of time sterilizing the bottles before we filled them. It must have been pretty good beer," he added, "because lots of Grandmother's friends would drop by to join her when she was drinking her daily allotment."

John, Jr., has some nostalgia-steeped memories of his grandmother's home in Nocona. "I loved going there," he said. "My grandmother had those big old feather beds that you'd sink down in. I remember how cold it got in the wintertime. I'd burrow down in that feather bed and, boy, it'd be great. It was a really big house. There was a grape arbor on one side, and on the other side of the lot was the playhouse my grandfather built for the kids, where they could have parties, dances, whatever they wanted to do. It was a big, open house with a porch all around it. That's where the Justin Leather Goods Company later got started. The kids got some of the scrap leather from the plant and started a leather goods business."

Meantime, business was growing steadily at the boot factory, primarily as a result of the success of the self-measuring system. This persuaded Justin to hit the road in search of new business. He began calling on merchants and department stores in cities throughout the western part of the country, offering them an opportunity to sell boots to their customers, using his self-measuring system. John Justin, Jr., described the deal Justin made with the merchants.

"My grandfather would go to a store such as A&L August in Fort Worth and leave some measuring blanks, and the merchant would get a dollar for measuring the customers and sending in the order. This put H. J. Justin into the wholesale business."

It also sold a lot of boots.

While he was on the road calling on merchants, Justin also carried samples with him and took orders from individuals living in the cities he visited. To let the public know he was available, he took out advertisements in local newspapers announcing when he'd be in town and where his samples could be seen. A typical advertisement declared, "H. J. Justin, manufacturer of Justin's Celebrated Cowboy Boots, will be in Duncan June 26 and 27 to take orders for my Celebrated Cowboy Boots. If you want a strictly high grade hand-made article, don't fail to see me. My cowboy boots have a wide reputation and have stood the test for many years."

Justin also tailored his ads for special occasions, such as a cattlemen's convention that was to be held in Fort Worth. Just prior to the convention, Justin took out the following ad in a Fort Worth newspaper:

> To the Visiting Stockmen. Try Justin's Celebrated Cowboy Boots. During the convention, I am located at 905 Main Street, Scott Building, where I will be pleased to see stockmen and others who want something durable in the way of footwear. The boots I make are the result of years of study, and that they are entirely satisfactory is proven by the fact that once a stockman becomes a customer of mine he remains one. I am here to take orders only. H. J. Justin, Nocona, Texas.

Recalling that era, John, Sr., said, "We sold thousands of pairs of good seventeen-inch, calfskin cowboy boots at $8.50 a pair." That the boots were passing muster with their wearers was attested in a letter from a satisfied customer who confessed, "I don't feel dressed up unless I have on a pair of Justin Boots."

The company's steady growth was noted in an article in the *Nocona News* in 1906 that quoted a letter written by H. J. Justin. In the letter, Justin noted that he was now shipping his cowboy boots to twenty-two states and the demand for them was steadily increasing. By 1908, annual boot production had topped the one thousand-pair mark, annual revenues had reached $12,000, and there were a dozen employees on the payroll. H. J. Justin was spending a great deal of time on the road lining up merchants to stock his company's products and was leaning more and more on his two oldest boys, John, twenty, and Earl, eighteen, to run the business while he was away. Both had literally grown up with the company.

It had always been Justin's dream to have his sons carry on the business after he was gone, and in 1908 he took the step to assure that it would happen. He informed John and Earl that he was taking them into the business as equal partners and changing the name of the company to H. J. Justin & Sons. As a memento of the historic occasion, he gave each son a $5 gold piece. A newspaper advertisement taking note of the change declared:

> Cowboys, Thank You! You wear the best boots in the world. You have made me increase my business year by year because you will wear the best boots. Your trade, like my boots, is the best, and we are growing along and prospering together. To keep step with this trade, I have young, active men with me in my business, and I will try during 1908 to give you even better service than before. With best wishes, H. J. Justin & Sons, The Cowboy Bootmakers. Nocona, Texas.

The newly ordained partners now found themselves dealing with the vicissitudes of running a business whose principal employees were itinerant bootmakers, craftsmen who wandered the countryside from one job to another, secure in the knowledge that somewhere down the road, a workbench in someone's boot shop was waiting to be filled.

"In those days," John Justin, Jr., explained, "your typical bootmaker was a drifter. He was also usually a heavy drinker. On a typical Monday morning in Nocona, when they had ten or twelve bootmakers working for them, my dad told me, not one would show up for work. Dad would have to go find them, bail some of them out of jail in Muenster and Wichita Falls, and try to sober up the others. It'd take a day or two to round them up and get them all back to work. Those old bootmakers had reputations that followed them around. This guy was a great stitcher or this guy was a great hand-laster. If you needed a hand, you tried to get him from wherever you could. My dad could look at a boot and tell you who the stitcher was."

Justin chuckled as he recalled one of his father's favorite stories of the Nocona era. "In those days, the banks were still kind of risky and my grandfather didn't trust them. He had a big old safe where he kept all the money. One day my grandfather got real sick and they had to take him to the hospital. It was payday and all the money was in the safe, and my grandfather wasn't available to open it. My dad had to go all the way to Wichita Falls, which was quite a trip at that time, to get a locksmith who could open the safe. When he finally opened it, the safe was just full of money, a lot of them big old greenbacks. My dad took the money out of the safe and put it all in the bank. He opened an account at the local bank."

One of H. J. Justin's first moves after taking his sons into the business was to mechanize the plant. Prior to that, Justin boots had been made primarily by hand, although a few Singer sewing machines had been used. Twenty-five pieces of machinery were added, allowing the factory to turn out more pairs of boots a day. The new equipment meant new employees were added to the payroll.

Despite the fact that the machinery was fitted to make both boots and shoes, shoemaking had never been a high priority with H. J. Justin, who had decided early on to concentrate all of his talents on making boots. The company did begin making a line of shoes after it moved to Nocona. But shortly after the boys came into the business, Justin sold his entire inventory of shoes to Warren Fooshee & Company and announced the company would henceforth direct all its attention to "the manufactory of its famous cowboy boots." The policy would remain in effect until after the company's move to Fort Worth in 1925.

By 1909, H. J. Justin & Sons boots were being sold in twenty-six states, Canada, Mexico and Cuba. When the *Nocona News* learned that the firm had just shipped a pair of boots to a customer in New York City, it commented, "No doubt some of our readers will wonder what a gentleman in New York City would want of these cowboy boots? Our idea is that a man don't [sic] have to be a cowboy to wear boots."

In a subsequent article in the summer of 1909, the newspaper emphasized the importance of the company to the Nocona economy. "No other institution in Nocona is bringing more money to the town than Justin's boot factory. That sounds like a big statement, but it is nonetheless altogether true, and it is time for us to tell our home people something about this factory which they probably do not know."

The editor ended with a gratuitous footnote. "There are today on the ranges of the West thousands of cowboys who would give you the big 'horse-laugh' if the suggestion was made that they wear anything else but Justin boots; and if the increase in business for this firm continues in the next 30 years as it has in the past few years, it will become a crime in some states for a bronco buster to shod his feet in anything which does not bear the already familiar Justin trademark."

H. J. Justin's penchant for publicity stood him in good stead when he was on the road. Wherever he traveled, he made certain that the local newspaper was apprised of the fact that he was in town. This resulted in a flood of news items, which Justin supplemented with advertisements such as one in the June 18, 1914, *Fort Worth Daily Livestock Reporter*. The ad waxed poetic over the company's products. The rhyming may have left something to be desired, but the message came through loud and clear— if you wanted the best, you had to wear Justins:

At the Mess Table, a Cowboy Speaks Thusly

> Come boys this business is slow,
> The dance at the Ranch house for me,
> I'll saddle my pony and away I go,
> What a time I'll have, Oh Gee.
>
> I will call for my gal at 8 p. m.,
> Then across the prairie we'll fly,
> She's riding Daisy—I'm riding Jim,
> Just watch us—we'll 'get by.'
>
> My gal's dolled up in a tailored suit,
> Hurry boys, let's begin the whirl,
> For I am wearing JUSTIN BOOTS,
> They are the best boots in the world.

If you are going to wear boots, why not wear the best? Why pay more when you can get the best for less money? Send us your address on a postal card, and we will mail you our catalogue with self-measuring system.

Yours for the best Cowboy Boots Made.

H. J. Justin & Sons
Mfrs. Justin's Celebrated Cowboy Boots
Nocona, Texas

By 1915, the Justins were employing twenty-five bootmakers who were turning out twenty-five pairs of boots daily, and the firm's weekly payroll had grown to $400. Boots were being shipped to thirty-six states and as far away as Australia. In one day in August 1915, sixteen money orders from self-measured customers were received at the plant, two from Cuba, one from Canada and thirteen from eleven different states. Such was the reputation of the company that each boot order was fully paid for, at an average price of $12 before a scrap of leather was cut or a stitch taken.

No one worked longer hours at the plant than John, Sr. "My dad was a hard worker," John Justin, Jr., noted. "He got up at 4:30 every morning. He would go to the post office and get the mail and have it opened and separated, the orders and the checks ready, by 7:30 in the morning. By the same token, he went to bed early, no matter who was there visiting."

But John, Sr., who in 1915 was one of Nocona's most eligible bachelors, apparently found the time to cultivate one special visitor to town: Ruby Harrison of Marietta, Oklahoma, whom he met at a party. A whirlwind courtship across the Red River culminated in an afternoon wedding in the Methodist church in Marietta on April 26, 1916. The bride was given in marriage by her stepfather, H. W. Choate, the editor of the *Marietta Monitor*, a weekly newspaper.

John and Ruby set up housekeeping in a small frame house not far from the boot factory, and it was there that John Sullivan Justin, Jr, was born on January 17, 1917. The joyous event was marred by the fact that H. J. Justin, in failing health after being stricken with a creeping paralysis two years earlier, would never be able to romp with his grandson in the backyard playground of the big house, and the grandson would grow up always regretting that fate denied him the chance to know his fabled grandfather.

three

Sorrow in the playhouse

Joe Justin spent the last three years of his life trying to find a cure for the mysterious disease that began ravaging his body in 1915. He consulted the best specialists in the country, traveling to New York, Chicago, St. Louis, Los Angeles and the Mayo Clinic in Rochester, Minnesota, to no avail. Although he was on the road almost constantly in his quest for a cure, he kept up with the business through correspondence with his sons, who had taken over the day-to-day operations of the company.

Typical of the correspondence between Justin and his sons is a letter from John, Sr., to his father, dated February 15, 1917:

Dear Dad

Just a few lines this morning to let you know that everything is going real well, everything is running nicely. We have opened up four new accounts since you left, all good ones, too, well-rated firms, and in good places. We are shipping out lots of boots, but are still about as far behind as we were any time last fall.

Orders are coming in fine. They average about 25 a day. I never saw so many orders in my life at this time of the year. And job applications, you never saw the like, from three to twelve and fifteen in every mail.

Am about to land some more French Calf. We sure are making some boots now; look good, well I should say so, and running about 180 pairs a week. The 9-hour business is working good, does not seem like the same crew. We are trying to get another man, and think we can run on an average of 200 pairs a week. Want to try to get a few stock boots on hand this summer, will have to do better than we are doing now, although we are making lots of boots, but are about four or five weeks behind.

Earl or I will probably go to Fort Worth during the Rodeo, as there are going to be about 500 bronc riders. Not that we need the work, but just to keep the other fellows from getting the bulge on us. Think it is a good idea, and we are arranged so we can spare one or the other of us for a day or so.

Had a dandy rain here night before last, just a slow, steady rain all night. Looked like it was going to get cold last night but it just barely froze. The sun is shining bright this morning and it is as clear as a bell. Sure is pretty outside.

Must get to booking the orders now, keep pretty well up with them.

Will let you hear from us frequently. Rest no uneasiness, we are getting along fine. Earl's and my policy is early to bed, early to rise, work like hell and advertise. It's $150,000 this year or bust. We will not be satisfied 'til we get it.

P. S. Ruby and J. S. Jr. are doing fine, am going to have to buy him some more clothes; he is about to outgrow all he has, one can almost see him grow, and fat, gee; you can't hardly see his eyes, he is so fat. Enid's baby looks like a dwarf beside him.

On March 24, 1917, Justin wrote a return letter to John:

Received your kind and welcome letter and was sure enough glad to hear from you. It was the first I heard from anyone for over a week. I have not gotten the *Nocona News* in three weeks. Have they quit publishing it?

It has been two months today since I left home. I am feeling just about the same as I did when I left there, no better or worse, about holding my own, and I think I will get all right.

I have studied some about the new building and my idea is that if we build it, to have it 30 feet in the clear and 80 feet long and two stories high, and to figure on a concrete floor for the first floor with iron ceilings, and a smooth brick wall on the inside so that it can be painted.

I will leave here next week and don't know what my address will be. You can continue to send me mail to Phoenix, c/o N. Porter & Company, and I will drop him a card as soon as I get located and have them to forward my mail to me. I don't know what to write about, as I have sent a letter to the *Nocona News* and told them all I knew.

With love to all, I am Daddy Joe.

P. S. Have Anis send me statements of the business, and my individual balance with the bank on the first of the month, and the pay roll, the men on it, giving the salaries of each man, and also how many there are on the pay roll, how much work you turn out per week on an average. That ought to give me a pretty good idea whether or not you are doing business on the safe side of the ledger.

Justin also carried on a regular correspondence with T. R. Stump, the editor of the *Nocona News*, and maintained a correspondence with his banker, W. A. McCall, president of the Farmers & Merchants National Bank of Nocona. McCall periodically gave Justin updates on the company's financial position.

When the United States entered the war against Germany, Justin wrote John, "I was very much pleased to note in the News that my boys were among the first to show their patriotism by putting 'Old Glory' over our shop."

On July 22, 1917, with the youngest Justin son, Avis, in the army, Earl complained to his father about the war-induced inflation that was pushing the cost of food in Nocona skyward. "Potatoes are selling for $3 per bushel and are scarce at this price. Pork is 30 cents per pound, steak 27 cents, everything else in proportion. Suppose you find everything high out there. What do you pay for bread?"

Justin was interspersing medical treatments with sightseeing. A bill in the amount of $100 from The Vito-Nuevo Treatment in Long Beach, California, received in Nocona in April 1917, indicated that he was now desperate enough to try some offbeat remedies. The invoice advertised that the treatment "successfully reached" everything from rheumatism and kidney troubles to skin and blood disorders.

The war in Europe was beginning to impact the boot business. Good leather was becoming scarce, especially French wax calfskin which virtually had disappeared from the marketplace by 1917. But thanks to H. J. Justin's forethought in buying a large shipment of the quality leather right after the outbreak of hostilities in Europe, the company's 1917 catalog was able to state, "We are using French Calf. Ask your bootmaker if he is."

Nevertheless, with supplies drying up and boot sales slumping as the nation reverted to a war footing, the Justin sons faced the problem of coping with a factory full of employees with nothing much to do. John, Sr., decided drastic measures were needed. He slashed prices, started the company's first daily newspaper advertising, and began selling boots directly off the factory racks. The tactics increased the cash flow sufficiently to permit the business to continue unabated while new sources of hides and chemicals were discovered. By 1918, the crisis had been alleviated and annual sales passed the $100,000 mark.

Meantime, H. J. Justin's condition continued to deteriorate steadily. "Medicine wasn't like it is now," John Justin, Jr., noted. "They didn't know too much and they simply couldn't help my granddad. One day, I remember my mother telling me, they got a telegram from my grandfather saying he was coming back to Nocona and that he would be on the train on a certain date and time. They all went to the station to meet him, but he didn't get off the train. The conductor had put down the step like they used to do.

"They asked him, 'Is that all of your passengers?'

"And he said, 'No, there's one more man aboard.'

"So they went inside and my grandfather was in the car, but he couldn't get up. He was unable to use his legs. So they got him off and took him home and put him to bed. He never walked again."

By now the Justin playhouse had been converted into a place to make bandages to be sent overseas. One day, while the elder Justin was seated on an easy chair in the playhouse, watching the ladies of Nocona roll bandages, the ten-year-old son of one of the volunteers came up to him and said, "Come on, Mr. Justin, get up and walk. You're bigger than me." It was one of the few times that anyone saw H. J. Justin cry.

He died on July 14, 1918, four months before the November 11 armistice that ended World War I. He was only fifty-nine years of age. Perhaps the principal legacy that H. J. Justin left behind him was incorporated in two quotations that would become a part of the company's heritage:

> No boot shall ever bear the Justin brand unless it is the very best that can be produced from the standpoint of material, style and workmanship.

and

> It is my wish that I might leave behind me an institution which will uphold the standards and spirit of the true West.

John Justin, Jr., was eighteen months old when his grandfather died. He retains no memory of the man responsible for making the Justin name synonymous with cowboy boots. But he does remember the thrill of accompanying his father to the boot factory as a wide-eyed toddler.

"We lived only a few blocks from the new plant that was built a couple of years after I was born," Justin recalled. "The new plant was a big improvement over the original rock building they moved into when they first arrived in Nocona. It was a fairly modern building with steel casement windows and a concrete floor. It's still standing. I remember going down to the factory as a little boy. I couldn't have been more than three or four. I'd go with my dad and watch them make boots. I thought that was a pretty big deal at the time."

The house that his parents moved into after he was born was located in the northeast part of Nocona. "It was really a little house," John, Jr., remembered, "but at that time it seemed pretty big to me. It had a big board fence. Behind us lived a brother and sister, neither of whom had married. They had a great big garden and they were always bringing my mother vegetables from it—beans, potatoes, berries."

John, Jr., recalled how people in Nocona were always concerned about the weather. "Nocona is located in the center of what they call Tornado Alley, running from Kansas through Oklahoma and into Texas," he explained. "Every night people would look out to the northwest, and if there were some black clouds in the sky they'd get real wary. My mother was really afraid of storms. There were some people who lived a block away from us who had a storm cellar. Who knows how many nights I spent in that storm cellar? But it was a lot, because at the first clap of thunder in the distance or the first flash of lightning, my mother would grab my hand and drag me off to the storm cellar. I didn't like it down there. It was damp and there were cobwebs. It didn't suit me at all, but that's what everybody did in those days. They headed for the storm cellar."

Another of his early memories is of his father's preoccupation with bringing the magic of radio into the house. "My grandmother gave my father one of the early radios," he recounted. "It was a box with a lot of dials on it. I can still see him tinkering with the radio every night. He had a wire on the radio that connected with an aerial outside the window. He'd put on his headset and he'd begin turning those dials trying to tune the radio in on stations around the country. Usually all he got was a lot of static. But the next morning he'd announce proudly, 'I got WGN in Chicago or KDKA in Pittsburgh or KOA in Denver last night.'"

His father was a strict taskmaster, John, Jr, said, a true chip off the old block. "He expected to be obeyed when he told me something, just as his father had. I used to go to Sunday school at the Methodist church in Nocona, and I had some cousins who went there, too. After Sunday school, we liked to go to my grandmother's house. She had a grape arbor where we liked to play. One time I was late to Sunday dinner because I'd been at my grandmother's house. The following Sunday morning, my father told me to come home directly from Sunday school so that I'd be on time for dinner. But my cousins urged me to go with them to my grandmother's house to play and I went with them against my father's orders.

> "So I was playing and having a good time when my grandmother came out to the grape arbor to tell me that I was wanted on the telephone. I went to the phone. It was one of those old crank-type phones. My father was on the line. "He said, 'John, Jr., are you there?'
> "I said, 'Yes.'

"There was a click on the line. I knew what that meant, so I started running home as fast as my legs could carry me. I was about five or six at the time. My father met me halfway. That was when they first had started using synthetic soles, and he was holding a sample of one that he had taken home for some reason. Boy, he swatted me each step that I took all the way home. He really helped me along. Needless to say, I didn't do that anymore."

John, Jr., also carries a vivid memory of the first car his father bought in the early 1920s. "The salesman brought the car from Wichita Falls to Nocona so that Dad could try it out. It was on a Sunday and my mother and I went along for the ride while Dad tried the car out to see if it could climb the hills around Nocona. There's also a lot of sand around Nocona, and he tried the car out on the sand to see if it could get through before he finally bought it." Justin doesn't remember the make or model, but he'll never forget the car and the exhilaration of that Sunday drive.

His fondest childhood memory, however, is the day he got to meet Tom Mix in person. At the height of his popularity in the 1920s, the former lawman and ranch hand was a national idol. On the silver screen, he was the epitome of the straight-shooting, square-dealing, clean-living good guy who stood for law and order and always won out against the bad guys. An uncompromising purist, Mix remained true to his role as a "real" cowboy, steadfastly refusing to sing or play a guitar, never kissing the girl, and always ordering sarsaparilla when the script called for him to enter the wicked confines of a saloon.

Mix favored sweeping sombreros, fancy, embroidered shirts, colorful bandanas, pearl-handled pistols and exotic footwear. His cowboy boots, made to order by the Justins, were his pride and joy. His boot orders were invariably marked "Rush," but the Justins were only too happy to comply. Tom Mix was their best salesman, a real live billboard for the Justin brand.

Mix's boots were usually shipped to him in Hollywood, but on one memorable occasion he picked up an order in person at the plant in Nocona. "I was about five or six," Justin recalled. "I was at home with my mother when the telephone rang. It was my dad on the line and he was all excited. 'Quick, bring John, Jr., over right away,' he told my mother.

"So she grabbed my hand and we ran the five or six blocks to the plant. When we got there, there was a big crowd milling around out in front. When we got inside, my father was waiting for me. 'There's someone I want you to meet,' he said to me. Then he led me into the office where Tom Mix was standing holding a pair of boots. I recognized him right away. I couldn't believe my own eyes. He had wired ahead to say he was going to be on a certain train coming through Nocona on a certain day and that he hoped his boots would be ready. The train station was only a block from the boot factory. So they held the train for him while he went over to the plant to pick up his boots from my father. And that's how I met the famous movie cowboy, Tom Mix. I still have a picture somewhere of us standing together."

In the company's archives, there is a telegram from Mix from Grand Canyon, Arizona, dated September 22, 1921, and addressed to "Justins. Boot Maker. Nocona, Texas." The wire reads: "Please make two pairs of boots same as the first pair. Ship to Los Angeles. Make them as soon as you can as I am sorely in need of them. This Grand Canyon is sure grand but hard on boots. Obliged. Tom Mix."

John, Jr., began helping out in the plant at the age of six as an unpaid assistant to his cousin, Bill Justin, putting laces in a new line of lace-up boots that were favorites of oilfield workers in the area. "There was a great amount of oil activity around Nocona," he related. "There was such a demand for oilfield workers that there weren't enough places for them to stay in town. My folks rented out a front bedroom in our house to two guys who worked in the oil fields. They worked twelve-hour shifts, so someone was sleeping there around the clock.

"I started putting laces in those big, old sixteen-inch lace boots that came up clear over your calf. The oilfield workers really loved them because they were great in mud and working around the wells. They really filled a need. I wasn't paid anything for putting in those laces. My father and my uncles also made an eight-inch driller boot that was great for working around the drilling rigs."

John, Jr., also remembered pasting H. J. Justin & Sons decals on compasses that the company gave away free to people who wrote in for them.

"My father had gotten a large supply of those compasses at a very distressed price and decided to use them as a sales promotion gimmick. They advertised the free compasses in two-inch magazine ads, and they couldn't believe the response those ads got. They received thousands of requests in the mail from all over the country. That gave them a lot of new names for their catalog. I about wore out my fingers pasting on those decals."

By then, Earl Justin and his brother-in-law, G. W. Humphreys, had established a leather goods business as an offshoot of the boot company. The move into leather goods resulted from the necessity of saving leather scraps during the war. Tanned leathers were in extremely short supply. Instead of incinerating the scraps that remained after the boot tops and soles were stamped out, they began utilizing the trimmings to make purses, billfolds and other products. In 1919, the Justin Leather Goods Company was organized and set up shop in the former Justin Clubhouse. A year later, the company moved from the clubhouse into the old boot company building that was vacated when the new H. J. Justin & Sons plant opened. The company was sold to H. J. Justin & Sons in 1955 and was later closed.

Meantime, sales at the boot company reached an all-time high in 1920 as the postwar economy began to heat up, fueled by a wildly speculative stock market. The company's balance sheet now showed total assets of $127,228, which included cash, U. S. bonds, accounts receivable, inventories, machinery and manufacturing equipment, and real estate—factory buildings and warehouse.

However, 1921 proved to be a disappointing year, with sales suffering a drastic decline and the bottom line showing a net loss of $256. The bad news was felt throughout the country, as well as in Nocona. Sales, however, rose sharply again in 1922 and a spirit of optimism prevailed.

The Justin plant in Nocona now employed thirty-six people. In 1922, the company turned out nine thousand pairs of boots, producing a pair every ten to twelve minutes. From the time a pair of boots started on the production line until it was finished required twelve days. The boots were selling for $16 to $22, although some fancy boots went for as much as $68 a pair.

The Justin brothers began facing questions from the media and others asking whether moving the company to a larger city would be beneficial to the growth of the business. Invariably, they shook their heads and pointed out that in Nocona they were able to train their own workers and were not bothered by labor troubles. Little did the Justins know that in

Fort Worth, while they were professing their loyalty to Nocona, a group of civic boosters committed to bringing new payrolls to the growing city already had H. J. Justin & Sons in its sights and would soon come a-courting.

Founder H. J. Justin, early 1900s.

An artist's rendering of the first Justin shop in Spanish Fort.

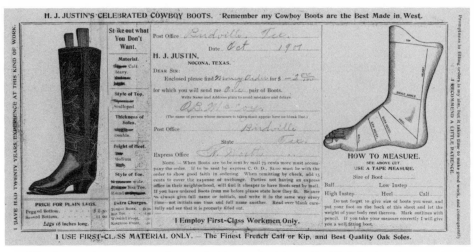

The first made-to-measure chart and order card originated by H. J. Justin prior to 1900.

A 1910 photo of the Nocona plant and Justin workers.

The Nocona plant before the introduction of modern machinery, early 1900s.

Inside the Nocona plant. H. J. Justin is in the foreground.

An envelope from the Justin boot factory in Nocona.

The packing room in the Nocona factory.

42

The Justin family, including children and grandchilren, in the summer of 1916. From left: Fern Justin Senter, holding her youngest child Mavis; Jess Senter with daughter Helen standing in front of the Senters; Florence Justin, holding Ruth; Maurine and Myrl stand in front of Earl Justin; to Earl's left are Mr. and Mrs. H. J. Justin; Enid Justin Stelzer and Julius Stelzer; Anis Justin; Sam Justin; Ruby Harrison Justin; and John Justin, Sr.

Mrs. H. J. Justin took a great interest in the boot business from the time she married Joe in 1886 until her death in 1939. While the shop was still in Spanish Fort, she developed the self-measuring kit that put Justin in the mail order business.

H.J. Justin

44

Screen actor Tom Mix is one of the many famous personalities who has worn Justin boots. This photo was taken in the 1920s.

This office space was added to the factory in Nocona around the turn of the century. In this early 1920s photo, Earl Justin is in fore-ground (wearing cap) and John sits at a desk in the rear.

four

A new home in Cowtown

In the summer of 1924, the superintendent of one of the large shoe factories in Brockton, Massachusetts, was visiting with one of his company's retail customers in Fort Worth when his eye fell on a cowboy boot displayed on a counter in the store's boot and shoe department. Picking up the boot, the veteran shoe manufacturer was bowled over by the fancy scroll stitching on the front quarter and vamp. When he asked who made the boot, he was told it came from a company named Justin in Nocona, Texas. The man from Massachusetts said he could hardly believe that the stitching was done in Texas, because he didn't think workmanship like that was found anywhere outside of New England.

The incident was cited by G. M. Knebel, the executive vice president of the Texas State Manufacturers' Association, in an article about H. J. Justin & Sons that appeared in the November 15, 1924, issue of the *Texas Commercial News*. Knebel had come to Nocona for a first hand look at the Justin plant because he felt the company could play a major role in the development of shoe and boot manufacturing in Texas. It was Knebel's view that Texas should capitalize on its huge livestock production by tanning its own hides and converting them into boots and shoes. He foresaw an annual market, in Texas alone, for some fourteen million pairs.

Commenting on the growth the company had enjoyed since its founding, Knebel noted that since the death of H. J. Justin in 1918, "his sons have had a desire to make the company serve more people than Mr. Justin ever anticipated. Believing that the best way to do this was to take to every man and woman interested in boots a complete picture story, they conceived the idea of building a catalog so far ahead and superior to anything that had ever been put out that there would be no question left unanswered about Justin boots."

The catalog, which made its debut in 1923, was a slick six-by-nine-inch fifty-page paper publication that featured a four-color sketch of an elderly Indian, peace pipe in hand, seated on the edge of a promontory and staring out reflectively over a western landscape dotted with grazing buffalo on its cover. The cover contained only two words: "Justin Boots." The inside cover carried a dedication "To the late H. J. Justin, creator of Justin's Celebrated Cowboy Boots, and to that iron-nerved cavalier of the range—The American Cowboy."

On the facing page was a photograph of H. J. Justin and his oft-quoted credo ". . .that I might leave behind me an institution which will uphold the standards and the spirit of the true West." Testimonials by Tom Mix, western artist Charles M. Russell and famed Texas Rangers' Captain Tom R. Hickman added a touch of glamour. A boot named the "Tom Mix" boasted a black kid top inlaid with a white tulip design. Russell was represented by a reproduction of a letter he wrote to the Justins thanking them for their "fine footwear." The letter, dated December 28, 1921, was written on Russell's personal stationery decorated with a color sketch of the artist seated on his horse and doffing his hat. In his own vernacular and minus punctuation, Russell avowed:

Dear Sirs

My hats off to you and your boot builders I have worn boots most of my life an I'm here to tell every man that yours are real regular boots for riding men and women both my wife and I thank you for the fine foot wear.

Wishing you all a Happy New Year

Yours with thanks
C M Russell

Tom Hickman, one of the best-known lawmen of the era, was another valuable promoter of the Justin brand. His greatest feat was the capture of the famous "Santa Claus" bandits, who had robbed a bank in Cisco, Texas, two days before Christmas while wearing Santa Claus costumes. Hickman always wore his twin .45s on his hips and his Justin boots with his pants legs tucked inside, and that's how he appeared in the catalog, the archetypical wearer of the badge.

The 1923 catalog was the culmination of an aggressive direct mail campaign aimed at individuals and retailers and launched after the end of World War I. Direct mail also was used to build the company's repair business and to build its dealer network. A stream of letters flowed out of Nocona to merchants throughout the West. By the early 1920s, however, it was apparent that direct mail couldn't do the job by itself, that there was room in the marketing mix for savvy salesmen who knew the product line and how to garner orders. This admission was akin to heresy for a company that had over the years proudly advertised the fact that it did not employ any traveling salesmen. "Our goods are our representatives," Justin advertisements and sales literature had proclaimed. "They speak for themselves."

Soon, there was a cadre of salesmen carrying the Justin word near and far, men like the legendary Jack Hamilton, who cranked up their Model T Fords and Reos and braved the rigors of unpaved roads, fleabag hostelries and greasy spoon eateries to peddle their wares in cities, towns and hamlets throughout the West.

Hamilton was twenty-six, out of work and deep in debt, when he strode into John Justin, Sr.'s, office one day in 1924 and asked for a job. He had spent his youth learning the retail business working for his uncle who owned a chain of department stores in North Texas and had finally begun operating a small mercantile store of his own in Burkburnett when the business went belly up due to a slowdown in oil drilling in the area. Hamilton owed money to H. J. Justin & Sons, mostly for a large quantity of lace boots for oil-field workers that had gone unsold.

Hamilton told John, Sr., that he knew he could sell boots. All he wanted was a chance to do that and, at the same time, pay off his indebtedness.

"The story I always heard," John Justin, Jr., related, "was that he told my dad, 'I want to sell Justin boots.' My dad didn't hire him. Jack just told him he was gonna sell boots for him and he started selling Justin boots."

As it turned out, Hamilton was a boot-selling natural, who not only quickly paid off his debt but became the first Justin sales representative to sell $100,000 worth of boots in a single year and the first to top the $1 million mark in career sales.

"I love to sell," he said in an interview in the *Daily Oklahoman* in 1980, when he celebrated his fifty-fifth anniversary as a Justin employee. At the age of eighty-two, he was still going strong as the nation's oldest traveling boot salesman. Hamilton believed that getting a merchant's undivided attention was the first step towards making a sale.

"Most of the stores he called on in those little country towns had wooden floors," John, Jr., recounted. "When the merchants swept the floors, they used some stuff that had oil in it to pick up the dust. This made the floors nice and shiny and slick. In those days, the company provided salesmen with fiber sample cases that had metal feet on them. They were long cases. Jack would bang open the front door and slide that long sample case right into the store and he'd follow right behind announcing, 'Watch out, boys, here comes Jack Hamilton, the world's greatest cowboy boot salesman. I've got the biggest house and the biggest mortgage in Oklahoma City. And I'm here to sell you some boots—Justin boots."

Jack Hamilton stories abound in company lore, but the most famous is the saga of the trick pulled on him by one of his customers back in the 1930s. In anticipation of Hamilton's arrival on one of his regular sales calls, the merchant had rigged up a microphone attachment to a radio located at the front of the store near the cash register. While Hamilton was on the premises passing the time of day in his usual effusive manner with a group of customers and store employees, an excited voice suddenly rose out of the radio: "We interrupt this program to bring you a news bulletin," the voice resounding with doom blared out. "A huge fire is now raging at the Justin Boot Company plant in Fort Worth. As we speak, fire trucks are on the scene unsuccessfully trying to stem the conflagration. It would appear that the building and everyone inside is doomed." Ashen-faced and, for once, stunned speechless, Hamilton raced to a nearby telephone and dialed the boot company number in Fort Worth. In those days, people answered their own telephones in the company offices, and Bert Fisch, the sales manager, picked up the phone.

"Hello," he said.

"Bert," Jack screamed, "the building's on fire. Save yourself. Get out while you can."

In 1924, with sales exceeding $200,000, H. J. Justin & Sons was restructured as a corporation. John Justin, Sr., Earl Justin and Avis Justin were elected to the firm's initial board of directors. Original shareholders were: Mrs. H. J. Justin; J. S. Justin, Sr.; W. E. Justin; S. A. Justin; Myrl Justin; Enid Justin Stelzer; Fern Justin Senter; Anis Justin Lemon; Helen Senter; Mavis Senter; J. S. Justin, Jr.; Maurine Justin; and Ruth Justin.

Article III of the incorporation document carried a statement that soon would assume special significance, "The principal office and place of business of this corporation shall be at Nocona, in Montague County, Texas, but this corporation may maintain business offices at such other places as may be necessary or convenient."

Less than a year later, this provision would be invoked to permit the company to move to Fort Worth, a fast-growing city of 125,000, some ninety miles south of Nocona.

What was behind the move? Reminiscing about it in later years to his son, John, Sr., pointed to the fact that the company had outgrown Nocona. "They moved the business to Fort Worth in 1925," John, Jr., explained, "in order to have better banking facilities, better freight facilities and a better chance for labor. The plant was growing, and the labor situation in Nocona was largely used up."

John, Jr., further noted, "The railroad ran only east and west through Nocona. Anything shipped from Nocona had to be shipped to Gainesville or Wichita Falls in order to get it on a railroad going north or south. Fort Worth, on the other hand, was a rail hub with trunk lines going out from it in all directions."

Numerous cities in Texas seeking new payrolls and additions to their tax rolls had been courting the Justins for a number of years prior to their decision to relocate to Fort Worth. One of the earliest suitors, according to a May 1911 story in the *Nocona News*, was Fort Worth's arch rival— Dallas. As the *News* told it, a representative of the *Dallas Morning News*, who was in Nocona on a business trip, dropped in at the Justin boot factory. The Dallas man was surprised that Nocona possessed any such enterprise and said so in no unmeasured terms. He offered Mr. Justin a large bonus to move his factory to Dallas. At that time, the company was firmly rooted in Nocona.

John, Jr., recalled that a number of cities had made passes at the company over the years. "They looked at Abilene, they looked at Waco, they looked at Dallas," he added. "Finally, Fort Worth made them the best deal."

The details of the deal were spelled out in a letter from B. B. Buckeridge, manager of the Manufacturers and Wholesalers Association of Fort Worth, dated April 13, 1925, to H. J. Justin & Sons, Inc., pledging the purchase of $50,000 in eight percent cumulative participating preferred Justin stock "in part consideration of removing the boot and shoe factory now located in Nocona, Texas, to Fort Worth." The association also agreed to reimburse Justin for the cost of moving machinery, equipment and stocks from Nocona to Fort Worth, "it being understood that the limit estimate of $5,000 will be not exceeded." Other provisions of the deal included furnishing Justin with a factory building rent-free for a period of one year and providing the company and its products with "a great amount of publicity" in the local newspapers.

On April 23, 1925, Justin stockholders met in Nocona and unanimously passed a motion to move the factory and offices to Fort Worth. The announcement hit the front page of the *Fort Worth Star-Telegram* on April 24, with a headline that trumpeted the news: Justin Boot Factory Comes to Ft. Worth.

The *Star-Telegram* reported that work on the firm's factory building would commence within the next few weeks on a site near the Worth Mills in South Fort Worth. About six hundred people would move from Nocona to Fort Worth with the factory, including seventy employees in the plant and their families, the article said.

The *Fort Worth Press* pulled out all stops in its front page story on the afternoon of April 24:

> With bands, banners, cheers, eclat, the famous shoe and boot factory of H. J. Justin & Sons will be moved to Fort Worth from Nocona, Texas, by truck, probably within 60 days. Plans for an elaborate cavalcade of motor trucks, bannered and decorated, to move the equipment from the Nocona plant are being made by the Manufacturers and Wholesalers Association.

On June 22, a Justin mailing piece from Nocona announced that after August 1, 1925, the company would be located in Fort Worth at 320 South Lake Street.

Not everyone in the Justin family was elated over the prospect of the move to Fort Worth, however. "When they decided to make the move from Nocona to Fort Worth," John, Jr., recounted, "everybody agreed to it except my Aunt Enid."

Actually, Enid Justin, who was then married to J. L. Stelzer, voted her fifty-six Justin shares in favor of the move to Fort Worth. She then underwent a change of heart.

"When the time came for her to move to Fort Worth, along with my father and uncles, she told them she needed more time, that she wasn't quite ready to leave," John, Jr., related. "She kept on delaying until she finally said she was going to remain in Nocona and open her own boot factory. It turned out that she had been stockpiling boot-making machinery in a warehouse in Gainesville all that time."

In her memoir published in 1985, Miss Enid gave her account of what transpired:

> Fort Worth was a thriving town and people from there kept coming to

Nocona to convince my brothers the boot company would do better in Fort Worth . . . . They took all my father's equipment with them, along with most of the employees. I wasn't happy with them moving out of Nocona.

When they announced to me they were going to take the factory to Fort Worth, I just bowed my neck and told them I wasn't going . . . .

Well, that got a response real quick from oldest brother, Johnny. He said, 'You're going to lose every damned cent you've got in six months.'

I said, 'Well, Johnny, if I do, Mother's taught me how to wash and iron and sew and cook and scrub; and if I go broke, I'll just do something else.' I'll never forget what my brother, Earl, said at that point. He looked at me with real sad eyes and said, 'Hon, don't you know it won't be much longer when there won't be any cowboy boots worn at all?'

I replied, 'Why, Earl, we'll always eat meat and the cowboys will always have to ride the range.' I've often thought in the last few years about what he said, now that Western wear and cowboy boots are so popular everywhere. Johnny and Earl both tried to get me to go with them to Fort Worth. I've always been glad I didn't.

Immediately after the move to Fort Worth, Miss Enid started the Nocona Boot Company. "She never called it the Justin Boot Company," John, Jr., said, "but all of her sales literature and ads carried the words, 'Enid Justin, President,' and she made sure that the Justin name was always a lot bigger than the Nocona name. She finally took enough liberties with the Justin name that they filed a lawsuit against her. They got Sidney Samuels, one of Fort Worth's top attorneys, to represent them. He felt he had a good case against her. But she came down and pleaded with her brothers to drop the suit. My dad felt business was business. But my Uncle Avis finally convinced my Uncle Earl that they should not go ahead with the suit and they finally withdrew it. Mr. Samuels was very unhappy about it."

Miss Enid would continue to be a tough and determined competitor of H. J. Justin & Sons and a thorn in John, Jr.'s, side after he assumed control of the company. There would be a pair of lawsuits and a number of other confrontations over the years. The rivalry finally came to an end in 1981, when Miss Enid capitulated and the Nocona Boot Company was merged into Justin Industries. The Nocona Boot Company continues to flourish in Nocona today, maintaining a relationship with the Justin brand that has lasted for more than a century.

five

A perfect fit

Justin and Fort Worth made a perfect fit. Cowboy boots and Cowtown. Fort Worth wore its "Cowtown" appellation proudly, basking in the authenticity of its western heritage, as opposed to its pretentious neighbor to the east, Dallas, which preferred a more cosmopolitan image.

Fort Worth's history was steeped in the lore of the Old West—Indians and dragoons, gun-slinging badmen and badge-wearing marshals, carousing cowboys and herds of Longhorns. Begun as one of a line of forts established by the army from Mexico to the Indian Territory, Fort Worth was rescued from the devastation of the Civil War by the great cattle drives. The Chisholm Trail ran smack through the heart of town, and Fort Worth began to flourish as a provider of hospitality to the cowboys moving the herds to market.

Fort Worth enjoyed even more rapid growth with the arrival of the railroad in 1876. Cattle shipping became its major industry. The city's business leaders, however, remained convinced that a large-scale meat packing operation was a necessity for the city's continued growth. A "pot" of $100,000 was raised and offered as a lure to any meat packing company that agreed to locate its operations in Fort Worth. In 1902, Swift and Armour, the Chicago-based meat-packing behemoths, agreed to open plants in Fort Worth, and the $100,000 was divided between them.

A quarter of a century later, history would repeat itself with the raising of the $50,000 pot that lured H. J. Justin & Sons to Cowtown.

In 1925, Fort Worth was still very much Cowtown. Four packing houses operated around the clock. The livestock exchange was one of the nation's busiest. Exchange Avenue, in the heart of the sprawling stock-yards area on the city's north side, resembled a giant western movie lot, with horses, cattle, saloons, colorful storefronts and walk-up hotels. But when the wind howled in from the north, the pungent aromas emanating from the stockyards left no doubt that Fort Worth's Cowtown image was no Hollywood hype.

The city had an estimated population of 125,000 and was in the midst of an epidemic of oil fever, with fortunes being made and lost daily. Although no oil had ever been found in Fort Worth, it was the nearest major city to oil fields that were discovered in West Texas on the W. T. Waggoner Ranch near Wichita Falls in 1911, at Ranger in 1917 and at Desdemona and Burkburnett in 1918. Fort Worth became a hotbed of the booming petroleum industry. Thousands of people jammed into the city. New companies were born daily. By 1925, seven oil refineries were oper-ating full blast. Between 1915 and 1925, the tax value of property in the city more than doubled to $152 million.

According to the 1925 city directory, there were 416 factories in Fort Worth employing 18,000 people with an annual payroll of $20 million. A downtown building boom that had begun with the end of World War I dramatically augmented the city's skyline. The principal addition was the twenty-four-story Farmers & Mechanics National Bank Building, which was proclaimed by its owners as the tallest building in the Southwest when it opened in 1921. In 1925, there were signs of construction throughout the city's downtown area, with new buildings poking their heads skyward. This was the city that welcomed the Justins to town.

The new home of H. J. Justin & Sons was a brick building at 320 South Lake Street on the city's blue-collar south side previously occupied by the Double Seal Piston Ring Company. The company signed a three-year lease on the building at a rental of $300 per month.

John, Jr., who was seven years old at the time of the move to Fort Worth, recalled the old Lake Street facility. "There were two big buildings over there, side by side. They occupied only one of the buildings at first, installing the manufacturing equipment in the back and putting the stock room up front. Then, as they began growing, they took the back half of the other building. And, finally, they took all of the second building, too. That's when they were really going to town making boots and shoes."

John, Jr., also remembered the caravan of trucks that hauled the machinery from the Nocona plant to Fort Worth. "The machinery wasn't real big then, but before they moved it, my father and my uncles came down and marked out their production lines," he recounted. "Then the machines were brought in and set down on the markings. At that time, the machines didn't have individual motors. So they used one big wheel with a large belt on it to provide the power to the various machines. The big wheel was installed overhead at one end of the line and they put the big belt onto a machine. There were as many as ten other machines running off that same motor."

Justin recalled his first home in Fort Worth, a boardinghouse run by a Mrs. Allen on Fifth Avenue, not far from the boot and shoe plant on South Lake Street. "Mrs. Allen was a widow, a really fine woman, a hard worker and a wonderful cook," Justin recalled. "The house had kind of a back porch that she had boxed in, had made a big room out of it, and had built in a little bathroom, and that's where my mother and dad and I lived. We just had that one big room. The bathroom was ours. It was a big, two-story house and she rented out rooms. She cooked for the renters and she also had some boarders who didn't live there but still ate there. One of the boarders was Lee Larsen, a building inspector for the city who later became a high-ranking city official. Another was Simon W. Freese of the Freese & Nichols engineering firm. He had a little apartment down the street, but he ate at Mrs. Allen's.

"One time the men, Lee and Si and my dad and two or three others who ate at Mrs. Allen's, decided they'd have a stag party and cook their own meal. They had the party at Freese's apartment and I got to go with them. Their cooking wasn't all that good, as I well remember. They wanted to make creamed corn. They opened a couple of cans of corn that they probably should have put, maybe, a half a cup of milk into. Instead, they put about a quart of milk into the corn. It didn't turn out so good. Corn-flavored milk is what it was. We drank the corn out of a cup. I remember how funny it was and what a laugh we got out of drinking the corn. I told my mother about it and she broke up laughing."

John, Jr., began attending the DeZavala Elementary School on College Avenue, near Mrs. Allen's boardinghouse. He still bears a memento acquired in the school's playground. "That's where I broke off part of my front tooth," he reported. "It was during recess and I was on a seesaw in the playground. The guy on the other end wanted to play around and he jumped the board a little and threw me off my end of the board. When I came down, my hands missed the board and I landed on my face."

He attended DeZavala for a couple of years before he began going to

Lily B. Clayton Elementary Echool on Park Place in a more affluent part of town. During this period, the family moved numerous times. "First we moved across the street and into the next block, where we rented a room that was a little bit larger than the one we had at Mrs. Allen's place," John Jr., recounted. "My father didn't believe in owning property. He thought that paying taxes was terrible and if you owned property, you had to pay taxes. He didn't take into consideration that you're paying them anyway. In those days, there were lots of houses for rent. So we moved very frequently.

"My mother could always find a house she liked better than the one we were living in. I remember she found a place over on Magnolia just past Jerome. She loved it. My dad always wanted to please my mother, so he rented the house. The company had an old panel truck, and I was helping my dad move my mother's dishes and household goods into the house. While we were moving in, she was out scouting the neighborhood. We hadn't even finished unloading the truck, when my mother found a house that she just loved over on Harrison, a block away. She wanted that house so much, she finally got my dad to agree to rent it. Unfortunately, he had already paid the first and last month's rent in advance on the house we had begun moving into. He was pretty upset that he was going to lose that rent without ever living there.

"The house on Harrison was really nice, with a basement and a furnace and a tile roof. A bootlegger had apparently once lived there, because periodically, someone would knock on the door at two o'clock in the morning and ask for a pint of bootleg whiskey. My dad would run him off."

John, Jr., had looked forward to getting a job in the new plant. But when he broached the idea to his father, John, Sr., turned him down. That didn't faze him.

"The thing is that I always wanted to work," John, Jr., asserted. "And since my father wouldn't give me a job, I just went into business for myself selling soda pop to the employees in the factory. The Ballard Ice Company was located right next door to the plant on South Lake Street. They had these huge three hundred-pound blocks of ice that they sawed and scored into smaller pieces before loading them on trucks for delivery to their customers. They had this big old saw that left a great mound of snow from the shavings from those big blocks of ice. Ballard also sold soda water by the case. So what I did was get myself two five-gallon buckets and a big half barrel. First, I would fill that half barrel with snow. Next I'd go inside and buy the soda. I'd fill up the buckets with that pretty snow and put the bottles of soft drinks in them and then I'd go over to the plant and sell the chilled soda pop to the workers for a nickel a bottle.

"I got to know pretty quickly what people wanted to drink. Some people drank grape, some drank cream soda. So when I went into a certain part of the factory, I knew which drinks to carry with me. This saved me from having to carry a bunch of stuff that I didn't need. I'd make the rounds and sell the soda pop. One thing still sticks in my mind after all these years. It always bugged me that I had to pay eighty cents a case for Coca-Cola and everything else was sixty cents a case—grape or orange or cream soda. Coca-Cola cost me more to buy, but I still got just a nickel a bottle, the same as I did for the plain old soda. I hated to sell Coca-Cola because I didn't make as much money off it, but I had to carry it for the people who asked for it."

John, Jr, continued to sell soda pop at the Justin plant until he began attending Jennings Avenue Junior High School. He then took a job as a delivery boy for the TCU Pharmacy, where he soon was clearing as much as $5.75 a week. "I worked after school from 5:30 to eleven o'clock at night, and I had to clean the store before I could go home," Justin recalled.

"Every once in a while, I'd get a tip. People didn't tip much in those days, maybe a nickel. Then I met some guys who had a paper route for the *Star-Telegram*. They really liked what they were doing and were making a lot more money than I was delivering drugs, so I made an application for a paper route. They didn't have any openings at first. Then one of the carriers left on a month's vacation and I threw his route for a month as a substitute. It was a bad time of year, raining every day. But I didn't mind getting wet because I figured if I did a good job, I'd get the next opening. The route was in the Berkeley area, a very nice part of town where my folks later rented a house."

When a permanent route finally became available in the Forest Park area, the *Star-Telegram* district manager offered it to Justin, who had impressed him with his hustle on his temporary assignment. The route included the Forest Park Apartments, a luxury high-rise overlooking the park, which by itself would have been a lucrative piece of business. But not for Justin.

"The manager kept the apartments for himself," John, Jr., reported. "All he had to do was give the papers to the elevator operator to deliver to the tenants."

Justin's daily schedule was to arise at 4:15 to throw the morning paper and then work the route again after school to deliver the evening edition. "I got so that I could really work that route," Justin recounted. "When I started out, I was making $45 or $50 a month. But I really worked on developing new customers. Most of the people on my route in those days had help who lived in quarters behind the house. The women worked as maids and cooks in the house and their husbands usually had jobs some-where else. The custom at that time was for the people who lived in the big house to give the newspapers to the servants after they'd finished with them and the help would then read them. I got the bright idea that those people ought not to be reading somebody else's newspaper. They ought to be reading their own paper. So what I began doing on Saturdays was knock on the door of the servants' quarters and try to sign them up to take the *Star-Telegram*. I'd tell the man of the house, 'Why read an old paper when I can deliver a fresh one to you every morning, evening and Sunday for $1 a month.' I got a lot of new customers that way. I also learned that it was better to collect twenty-five cents a week from my customers rather than one dollar once a month, because there were fifty-two weeks in the year versus only twelve months. Pretty soon I had everybody on that route taking all editions of the paper, and I was collecting from them weekly and making $125 to $130 a month, which wasn't bad in the early '30s during the Depression. Lots of people with families weren't making that much money, if they were working at all. I really accumulated some money. But I had to go out every Saturday to collect those quarters."

Justin continued throwing his paper route when he entered Central High School in 1932. This was the year the Great Depression reached its nadir, with the stock market falling to an all-time low and unemployment rising to an all-time high. The presidential election in November 1932 was no contest. Franklin Delano Roosevelt swept into office in a landslide that netted him the electoral votes of all but two states, Maine and Vermont, and spawned a play on words changing the old political bromide from, "As Maine goes, so goes the nation" to "As Maine goes, so goes Vermont."

FDR's inauguration, on March 4, 1933, precipitated another landslide, this one of government programs with which the new administration hoped to recharge the comatose economy. Alphabet agencies sprang into existence like Johnson grass in Texas after a spring gully-washer: Works Progress Administration, Public Works Administration, Reconstruction Finance Corporation, Civilian Conservation Corps, Securities and Exchange Commission, National Recovery Act.

John Justin, Jr., was sixteen and attending Central High School in Fort

Worth when Washington, D. C., became the center of a maelstrom of legislation and executive decrees. The nation's capital was where the action was, and, inexplicably, it beckoned seductively to the impressionable Justin, who felt "hamstrung" over the fact that he still couldn't persuade his father to give him a job.

"All I know," he remembered, "is that all I wanted to do was go to Washington."

What was his motivation? It might have been his frustration with his inability to persuade his father to give him a job. It could have been that he felt he had no more worlds to conquer on his paper route. Plus the fact he wasn't exactly setting the woods afire academically.

"I wasn't too happy in school and I wasn't doing too well," he conceded. "A lot of it I liked, and a lot of it I didn't like."

The idea of going to Washington came from one of John, Jr.'s, colleagues on a *Star-Telegram* paper route, Scotty Coleman. "Scotty wanted to go to Washington, D. C., worse than anything," Justin related. "My mother and father knew a man, Henry Bagley, who used to own the old *Fort Worth Record*. He was the brother-in-law of Josephus Daniels of North Carolina, one of the big politicians in Washington. So I had Scotty get in touch with Mr. Bagley and Mr. Bagley got him a job. Scotty wanted me to go up there with him and get a job. I talked to my dad and my dad, of course, wasn't too much for it. But I wouldn't give up. I hounded him to death, almost, and he finally said, 'I'll buy you an excursion ticket on the train.' You could buy one of those round-trip excursion tickets for almost nothing in those days. And he said, 'I'll give you enough money to keep you while you're up there. But when that excursion ticket runs out, then you better come back or it's adios, amigo. If you stay after that, you're on your own.' I think the excursion ticket was good for something like two or three weeks. My dad was obviously thinking in terms of my taking a short trip, but I wanted to go so badly that I took him up on it."

So Justin boarded the train at the old Santa Fe Depot in Fort Worth and rode it to Washington, D. C. Suitcase in hand, he disembarked and began looking for a place to stay that he felt he could afford. After several hours of looking at rooms, he finally settled for one on the fourth floor of a narrow row house in an inner-city residential area.

"This woman had this house and she rented out rooms. The room I rented was kind of her attic," Justin recalled. He paid the landlady a week's rent in advance and began looking for a job. "Of course, things up there then were just as they are now," Justin claimed. "If you didn't have connections you were out of luck. My friend, Scotty Coleman, had gotten a job as a messenger in the messenger pool that served the Department of Commerce Building. The different agencies in the building would call the pool and ask for a messenger. A fellow named Phil Handler was in charge of the pool. I got to know him through Scotty and he began trying to help me get a job. He told me to hang around there. What he would do when somebody ordered a messenger too often was encourage them to hire someone from the pool as their own full-time messenger.

"Handler told me about an office that had been calling regularly and really needed its own messenger. He said he was going to try to get them to hire me the next time they called. So I was hanging around there when they called. Boy, he got me and he said, 'Go up there and do whatever they want you to do with a smile on your face and, maybe, they'll hire you.'

"So I went up to see this guy named Lawrence J. Martin. He was the brother of Pete Martin, who used to write for the *Saturday Evening Post*. Lawrence Martin headed one of the code agencies in the NRA, which was just getting started then. He was a big, hearty guy. He got a kick out of my Texas accent, and he really got on me pretty good about it.

"Hey, Texas, where you from?' he asked me. I told him, 'Fort Worth.' 'Okay, Fort Worth,' he said. 'Let's see if you can deliver this package for me.'

"Man, I hooked off, did what he wanted and came back as fast as I could, all the while remembering to keep a big smile on my face. He gave me something else to deliver. I did two or three more deliveries. He used me pretty heavily right there.

Then he said, 'We may need a full-time messenger here. I may get you transferred from the pool.'

"And I said, 'I'm not in the pool.'

"He said, 'What are you doing here?'

"And I said, 'I'm trying to find a job.'

"He thought that was extremely funny and he began laughing real hard. He was an extremely profane man. He couldn't say, 'Good morning,' without calling it a 'blankety-blank morning.' But he knew all the right people. He knew the Roosevelts and everybody. So he called Handler and told him, 'What are you doing sending me a guy who's not even an employee?' And Handler said, 'Well, I thought you might need him. He's a good boy,' or something like that.

"Each agency had a chief clerk who handled the payroll. So Martin called in his chief clerk and said, 'I want to hire this boy as my messenger. Sign him up.' Boy, you talk about being elated. I was in seventh heaven. That was the last day my railroad ticket was good. The day before, I'd packed my bag, and I was crying because I was so upset. I felt I'd failed. I'll never forget holding that ticket in my hand and crying. I got so mad that I tore the ticket up so I wouldn't be able to use it. Then I really hustled back down to the messenger pool and the next day I got a job."

Justin doesn't remember what he got paid, except that "it wasn't much." But he had already figured out a way of making do with one meal a day to hold down his living expenses. He found a Chinese restaurant near the Department of Commerce Building that featured a chow mein lunch with all the bread you could eat. Justin began eating there every day, filling up on bread. This enabled him to skip breakfast and dinner.

"This went on until a group of us got together with Handler, who rented a house, and we all chipped in on the rent and the food," Justin reported. "There were eight or ten of us in the house, and Handler did the cooking. He could make a meal for practically nothing. He had a dish he called meat and noodles into which he put a whole lot of noodles and a little bit of meat. It was good."

Handler took a delight in showing the group of youngsters the sights of Washington and the surrounding area. One weekend, the group would tour Annapolis, the next weekend Gettysburg. Another time it would be Mount Vernon or Monticello. One evening after dinner, Handler informed the group that the following weekend he was going to show them New York. Justin could hardly wait for the week to pass.

"Everybody put in twenty-five bucks and Handler rented a car," Justin recalled. "He rented a big sedan as cheaply as he could and six or eight of us went. He'd gotten us a cheap place to stay. We saw all the sights, the Statue of Liberty, the Empire State Building.

"Handler had bought a big silver plate on which he'd attached two gold-colored letters that said, 'U. S.' We'd screwed the plate with the letters on the front of the car. I'll never forget, we drove the car into Times Square and, of course, there was a sea of no-parking signs.

"Handler asked a policeman, 'Officer, is there any place we can leave our car around here?'

"The policeman saw the letters 'U. S.' on the plate on the front of the car and said, 'Oh, yes, sir, you can pull in right here,' and he moved one of the barricades to permit us to park. It worked wherever we went all over New York. It was always, 'Yes, sir, you can park your car right here. Come right in.'"

Justin had been attending night classes while working during the day. Finally, he had amassed enough credits to graduate from high school. Graduation day remains a poignant memory. "The night they had the graduation ceremonies, I didn't have any family. I went there, and I was completely by myself. Everybody else was surrounded by family members, parents, brothers and sisters, aunts and uncles. I got so blue that I said 'to hell with it,' and left. They mailed my graduation certificate to me."

After working as a messenger for about a year, Justin began looking for another job within the NRA that paid a little more money. "There was a guy who was helping me find another position," Justin recalled, "and he said to me, 'I've got openings I'm going to send you out on; but don't ever admit you can't do anything. If they ask if you can flap your wings and fly, say 'yes, sir, that's my long suit.'"

A day or two later, one of the agencies called and said that it needed a comptometer operator. Justin was sent over to interview for the job. "I didn't even know what a comptometer was," he admitted. "I sat down with the chief clerk of the agency and he asked, 'Are you an experienced comptometer operator?' And I said, 'Oh, yes, sure, that's my main thing.' He hired me on the spot.

"He took me back to this huge room with a lot of people in it. Everyone had a desk and a comptometer and a big stack of papers. The comptometer was a big calculating machine with lots of keys on it. It was a kind of mechanical computer. Well, this guy sat me down at this desk and said, 'Here's your machine and here's your paper,' and he left."

Justin began "monkeying around" with the comptometer until a woman sitting at a desk next to his interrupted him with a question, "Do you know how to operate one of these?" Justin informed her that he had never seen one before in his life.

The woman said, "Fake it for a little while and after quitting time, I'll brief you on it."

When the bell rang at five o'clock, Justin recalled, "everybody took off like a covey of quail." But the woman who had offered to teach him the ropes stayed and showed him how to operate the machine. "By the time I left that night," Justin said, "I could do it. The next morning, there was another stack of papers on my desk."

John had been working in Washington for about two years when the NRA was regionalized. His boss called him in and said, "I've got openings all over the country, Seattle, San Francisco, you name it." He handed Justin a list of openings and said, "Take your pick."

There was an opening in Dallas for a clerical worker, and Justin took it. He was ready to come home to Texas. He rented a room in a boarding-house just off Oak Lawn Avenue in Dallas. His stay there was uneventful except for one incident that has remained vivid in his memory over the years.

"One of the boarders was a very unusual woman," he recounted. "She was a name-dropper, always trying to impress the other boarders. People tried to avoid her, but you'd sit down at the table and she'd monopolize it. She had a full-length fur coat which was her pride and joy. She wore it all the time, even in warm weather. I really didn't think it was real fur. I suspected it might be rabbit or something.

"Anyway, one night we had this fire in the house. I woke up in the middle of the night and smelled smoke. I got out in the yard. Everybody did. There was smoke everywhere. There was a lot of heat but no big flames. It was a big old frame house, and it's a wonder that it didn't burn to the ground. The firemen got there and put out the fire, but they had to get two people out of the house who had been overcome by the smoke. There were no fatalities.

"But this woman was screaming and trying to get back in the house. Her fur coat was still in there. The firemen had to restrain her from going back into the house to get it. Finally, one of the firemen went in after it wearing a mask. When he came out with the coat, it had shrunk to something that would fit a doll. The woman was just distraught. I was never so sorry for anyone in my life."

Justin continued working in Dallas until the NRA was declared unconstitutional by the United States Supreme Court in 1935. That spelled the end of the agency and the end of Justin's tenure as a federal employee. It was no great blow since he was ready to come back home anyway. He had shown he could make it on his own. But his father still wasn't ready to offer him a job in the family business.

"My dad kept telling me that I ought to go to college," John, Jr., said. "He didn't believe in coeducational schools, so he wanted me to go to Texas A&M. But A&M just didn't appeal to me. I had a friend I had met in Washington, Jim Edgecomb, who had gone to Oklahoma A&M in Stillwater. Like all old grads, he wanted me to go to his school. Of course, the name A&M pleased my dad. So I went there for my freshman year. I did fairly well, but it was a long way up there, especially when I had to

hitchhike back and forth to Stillwater, which wasn't even on a main highway. And that year they had one of their coldest winters on record.

"I had pledged a fraternity, Kappa Sigma, and the fraternity house had
a screened-in sleeping porch, and we slept out there. Boy, it was cold. I
think it was the coldest winter they'd ever had in Stillwater. I nearly froze
to death. That's when I decided I wanted to come back home to Fort
Worth."

Justin attended Oklahoma A&M, now Oklahoma State University, for
one year and then transferred to Texas Christian University in Fort
Worth. There he renewed his acquaintance with a boyhood friend and
another budding entrepreneur, Charles D. Tandy, the founder of Tandy
Corporation, who would go on to make marketing history by building
Tandy's Radio Shack into the world's largest consumer electronics chain.

"I had known Charlie for a long time," Justin revealed. "We grew up
running into each other. Our fathers were kind of frugal with us, so
Charlie kept coming up with ideas for making some money. He was always
thinking. It was his idea for us to go into the ladies' belt business together. He said that with all the scrap leather that was available down at my
father's boot factory, we ought to be able to do something with it.

"So I got an old cutting block from the boot factory that they'd discarded. And I found an old sixteen-pound mallet that they used for cutting out leather. And we bought a die. It was kind of oblong-shaped with
the corners cut off and had four holes, two at each end. I'd bring all this
heavy scrap leather home from the boot factory, and we'd go out to my
garage on Lofton Terrace in Park Hill, not far from where Charles lived.
That was the first house that Dad bought.

"We worked in my garage. We'd start pounding that die with the sixteen-pound mallet, cutting out belts in the shapes we wanted. We'd place
the die on the piece of leather and pound on it. One of us would hit that
thing until our arm would just give out. Then the other guy would begin
to hit. If you didn't hit the die hard enough with the mallet, it wouldn't
cut through the leather and you'd have to hit it again. Charlie and I sometimes stayed in my garage damn near all night knocking those belts out,
particularly when we had orders. Charlie liked to work."

Justin and Tandy used an old burning needle to decorate the belts with
cattle brands from a book of brands they acquired somewhere. Later, they
developed designs of their own. They sold the belts to department and
specialty stores in downtown Fort Worth. Business was good in the
Depression year of 1937.

"We were getting a buck or two apiece for our belts and they were selling in the stores for around $4," Justin remembered. "Pretty soon, they got to be quite a fashion item around town. Women wore them as a sort of novelty-type thing, because the belts came without buckles. We'd put some strip leather through the holes at each end of the belt, and the women would just tie the belts in front instead of using a buckle.

"It was a nice little business while it lasted," Justin said. "The leather was free and the labor was free. We made a little money."

six

The romance of leather

In 1926, men's dress shoes were added to the Justin inventory to augment the line of men's work shoes instituted shortly before the move from Nocona. There was no problem as far as the plant was concerned. With a capacity of six hundred pairs a day, only about one-fourth that many were coming off the production line. Management had as its goal that total sales for the year would reach between sixty thousand and seventy thousand pairs of all kinds. Of this number, there would probably be ten thousand or twelve thousand western boots and fifteen thousand lace boots produced. Work shoes would account for the greatest number of pairs, however, even though the greatest value would continue to be in cowboy boots, whose average retail price of $20 far outstripped the other categories.

But the fact that work shoes were now coming off the Justin production line in greater volume than cowboy boots strongly confirmed the fact that H. J. Justin's faith in the future of the cowboy boot business was not shared by his sons. They had become increasingly concerned after their father's death over the company's dependence on a single product, cowboy boots, at a time when the cowboy was rapidly becoming an endangered species, even in the West.

Reluctantly, John, Sr., Earl and Sam concluded that a major change in their focus, from boots to shoes, was essential to the company's survival. Their decision was buttressed by the growing popularity of their work shoes and work boots, particularly lace-ups and drillers. Furthermore, at the time of the move to Fort Worth, there were no other shoe factories in the entire Southwest.

John, Jr., recalled his father's concern over the future of the cowboy boot business. "My dad always felt that the boot business was an obsolete business, a dying business," he said. "He felt that with automobiles and sidewalks, people wouldn't need boots any more. He just sort of felt that boots were a lost cause. So they began playing down the cowboy boot side of the business and they began concentrating on work boots and on making shoes."

Along with work boots, Justin also moved into the production of a cowboy shoe called "The Dogie," which it advertised as "a shoe for men who like the feel and comfort of the cowboy last and heel." The Justins also began turning out military boots and fancy riding boots. The company also produced a line of English riding boots which ranged in price from $20 to $28 and were available directly from the factory.

But, whether they liked it or not, the Justin name still remained synonymous with cowboys and continued to conjure up memories of the Old West, as was demonstrated by a column by John Sorrells in the *Fort Worth Press* on April 30, 1928.

. . . . There is something typically Texan about these boots . . . something that seems to catch and hold the spirit of the old west and the men who followed its trails. One can take a pair in his hand, and vision the man who will wear it . . . imagine the men who have worn them in the years gone by. One will be studded with silver conches, reared on a towering heel . . . and one can see the frontier dandy with that boot, a sheik of the roundup and the dance hall; a tall, lean youth with clinking spurs and bold eyes. There are other boots with plain stitching, some with flowered design, some with steers cut into the leather. But all give to the lonely man of the trail that same pride in personal appearance which the fancy vest or the spats will give to the man who treads the canyons of the great city. They wear these boots everywhere . . . everywhere that men are in the open, and are faced with the necessity of secure footing and protection. To old Mexico go the boots with silver conches and elaborate stitching; in Canada, the Mounted Police wear them; in Cuba,they are worn, and Sandino the Nicaraguan probably has a pair on his feet. The burning sands of India crumple into flaky bits under the heavy sole of these boots, and in South America the vaqueros ride the pampas with their feet in boot leather from Fort Worth. . . .

There's an old book out at the Justin plant. And from this book they catch the romance of the thing which they are doing. It is an old order book that H. J. Justin had years ago. Its leaves are yellowed and some of the writing is faded. But it tells a story. It's one facet of the history of the Lone Star

State. One order may give a little something of the history of the man who wants them . . . he has settled on a little plot now, and expects to have his wife and family out from Iowa next year . . . Another may tell about the arrival of a son and heir with his order . . . another of a long trek with covered wagon to the little valley where he stops and builds his home. The cattle thief dies with a rope around his neck . . . and his feet in Justin boots. And the posse which strung him followed him with Justin boots thumping against the stirrup strap. If your business ever palls on you, and there seems nothing in it but a routine of invoices and bills of lading and statistics, go out and let Earl Justin tell you about the boot business. You'll go back and see your own business with a different eye. For if Earl can breathe romance into a piece of leather and some wax thread, there are infinite possibilities in every other line of endeavor.

In 1926, the first full year of operations in Fort Worth, sales were high, but expenses incurred as a result of the move from Nocona had taken their toll on the bottom line, resulting in a net loss for the year. The following year, with sales up appreciably, operations had returned to the black. In 1928, with sales topping $300,000 for the first time and net income at an all-time high, the future looked rosier than ever.

As the final year of the "Roaring Twenties" began, optimism continued to abound from Wall Street to Main Street. People played the stock market with the reckless abandon of a crapshooter on a hot streak. Stories of millionaires being made overnight fueled the fire. "I should have known that things had gotten out of hand," one former speculator would later sigh retrospectively, "when I began buying stocks on tips from my shoeshine boy."

As new record highs became daily phenomena on Wall Street, as the market manipulators worked their legerdemain, and small investors continued to commit their life's savings to buying stocks on margin, there were occasional notes of warning. But no one really listened. People much preferred Herbert Hoover's optimistic vision of the future, as exemplified by the slogan that had helped him soundly thrash Governor Al Smith of New York in the 1928 presidential election: "A chicken in every pot and a car in every garage."

This was the setting as H. J. Justin & Sons prepared to celebrate its fiftieth anniversary in 1929. In observance of the event, the company published an elaborate mailing piece aimed at its oldest and staunchest customer, and featuring a boot called "The Longhorn," with a black calf vamp and a hand-stamped upper that featured a cowboy riding a bucking bronco on one side and astride a Longhorn steer on the other side. At the top front was the head of a Longhorn embossed in natural color steer leather on a black background. The boot carried a price tag of $60 a pair, a premium price for a pair of boots at the time.

"The Longhorn" sold briskly after its introduction in early 1929. But in the Great Depression that followed the stock market crash on "Black Thursday," October 29, 1929, $60 cowboy boots were destined to go the way of other extravangances. In 1929, Justin sales hit an all-time high and net income set another record. The company was riding tall in the saddle. The fact that Wall Street had laid an egg had failed to dampen the Justins' outlook. They told themselves that even in bad times, people still needed to wear something on their feet.

The crash caught the Justins in the middle of an expansion program. Banks of new shoe-making machinery had been installed in the South Lake Street factory, necessitating an expansion into the adjoining building and the hiring of additional workers as production began on a new line of dress and casual shoes known as the Justin "Easy Walkers."

The Justins' intent was to go into direct competition with Florsheim, Jarman and other established names in the shoe business. The new line, which made its debut in time for the spring and summer selling season in 1930, even included golf shoes, a product it is doubtful H. J. Justin had ever seen, much less deigned to make.

The Justin golf shoe never became de rigeur at country club pro shops and eventually vanished from the scene during the depths of the Depression, when a hole in one's sole—rather than a pair of cleats—became a symbol of the times. Years after the disappearance of the golf shoe, the ill-fated venture had a successful offshoot involving Governor Dan Thornton of Colorado, a transplanted Texan. The result was a publicity bonanza for Justin boots in the lucrative Rocky Mountain market.

Governor Thornton made an appearance at a Justin sales meeting in Denver in January 1954. John Justin, Jr., had written Thornton advising him of the Denver meeting and inviting him to drop by and deliver a few welcoming remarks, if his schedule permitted. Justin had received no reply to his letter and had written off the governor's presence on the program. "I'll have to admit," he said, "that I was a little surprised that I hadn't even gotten an answer to my invitation. Anyway, I had just opened the meeting and was standing at the podium, when the door to the room burst open and the governor appeared. I recognized him right away. Well, he strode up to the front of the room and greeted me like a long-lost brother, 'John, it's great to see you. How's your father?' Then he asked me if it would be all right for him to say a few words. I said, 'Sure.' And he proceeded to make a fifteen-minute speech about the heritage of Justin boots and how it represented the American free enterprise system at its very best. Man, he couldn't have said it any better if we'd had a speech written for him. All of our people were absolutely bowled over.

"Then he told how he always wore cowboy boots, even on formal occasions. 'The only time I don't wear boots,' he said, 'is when I play golf.'" Upon Justin's return to Fort Worth, he contacted an aide to the governor who had accompanied his boss to the sales meeting and secured Thornton's shoe size. Justin then had the plant superintendent, Ruff Lemon, craft a pair of cleated cowboy boots for the Colorado governor.

The next step was to arrange a presentation ceremony. A date was set for a Saturday morning in July, when Thornton would be playing in his regular foursome at Cherry Hills Country Club in Denver.

"You be at the number ten tee at Cherry Hills at ten o'clock," Justin was told.

At the appointed time, Justin was waiting, boots in hand, when the governor arrived at the tee, having just completed the front nine. Trailing behind him was a melange of television news cameramen and assorted other radio and print media types to record the event. Thornton hammed it up for the cameras as he discarded his golf shoes and pulled on his new golf cowboy boots. He then strode to the tee and promptly hammered a 250-yard drive down the middle of the fairway.

"You've cured my slice," Thornton exulted to Justin. "I'll never wear a pair of golf shoes again."

The Justin "Easy Walkers" that began rolling off the assembly line in Fort Worth in the spring of 1930 were endowed with the traditional Justin quality, but they lacked one important ingredient—style, John, Jr., contended. "My father and my uncles made a wonderful shoe, quality-wise," he noted. "The Easy Walkers were as good as a $25 shoe of that era, as good as a J&M, a very fine shoe. But it had no styling, or 'snap,' as I call it, something to catch your eye. The shoes just didn't have that. So to sell them, they had to price them below their competitors. They were selling them to their customers, the retailers, for three and a quarter a pair, so that the retailers could sell them to the public at $5 a pair. But it was costing them four and a quarter a pair to make them. So they were losing a dollar on every pair of shoes they sold."

On the other hand, cowboy boot operations continued to be profitable, and cowboy boot sales held steady right through the Depression years. As unemployment reached twenty-five percent of the nation's work force, not a single employee of H. J. Justin & Sons left the payroll. "In the early '30s, when times really got bad, we operated the plant three days a week in order to give the employees something to eat on," John Justin, Sr., recalled in newspaper interviews. In January 1932, H. J. Justin & Sons began publishing a house organ for its salesmen, entitled "Boot Filosophy," that attempted to buoy up the sagging spirits of the men in the field and offer them advice on moving merchandise. The articles offer a rare insight into the struggle for survival that marked the Great Depression years.

One issue discussed was the craze for volume, even without profit, a craze that afflicted many executives and was closing the doors of more business houses than ever in the annals of American history. Justin wanted its salesmen to see their mission as, at least in part, helping customers realize the importance of profit. Price cutters, the article said, constantly hammer and chisel for lower prices. Factories then cut quality, cut this and cut that and were finally forced to cut wages.

Another article noted that salesmen for tire manufacturers talked to their customers on a basis of replacement and were smart enough to get a lot of newspaper publicity on the subject. "What about the replacement of worn boots and shoes?" the article asked.

Still another issue discussed was complaints received over a twelve-pair lot deal on cowboy boots to combat chain store competition. The senior Justin fired back this salvo: "A dozen pairs of these boots cost but $82.20, no more than a dozen pairs of high-priced dress shoes, and there are lots of dress shoes costing much more. If a buyer is really a buyer, he should buy, at the outset, at least twenty-four pairs, and better still, thirty pairs. That is only $200 worth of boots. This way he can get three and four pairs of a size in his best sizes and when his stock runs down to twelve or fifteen pairs, he will still have sizes and can conveniently order twelve additional pairs and get the benefit of the special price on this lot."

Pussyfooting at the beginning never got a salesman anywhere, according to Justin. But the company was trying hard to help both its employees and its factory personnel through the hard times . . . and at the same time, keep its head above water.

seven

A break with the family business

As the Depression persisted, despite the seemingly endless parade of alphabet agency panaceas that emanated from the White House, H. J. Justin & Sons managed to keep its head above the waters that were engulfing so many other business enterprises. Astoundingly, in 1934, the company actually began to experience an upturn in cowboy boot sales. Behind this totally unexpected but exceedingly welcome development was a new phenomenon—the emergence of dude ranching—that created new cadres of customers for western wear.

The dude ranch was an outgrowth of the hard times that had assailed the cattle business. No one knows for certain which hard-pressed cattle baron originated the idea of offering eastern dudes an opportunity to experience life on the range—for a price, of course. But the idea caught on.

By dictionary definition, a "dude" is a person "excessively concerned with his clothes, grooming and manners." A second choice identifies him as an individual "raised in a large city." The emergence of the dude ranch in the mid-1930s created a third definition: "a person vacationing on a ranch."

Some of the comedians of the era had another, more pointed definition—"a dude is a $50,000-a-year executive who lets a $50-a-month wrangler boss him around." Despite the fact that all of the definitions seemed to identify dudes in the masculine gender, many women actually patronized the dude ranches that sprang up throughout the West.

Women, as well as men, it appeared could find fulfillment and recreation participating in roundups, trail riding, cookouts, and sleeping beneath the light of western stars.

To the ranch hands, the sight of dudes of both sexes paying good money to rough it on the range was little short of hilarious. But to the Justins and other purveyors of western garb, hats and footwear, the new craze was serious business and as welcome as a refreshing spring rain in West Texas.

The advent of the dude ranching phenomenon motivated the Justins to create a new line of cowboy boots specifically for women. It was a move that would continue to pay dividends over the years. Women, up to that time, had been obliged to satisfy their desire to own a pair of cowboy boots by buying men's boots—provided, of course, that they were available in the smaller sizes most women required. But, although the boots might have fit properly, most women still found them too heavy and too ungainly for real comfort. An untapped market for women's boots was waiting to be filled.

H. N. (Bert) Fisch, the Justin sales manager, recalled how he became interested in the development of a woman's boot after encountering a line of boots with lightweight soles during a western trip in 1934. "I came across these women's boots that were being made with the outsole stapled to the insole, thus eliminating the thickness of the welt.

"When I got back to Fort Worth," Fisch continued, "I contacted the United Shoe Machinery Corporation. They told me they could show us how we could make extremely lighweight welt boots that would be far more satisfactory than the ones I had seen. Our lightweight women's boots were the result of these trials."

The Justins also approached Krentler Brothers, a leading last-fabricating firm, about developing a last or form to shape the woman's boot. Orders were placed for the last in November 1934, and the new product line went into production soon after that.

The first woman's boot, called the "Western Gypsy," not only was light on the foot but also featured a top that provided the wearer with a glove-like feeling. The "Western Gypsy" was an instant hit. Although only a lightweight, it soon became a heavyweight in the marketplace.

And a growing marketplace it was. Cowboy boots, once relegated to the same category of obsolescence as the buggy whip, not only refused to fade away, but were making a comeback. By the late 1930s, the rebound in sales that had begun in 1934 was manifesting itself throughout the entire Justin cowboy boot line, as more and more people discovered that a well-fitted pair of cowboy boots could be as comfortable as a pair of soft bedroom slippers and offered sturdy arch support, firm footing and ankle and leg protection.

Although Texas continued to remain the Justins' largest dollar-volume state, large numbers of Justin boots were being shipped to all forty-eight states and abroad to Australia, New Zealand, France, Switzerland, Italy and Canada.

H. J. Justin's original customers, the hard-working, hard-riding, gun-toting denizens of the cattle ranges, would have found it difficult to believe that among the Justin clientele in 1939 was a New York City department store executive who not only wore his cowboy boots to the office every day but had a patent leather pair in his closet at home that he wore on formal occasions, plus a Galveston hotel owner whose wardrobe boasted an array of Justin boots in a wide range of colors from black to white, for wear with different-colored suits.

By 1939, the Justins were filling cowboy boot orders from a disparate group of customers that included a trackman on the Long Island Railroad, a sailor in San Diego, an Army Air Corps pilot in Maine, an airline captain in Chicago, a secretary in a bank in West Virginia, an electrician in Philadelphia, a housewife in Colorado, and a State Highway Department employee in Iowa who confided that the only time his feet didn't bother him was when he wore his Justin boots.

There seemed to be a universal truth lurking behind the comfort of a cowboy boot. Perhaps that was why the Justin files contained a number of laudatory letters from long-haul truck drivers, who swore to the therapeutic benefits of being well-shod in cowboy boots while spending long hours behind the wheel. Then there were celebrities who doted on their Justins, among them governors, congressmen, cabinet members and movie stars like Gene Autry, Wallace Beery, Leo Carillo, Bob Burns and Andy Devine. Will Rogers twirled his rope and offered his wisecracks about politicians' foibles while wearing a pair of fancy Justins. Paul Whiteman, the bandleader, avowed that his Justins were the most comfortable things he had ever put his feet into. And Amon Carter, the flamboyant Fort Worth newspaper publisher and Cowtown's number one civic booster, dusted off his Justins when he entertained visitors, ranging from heavyweight boxing champion Jack Dempsey to President Franklin D. Roosevelt, in his suite at the Fort Worth Club. FDR was a frequent visitor to Fort Worth by virtue of the fact his son, Elliott, had married a Fort Worth girl, Ruth Googins.

On March 7, 1939, the noted humorist, Irvin S. Cobb, wrote to the Justins from his home in Santa Monica, California, on his personal letter-head that featured a profile shot of the writer chomping on a cigar:

Gentlemen,

I have a complaint to enter. About three months ago you made for me, to order, a pair of boots at the behest of Mr. Jake Oshman of Houston, Texas, a place which the Honorable Amon Carter of your city would prob-ably describe as one of the more outlying suburbs of Fort Worth.

There is no fault to be found with the boots. They fit perfectly and they're so smart-looking I hate to take 'em off even for long enough to trim my toe-nails. The trouble is that the mere sight of them arouses the baser instincts of some of my friends in the moving picture set. Already Mr. Leo Carillo has made two deliberate attempts to abscond with my new boots and frequently I detect a look of low animal cunning in the envious eyes of that distinguished Arkansas cowboy, Mr. Bob Burns.

So, for fear of larceny, or earthquake, or such-like acts of God—and wicked men—I figure I'd better get me a second supply of your justly renowned output right away. This time I rather lean to the idea of a pair of brownish or tannish or reddish boots—whichever is the most stylish—adorned on the legs with a few fancy scallops or stitched scrollings in con-trasting colors. Then maybe I could wear your product to rodeos and so-called Wild West shows and not only enhance the landscape values but maybe deceive these Californians into thinking I was a real horseman. Of course I couldn't fool a horse but you probably know how gullible some peo-ple are, and especially native sons.

I assume you have on file my measurements. If so, please let me know what the price would be for the contemplated job? Incidentally you might also send along one of your catalogues or style sheets to guide me in select-ing the above-mentioned decorative effects. With my sincere compliments on the merits of your merchandise, I am,

Yours truly,
Irvin S. Cobb

P. S. Perhaps I should add that, under the present interpretation, a native son is anybody who's been out here long enough to see his trailer.

With business on the upswing and the general economic outlook appearing brighter than it had in nearly a decade, the Justins decided, in early 1939, the time was ripe to escape the cramped confines of the South

Lake Street plant. The company had been experiencing growing pains for several years and had flat run out of room for expansion. So when the opportunity presented itself to secure a favorable fifteen-year lease on a large two-story brick building at Hemphill and Daggett streets on the near South Side, the Justins jumped at it.

John Justin, Jr., recalled the new facility. "The building at Hemphill and Daggett, where the boot company plant still is located, had about 65,000 to seventy thousand square feet of sprinkled floor space. It had housed a big Exline-Reimers building. It was a pretty good building structurally, but it had some problems because of a WPA sewing room that had been in there. They'd sprayed the walls with calcimine paint and there were big sheets of that paint hanging down that had to be taken out." However, Justin added, the major problem that had to be overcome was replacing the floors.

"They were really in bad shape," Justin related. "But as part of the deal, my father and uncles got several carloads of factory maple from Canada, which in those days made the best kind of flooring. There was a railroad track ran directly behind the building. So they took out one of the tall windows at the rear of the building and parked the railroad cars right by that opening, laid boards down and carried in those carloads of maple flooring.

"They hired a guy named Simms who worked for the Chickasaw Lumber Company to put in the new floors. He took out the old floors, put down the screeds to which the maple was nailed, and put in the new maple flooring, polished it and waxed it. I still remember going in there and seeing that floor when it was finished. It was gorgeous. That factory maple is kind of an orange-yellow and it makes a beautiful floor.

"Then my father and uncles moved in the boot-and shoemaking equipment. In those days, they didn't have individual motors on each machine, as we do now. So, across the back and down one side of the plant, they had these big drive shafts that pulled the belts that worked the machines."

John, Jr., recounted the chain of events that eventually led to the purchase of the building by H. J. Justin & Sons in 1945, nine years before the expiration of the lease. "The building belonged to an insurance company, but the state legislature had passed a law that said insurance companies couldn't own any building except their own home office building. The way I understand it, some insurance companies had gotten into trouble and there had been some kind of fiasco or scandal. So all the insurance companies that owned buildings in Texas had to get rid of them on a time schedule.

"The Southland Life Insurance Company that owned the building wanted to sell it to my dad. He was always against owning property. But as the deadline for getting rid of the property got closer, the price the insurance company was asking came way down. So my dad and uncles finally bought the building for a very reasonable price. They paid something like $50,000, which was a lot less than the building was worth."

On October 16 and 17, 1939, in observance of the sixtieth anniversary of H. J. Justin & Sons, the Justins threw open the doors of their new home to show off the new facilities. One of the features of the evening open house was that the factory remained in full operation so that guests could see how boots and shoes were made, step by step.

Noticeably absent from the sixtieth anniversary celebration was John Justin, Jr., who was now a budding entrepreneur in his own right as a partner with W. D. Barton of Fort Worth in the Justin-Barton Belt Company. John, Jr., had left what he had considered to be a dead-end office job in the family boot factory a year earlier to go into business with Barton. He had financed the venture with a $1,500 bank loan, secured by several shares of H. J. Justin & Sons stock left to him by his grandmother.

John, Jr., had gone to work at the boot plant in late 1937 following the dissolution of the ladies' belt business he had operated out of his garage with Charles Tandy. "I had found myself staying up all night making belts in my garage and trying to go to TCU in the day," Justin recounted. "I simply wasn't getting my college work done. So I told Charlie I couldn't do that anymore. But I still needed to make some money, so I approached my father about a job in the plant. My dad was still not encouraging me to come into the family business. But when I told him how badly I wanted to work, he offered me a job making out work tickets. About that time, I also decided that I'd had all the schooling I wanted. What I really wanted to do was work. So I quit college and went to work full-time at the boot plant making out work tickets.

"In those days, the work tickets were made out manually. They were made of cardboard and were printed in a kind of yellowish tan. They carried little tags you could tear off for the different parts of the boots. The work ticket described the boot. It told what color it was, what stitch pattern it required, what kind of sole it had, and all of the different parts of the boot. You had to write in all of this information with a pen. Then there was the size scale. For example, if the order was for five pairs of boots, there would be one size 6, two of 6 1/2, or whatever. You'd write all of this in by hand. Today we do it with a computer. I did this for about a year, but

I didn't really feel I was doing anything important or getting any place. I got to where I could do the job in my sleep."

Justin was already disenchanted with his situation when something happened that led him to decide to seek opportunities elsewhere. Looking back from a perspective of more than half a century, Justin spoke feelingly about the incident that led him to leave the family business.

"In the factory," he related, "there was a machine called a 'lightning nailer,' which was used to nail the heels to the boots. The nails had to be hand-fed into the machine, and this job belonged to a woman who was really an expert at it. She worked with a big pan of nails. The nails had no heads on them, but one end was smaller than the other, and the nails had to be put in with the small end down. So to do the job fast, you had to put the nails in by feel. Not too many people could do that. It was a pretty tricky operation. I had often watched the woman doing it and had been impressed with her speed and dexterity.

"Well, one day the woman got sick and production in the plant came to standstill because nobody else could do the job. I was working in the office making out work orders, when I heard what had happened. So I went down in the plant. I was young, I was adept, and I felt I could put those nails in as fast as the woman could. So I went up to the foreman, a guy named Stephen Brady, and I told him I could do the job and get the factory running again. Figuring that he had nothing to lose, Mr. Brady let me try it. And I did the job. I got the production line running again. I did this for a week. I was feeling pretty good. After I finished in the plant, I would go back upstairs to the office at night and do my regular job making out work tickets.

"At the end of the week, Mr. Brady said to me, 'John, you've done a good job. I want to turn in your time. I think you ought to be paid for what you did.'

"I think the minimum wage then was about forty cents an hour, and I was making 10 cents an hour filling out work tickets. Anyway, Mr. Brady turned my time in.

"One of my uncles always took charge of the payroll, and when he saw the time sheet Mr. Brady had turned in for me, he tore it up right in front of me.

"He told me, 'You're being paid in the office. You can't be paid in the office and in the factory, too.'

"He didn't even say a word of thanks for what I'd done. That really discouraged me. There was never any encouragement for the things I wanted to do. That's when I decided to leave."

Justin had heard of a man named Barton in the belt business who might be interested in selling his company, which was located in the Ledger Building, an old building in a low-rent district at 5th and Calhoun streets downtown close to the building that housed the *Fort Worth Press*. So Justin went down to see Barton.

"I went in and here was this fine-looking man, very rotund, about 250 pounds and five foot six," Justin recalled. "He had on a neat apron like most leather workers wore in those days. He was at his workbench with a tablet in front of him doing some writing.

"I said, 'I'm looking for Mr. W. D. Barton.'

"He rose to his full height and said, 'I'm W. D. Barton.'

"I said, 'I'm John Justin. I've been wanting to meet you.'

"And he said, 'Oh, are you with Justin Boots?'

"I said, 'Yes, my father is in the boot business.'

"What can I do for you?"

"I told him, 'Well, I'm not happy in the boot business. I don't feel like I'm being given the right kind of opportunity. I'd like to get into some other type of business, and I wondered if you might be looking for a partner or want to sell this business?'

With that, Barton grabbed his head. Justin thought he was having a heart attack or a stroke and started to run around the other side of the workbench to help him. Barton finally caught his breath, and Justin asked him what had happened.

"He said, 'I can't believe this. Read what I've been writing on this tablet.'"

Barton handed the tablet to Justin. He had been composing a newspaper advertisement that read, "Wanted, young man to come into the belt business with an older man. . . ."

"Do you have any money?" Barton asked.

"Well, I really don't," Justin replied. "But I think I can get a little. What'll it take?"

"As much as you can get," Barton responded. "If we can buy a little leather, I think we can make a success out of this."

"Mr. Barton had once been a wealthy man and quite well known," Justin related. "I say well known, because he had developed Barton's Dye and Shine during World War I, which had been a very successful boot and shoe polish. But he'd drilled an awful lot of dry holes in the oil business after that and had bought a lot of cotton whose price promptly went down, and he had lost all of his money. He was a very fine leather worker. His father had been a leather worker before him and had made the saddle that had won first prize at the Chicago World's Fair in 1932."

Barton was losing money in his belt business, Justin said, "because he was making belts worth $10 and selling them for $1. By the time we joined forces, he didn't have any money or leather."

Justin's first stop after leaving Barton's office was at the Continental National Bank, where he approached Clarence Burke, a vice president and loan officer, about borrowing some money. "My grandmother had given me a few shares of Justin stock, and Mr. Burke told me he'd let me have $1,500 if I pledged my stock," Justin related. "So we were in business. Our official starting date was October 5, 1938. I was twenty-one years old."

With a little money in the bank, Justin and Barton drove to Dallas to buy some leather from a firm that Barton had done business with in the past. After selecting a quantity of leather, Justin was called to one side by the owner of the leather firm. "I can't sell you any leather," the man declared.

"Why?" a stunned Justin asked.

"Barton owes us $300."

"Will you take a check?" Justin demanded, whipping out his brand new checkbook.

"When Mr. Barton saw what was happening, he protested," Justin continued. "He said he didn't want me paying off his old debts. But I told him we were partners now and were in this together. So we took the leather back to Fort Worth and began making belts."

The Justin-Barton Belt Company line initially consisted of four styles of belts, which were tooled on old-fashioned hand-cranked embossing machines, originally built for embossing saddles. "All you had to do was wet the leather and turn the crank," Justin said, "and I could do that in my sleep. Slowly we made and modified our equipment until we had a pretty good shop put together."

The original shop was in a small workroom next to the office where Justin had first met Barton. Justin recalled the old hand-operated elevator in the Ledger Building. "It had a long rope that you really had to pull on to move the elevator."

After the business began to grow, the firm occupied two-thirds of the building. Justin quickly immersed himself in the sales end of the business. His first step was to enlist the services of Jack Hamilton and Bill Justin and other H. J. Justin and Sons boot salesmen to carry his line of belts. "I talked to my dad and uncles about it, and they agreed it was a pretty good idea. They saw it as a way for their salesmen, who were having a hard time during the Depression, to make some extra money. We paid them a ten percent commission. My cousin Bill Justin's first commission check was $15. So he gave the check to his wife, Eulala, and promised her he'd let her have all of his belt commissions. Pretty soon, after he began getting bigger checks from us, he decided that wasn't such a good idea. He told Eulala, 'Honey, you don't need that much money.'

"Bill and Jack thought they were doing me a favor," Justin added. "But, of course, they were making money at it, too."

As the company began to grow, Justin felt a sense of pride. "Neither my dad nor my grandfather had ever made belts," he explained. "I was succeeding at something new in my own right."

From the very beginning, the business exceeded Justin's expectations. "On October 5, 1938, when we began the business, we took an inventory," he reported. "And when I calculated everything up at the end of the year on December 31, we really hadn't made that much money. We made a profit of $8,000. But that was a lot to me. Before long, we were selling our belts all over the country and began making some really good money."

John, Jr., recalled an automobile trip he took with his parents during that period. "My mother and dad were going to take a vacation, and they invited me to go with them. My dad's idea of a vacation was to get in the car and drive as far as you could in a day, check into a motel, spend the night, and then drive as far as you could the next day. Of course, I did the driving. So we drove all the way to Cheyenne, Wyoming, where they were having the Frontier Days.

"Well, I had loaded some samples of my belts in the car. When we got to Cheyenne, my dad promised he'd let us spend a day there. So I went around to some of the stores with my samples and I sold belts like you wouldn't believe. In those days, an order for a dozen belts was a good sale. I'd go into a store, and they'd never seen belts like these. And these merchants would order twenty dozen of this and twenty dozen of that. I could hardly wait to get home and get those belts into production so we could ship them."

One of the Justin-Barton Belt Company's best-sellers was a man's belt they called the "Ranger."

"We considered it a generic name," Justin said. "It was a belt that tapered to a billet and was made for an overlay buckle. Well, we were selling them pretty good when we received a letter from Carl C. Welhausen, the head of Tex-Tan of Yoakum, a leading western leather goods company, informing us that we had no right to use the Ranger name and asking us to cease and desist. I talked to a leading patent attorney who said it was perfectly okay. So I went down to see Mr. Welhausen. He saw this kid and he really lit into me.

"Finally, I said, 'Mr. Welhausen, we may have a difference of opinion on this matter. My attorney says I can use the name. But why can't we be gentlemen about it. After all, I came down here to see you and I'm a guest in your home, so to speak.'

"He looked at me for a moment and then began to smile. "'You're right,' he said. 'Forget it.'

Justin-Barton made a quality product, John, Jr., said. "We began using a tannery in Asheville, North Carolina, that gave us excellent leather. I bet some of those belts we made are still being used."

The belt company also helped Justin establish himself as a businessman who met his obligations. After paying off his first loan at the Continental National Bank, he began borrowing additional funds from the bank to build more inventory, and again met his repayment schedule promptly. Before long, other major downtown banks, always on the lookout for new borrowing customers with growing checking account balances, were courting his business. One of those bankers was O. P. (Huck) Newberry, a vice president of the Fort Worth National Bank, the city's largest.

"If you ever find yourself needing help, let me know," Newberry told John, Jr.

Justin didn't realize it at the time, but several years later when the opportunity would present itself for him to acquire control of the family boot business, he would call in that pledge.

But first would come a three-year interlude at sea aboard liberty ships dodging German U-boat torpedoes in the North Atlantic as an officer in the U. S. Merchant Marine during World War II.

eight

Action in the North Atlantic

When the bombs began falling on Pearl Harbor on the Sunday morning of December 7, 1941, John Justin, Jr., was engrossed in building his belt business. At age twenty-four, he was now the sole proprietor of the Justin Belt Company, having bought out W. D. Barton's interest.

A licensed pilot who had learned to fly before the war, Justin looked forward to serving in the Army Air Corps, which was badly in need of pilots. "I wanted to go into the Air Transport Command," he said. "I'd always wanted to fly heavy equipment, so I went down to the recruiting office. They told me to report back in two weeks to sign up for the Air Transport Command."

Two weeks later, Justin returned, ready to sign the papers. But when he looked at the form, he was shocked to see there was no mention of the Air Transport Command. When he asked what was going on, he was informed that the quota for the Air Transport Command had already been filled and that he was slated to become a primary flight training instructor. Justin was devastated by the news.

"First of all," he said, "I knew that becoming an instructor wouldn't fit me at all. I knew that I was simply not cut out to be an instructor. Furthermore, I wasn't qualified to be an instructor. I'd have to go to instructors' school to become one. But most of all, I simply didn't want to become an instructor. But I needed to do something quickly because my draft board had informed me that my extension was up. I had a friend who was in the Merchant Marines, and he signed me up for the Merchant Marines."

Justin's friend in the Merchant Marines was working closely at the time with the United States Coast Guard, which had a recruiting office in Dallas. "The Coast Guard's mission was to provide the officers for the huge number of liberty ships that were being built," Justin related. "We'd get a call from Washington telling us how many guys they needed for deck school and how many they needed for engineering school. Our job was to process these applicants, get them their physicals, get them on the train and send them on. Eventually, our district expanded to where we had offices in San Antonio, Houston, El Paso and New Orleans."

It didn't take Justin long to become bored with the sameness of the office routine. As his monotony increased so did his desire to do what he had originally signed up with the Merchant Marines for—go to sea. "Certainly, I missed the challenges of running my business, but most of all I got really tired of what I was doing," Justin recounted. "So I told the Coast Guard that I would like to go to sea. They asked me what I was qualified to do—and I said that I was a businessman. That was all I'd ever done.

"They told me, 'You ought to be a purser. Every ship has got to have a purser.' So I took the purser test," Justin reported, "and it turned out that I qualified for a chief purser's license."

He was commissioned an ensign in the U. S. Merchant Marines and received orders to report for active duty on June 19, 1942, as the chief purser aboard a ship named the *Will R. Wood*, berthed in Galveston.

Justin now faced the problem of what to do about his belt company while he was away at sea. "I had a good business going and I didn't want to see it shut down because I was going into the service," he said. "I began looking for a manager to take over while I was away, but there was no one I found that I felt could fill the bill."

Finally, with his reporting date coming closer, Justin made a decision. He asked his mother to manage the business in his absence. Her initial reaction was negative, and Justin had to engage in some high-powered persuasion before she finally agreed to take the job until a more suitable manager could be found.

"She had some real understandable doubts about being able to run a business," Justin recalled. "It was something she knew very little about other than what she might have picked up from conversations with my dad about the boot company's problems over the years. But she also felt a loyalty to me that enabled me to convince her to take on the job."

As it turned out, a more suitable manager never materialized and Mrs.

Justin operated the Justin Belt Company until John, Jr.'s, return home at the war's end.

On June 19, 1942, Ensign John Justin, Jr., reported for active duty. "The *William R. Wood* was one of the older liberty ships," he recalled. His job as chief purser was to take care of the ship's payroll, sign the crew on and off, order supplies, and handle the ship's papers. Justin had never been to sea before. His introduction to life on the briny deep was less than auspicious.

"We shipped out of Galveston with a load of military equipment bound for England," Justin remembered, "and on our first day out we ran into a terrible hurricane that almost sank the ship. They didn't have the weather reports that we have today and the storm caught us totally unawares. It got so bad that we had to cut loose some Sherman tanks that we had on deck. They're still at the bottom of the Gulf of Mexico. We lost all of our lifeboats. We finally were able to get into Dry Tortuga, which is down below Key West, to get some emergency fittings. From there, we went up the Atlantic Coast to New York, hugging the coast as closely as we could because there were German submarines out there sinking ships every day off the eastern coastline.

"We finally got to New York and they put us in a yard up there. They put new lifeboats aboard to replace the ones that had been smashed or washed overboard and reprovisioned the ship and reloaded it. We'd lost all of our deck load. From there we went out in a convoy, with our destination England.

"Those liberty ships just wallowed along," Justin continued. "We were in a four-knot convoy. We had seaplanes over us, Navy PBYs, for part of the way and we had destroyers escorting us. Still, the Germans sank an awful lot of our ships. It wasn't pretty to watch, to see a torpedoed ship disintegrate before your eyes." Justin spent the next three years aboard a succession of liberty ships going back and forth across the North Atlantic. "It wasn't much fun," he asserted. "Shipboard life was a never-changing, on-duty and off-duty thing."

Occasionally, however, the routine was punctuated by the threat of imminent disaster. Justin recalled one particular incident. "We had a new device called a streamer installed on our ship to intercept torpedoes fired at us by German submarines. The streamers, which were about the size of a fire hose in circumference, were attached to the side of the ship at the bow, two to a side. One streamer was up to fifty feet long and the other only slightly shorter, and each was filled with six hundred pounds of TNT.

Each streamer had a device attached to its end that kept it afloat and made it maneuverable.

"There was a Navy crew on board manning the sonar equipment. When a sonar operator detected a torpedo heading our way, he would arm one of the streamers on the side of the ship from which the torpedo was coming. The theory was that the streamer would intercept the torpedo and explode, crushing the torpedo's innards and sinking it before it could hit the ship. The sonar operator would also immediately arm the other streamer on that side of the ship because the German submarines always fired two torpedoes. So when the second torpedo headed towards us, the other streamer would hopefully be ready to intercept it and sink it. As soon as both streamers exploded, the captain would begin turning the ship around so that we would be able to utilize the two streamers on the other side of the vessel in the event we were attacked again.

"One night, it must have been about two o'clock in the morning, we were out in the middle of the North Atlantic headed for England when we were attacked by a German submarine that launched two torpedoes at us. We never knew for certain what actually happened. But, somehow, the noses of the German torpedoes got tangled up with the streamers and floated perilously close to the ship. When the streamers went off, the torpedoes also went off. So we had twelve hundred pounds of TNT from the streamers, plus two torpedoes, exploding right off the side of the ship. The explosion crippled the ship so badly it almost keeled over.

"The hull was badly damaged and leaking. The explosion was so severe that the ship's big steel shaft was literally tied into a bow knot. The boilers were knocked out. We were sinking."

The heroics of the chief engineer saved the ship. He went below in the pitch darkness, with only a flashlight to help him see what he was doing. Somehow, he got one of the generators going, and that provided a little power. Other crew members then helped him get the pumps going that kept the ship afloat.

When it was touch-and-go as to whether the ship would survive, Justin was on the bridge with the captain. Prior to that, he had opened the ship's safe and placed its code books, other important papers and the cash aboard the vessel in a metal box. "The box had holes in it so that it would sink if thrown overboard," Justin said. "My job was to throw it overboard, at the captain's order, to keep its contents from falling into the enemy's hands if we had to abandon ship."

Fortunately, that order never had to be given.

At dawn the following morning, Justin went up on deck and found that the convoy, of which his ship had been a part, had continued steaming towards England. "The convoy had to leave us behind. That was the rule," Justin recounted. "They couldn't jeopardize hundreds of ships to save one that was crippled and unable to keep up. They did leave a destroyer escort with us. But it later had to go on, and we found ourselves all alone in the middle of the North Atlantic."

The crew, under the direction of the chief engineer, somehow managed to get the shaft straightened out by pounding on it with sledgehammers, and the ship eventually was able to get up enough steam to limp along at two or three knots.

"We were sitting ducks for U-boats," Justin related, "but, fortunately, none bothered us."

When the ship finally limped into British waters, it was directed to Milford Haven, a British naval base near Cardiff, Wales, where it put in for repairs and refitting. The layover permitted Justin and the ship's captain to receive a taste of Welsh hospitality. Justin particularly recalled several days he and the captain spent in a nearby village called Cowbridge.

"We rode a little bus to get there," he recalled. "We stayed at a picturesque little inn. Everybody in the village wanted to entertain us, to buy us a drink. No Americans had ever visited there before."

When the repairs to the ship were completed, Justin headed out into another adventure. This time, the ship sailed into the mine-infested waters of the English Channel, off the English coast. "It was a pitch-black night," Justin related. "We got a light challenge from shore that we answered properly, otherwise we'd have been blown out of the water. Then we got a signal: 'Cut engines immediately. Drop anchor,' to which we complied. The next morning, when the sun came up, we found ourselves completely surrounded by floating mines. There were so many mines out there just below the surface of the water that I could have walked all the way to shore by stepping on them."

Later that morning, a small boat carefully drew alongside Justin's ship and a pilot clambered aboard to navigate them into port. There they were loaded with bombs and received orders to proceed to Belgium and another harrowing experience.

"The bombs we were carrying were badly needed for bombing the German positions in France," Justin said. "When we got to Belgium, they had us steam into shallow river waters until we finally ran aground right next to where the Allies had built a runway. The planes were able to land right alongside our ship and load up with bombs. We were able to get rid of our entire cargo of bombs that way."

When the war in Europe ended with Germany's surrender in 1945, Justin found himself back in Galveston with a new assignment. "I'd been on liberty ships in the North Atlantic," he recalled. "Now I was assigned to a C2 tanker, which was really an elegant ship as far as the crew quarters were concerned. But it was a dangerous ship because it carried gasoline. We were going to sail out of Galveston and head for the Pacific through the Panama Canal. They told us we'd be gone for five years, no matter what."

The news had a chilling effect on Justin's morale. "I wasn't looking forward to being gone that long," he confessed. "On top of that, we kept hearing all these rumors about how the war with Japan would soon be over. I thought, 'If it's about over, I want to get back to my belt business. I sure don't want to be stuck in the South Pacific for five years.'

"Well, I sailed from Galveston aboard the tanker. We were about 150 miles into the Gulf of Mexico when we developed vibrations in the turbine that the chief engineer didn't like. So we turned around and went back to Galveston. I wanted to get off the ship, but they told me, 'No way, you're on to stay.' I pleaded, 'I've got no business in the South Pacific,' and they finally told me, 'If you can get someone qualified to take your place, we'll let you go.' Believe it or not, I found a guy who was qualified and who was willing to go to the South Pacific for an extended period. I was so elated and, yet, so fearful that something would go wrong that I immediately caught a bus from Galveston to Houston, where I checked into a hotel and spent the night. I was still very nervous that something would go wrong and they'd call me back. Then I got on the train in Houston the next morning and came to Fort Worth."

Justin didn't recognize the old place when he saw the belt factory for the first time upon his return. He found that a decidedly feminine touch had taken over the premises, and for good reason. The entire work force, with the exception of two boys, was made up of women, twenty-four in all. Nearly all had sons, brothers or husbands serving in the armed forces.

"We all got along fine together," Mrs. Justin was quoted in a *Star-Telegram* interview on July 10, 1945. "If we didn't, we couldn't have done what we did. We worked out a system under which we rotated on the various shop machines, so that the work wouldn't become monotonous and every employee could step into any phase of the operation. That gave me a better insight into labor problems. I'm proud of the fact that I never had to discharge a single employee."

The major significance of Mrs. Justin's feat of keeping her son's belt business afloat, of course, was that John, Jr., had a going enterprise to return to after the war. By 1950, with Justin Belt Company's sales reaching the $500,000 mark, he was positioned to take the steps that would lead to his assumption of the managerial reins of H. J. Justin & Sons.

When the war began, H. J. Justin & Sons' work force consisted of 160 people, of which a substantial number soon found themselves in uniform. Those who left were not replaced, since wartime production of boots and shoes for nonmilitary use was soon curtailed.

Early on, the Justin brothers made a decision not to pursue military orders, preferring that the company make its contribution to the war effort through its production of quality work shoes and boots for those employed in essential industries at home. Although military orders became only a small part of the company's sales volume, limited production of shoes for the armed forces in 1943 helped boost the company's sales past the $1 million mark for the first time. But as the shortage of leather increasingly impacted production, sales volumes declined in 1944 and again in 1945.

After the war, the company's promotional efforts with dealers continued to pay dividends. Nudie's of Hollywood, which billed itself as the "western outfitter to the stars," received nationwide publicity with a photograph of a coterie of its customers, Gene Autry, Roy Rogers, Rex Allen and Tex Williams, all sporting Justin boots.

Even President Harry S. Truman got into the act during the 1948 presidential campaign. While on a "whistle-stop" aboard his private train in Kearney, Nebraska, on Sunday, June 6, 1948, Truman was presented with a pair of Justin boots by the Kearney Junior Chamber of Commerce, courtesy of Claussens, the exclusive Justin dealer in Kearney.

"Now I can really ride herd on Congress," the president laughingly told the crowd. "You see, Grand Island gave me a pair of spurs on the way over here."

But of all of the postwar promotional activities, the one that impacted the company's sales and bottom line with the greatest effect stemmed from the square dance craze that swept the country in the late 1940s. Sam Justin, an avid square dancing aficionado, played a major role in the firm's tapping into the sales bonanza the craze created. Sam proposed to his brothers that Justin publish a "how-to" booklet on square dancing that would explain to the burgeoning ranks of would-be "do-si-doers" all they needed to know about the steps and the calls.

Called *Square Dancing Is Easy*, the booklet was noncommercial except for the copy on the back cover which stated, "You can dance all night and dance a little longer in easy-feeling Justin Boots." Initially distributed through Justin cowboy boot dealers across the country, the booklet was an instant hit. It was also perfectly timed.

Thousands of spectators watching others square dance yearned to get in on the fun. All they needed was to learn the steps. The Justin booklet provided the way to make participants, and cowboy boot wearers, out of spectators.

In the fall of 1948, Justin cautiously printed ten thousand booklets. The company sent a free copy with letter attached to about 2,000 of its retail dealers throughout the country, asking if they would like fifty free copies to be distributed to the stores' customers. About twenty-five percent of the dealers responded, and in two weeks the original supply of booklets was gone. Another 20,000 were printed and distributed to dealers at 5 cents per copy, or half the printing cost. Again the supply was quickly exhausted, with some dealers asking for up to one thousand copies. By the fall of 1949, more than one hundred thousand copies had been printed, with thousands more still to come as requests kept pouring in and the list of dealers expanded far beyond the original five hundred that initially climbed on the bandwagon.

nine

"I want to run this company"

October 5, 1950, should have been a normal workday at the Justin Belt Company. But a visitor arriving at the plant in downtown Fort Worth would have found the machines curiously silent and the long work tables startlingly clear of the normal accoutrements and paraphernalia of belt production. And in the place of the leathery odor that usually permeated the premises was the pungent, mouth-watering aroma of barbecued beef.

At the front door, a hand-lettered sign explained what was going on. The sign read, "Closed . . . Party in Progress." The Justin Belt Company was observing the twelfth anniversary of its humble beginning. At age thirty-three, John Justin, Jr., now the owner of a growing, profitable business with sales of $500,000, could be forgiven for throwing a party, even though participating cheerfully in the loss of a day's production was something of an anomaly for the hard-driving young entrepreneur.

The Justin Belt Company had come a long way from the spartan quarters it had initially occupied in the Ledger Building at 5th and Calhoun streets. It was now producing its lines of belts in a modern factory at 207 1/2 West 11th Street near the southern end of downtown. The company's offices and factory were on the second floor of the building above a restaurant, recalled Dorothy Morell, John, Jr.'s, longtime secretary, who began working for the Justin Belt Company in October 1948. She retired from Justin Industries in 1989.

"There were two other women employed in the office at that time, and we had a shipping manager and a factory manager," Mrs. Morell remembered. "There were, maybe, two dozen people working in the factory. The factory wasn't large, but we did produce a lot of belts, all kinds of western belts for men and women and we also sold buckles to go with the belts.

"I think Mr. Justin was making money," she added, "but, mostly, he was trying to build the business, trying to expand by getting more customers. He worked very hard and put in long hours. He traveled with the salesmen an awful lot and he also did most of the leather buying."

Early on, Mrs. Morell learned that her boss had a sense of humor. "We had two customers located in different parts of the country who had the same name," she related. "One day a check came into the office from one of the customers and I credited it to the other company's account. The customer that had mailed us the check called in to complain after he received his next statement. Mr. Justin called me into his office and said to me very seriously that if something like that happened again, he would have to fire me. I was really upset. I began apologizing. Then he began to laugh and he said to me, 'As long as you're breathing, you're going to make mistakes. But we learn from them.'

"That's when I found out what kind of a person he was. He was an easy person to work for. His office was always open to people. He was never sarcastic and he never spoke harshly to any of the employees. If he criticized you, it was only with good reason. If he felt you were doing the best that you could, that was good enough for him."

The fall of 1950 was a heady time for John, Jr. "I was happy," he confided. "I was running my own company. I could go where I wanted to when I wanted to, do as I wanted to. Whatever I made was mine. The business was mine entirely. I didn't have to answer to anyone. I really had as good a life as I could want. We were selling a lot of belts, our manufacturing processes were good, and I was making good money doing it."

Still, he admitted, despite the success he was achieving with his own company, he continued to experience a discontent that he was unable to shake. Always tempering his euphoria over the progress of the Justin Belt Company was his unrequited desire, dating back to his early boyhood, to run the family boot business. The cowboy boot business pioneered by his grandfather stood grandly in his imagination, beckoning to him with irresistible appeal.

"All of my life," Justin confessed, "I had my heart set on running the boot company." He recalled an incident that occurred several years after the move of H. J. Justin & Sons to Fort Worth. "There was a place out south of town called Two Bucks," he related. "It was a kind of a nightclub, and the company had an employees' dinner out there as a kind of a reward for the reasonably good year the company had enjoyed. There were, maybe, fifty or sixty employees there with their wives and husbands.

"I was just a little kid then. I was sitting at the head table with my parents. My father and my uncles spoke and then my Grandmother Justin was introduced and she got up and spoke. While she was speaking to the group, I'll never forget this, she looked over at me and said, 'Now, John, Jr., what do you want to do when you grow up?' Well, it was a completely spontaneous thing on my part. I felt like an idiot after I'd done it. But I looked up at her and said with all seriousness, 'I want to run this company.'

"As you might expect, everybody just roared. They thought it was a pretty hilarious remark coming from a little kid. But I wasn't kidding. Going back as far as I can remember, running the company was what I wanted to do."

By 1950, however, John, Jr., had pretty much despaired of ever achieving his ambition. The disappointment he had experienced in his attempts to carve out a niche for himself in the family business had left him with scars he would always carry. Exacerbating Justin's frustration was the fact that from his vantage point as a member of the family and as a minority stockholder, he was fully aware that, because of a lack of a strong hand at the helm, H. J. Justin & Sons was floundering, losing ground in the marketplace.

The power vacuum in the company's top management was the result of years of internecine conflicts among the three Justin brothers. H. J. Justin, before his death, had never decreed a line of succession. The result sometimes bordered on chaos. From firsthand experience, John, Jr., knew all about the internal bickering and backbiting that had become a tradition in the boot company's executive office. Operations were frequently hamstrung as decisions were second-guessed and orders countermanded by one of the brothers.

"No one was in charge, no one had the final word," Justin related. "My father and uncles were always changing titles. One of them would be president for a while, then another one. And they were always arguing about something. Rhubarbs were common. They never seemed to agree on anything.

"If my dad decided they needed to buy some leather, Uncle Avis would say, 'We don't need any more leather.' So they would have to hold a directors' meeting to decide whether they needed to buy leather or not."

John, Jr., was not alone in his recognition of what was ailing the company. Over the years, Earl Justin had become increasingly concerned over the lack of direction at the top. He was convinced that the firm desperately needed strong new leadership. He stewed about the problem, while the situation continued to deteriorate, until he finally decided to take the bull by the horns. He had been watching the success that John, Jr., had achieved with his belt company and had come to the conclusion that John, Jr., had the potential to come in and take over the management of the company. In the late summer of 1950, Earl approached his nephew with a proposal.

"Uncle Earl came to me and poured his heart out," John, Jr., revealed. "He told me how badly things were going and he made this impassioned plea. He said, 'John, we really have to have some new blood. We really need somebody like you to take over and run the company.'

"Of course, that was what I wanted to hear, what I had always wanted to do," John, Jr., said. He was also fully aware of the pitfalls that faced him if he accepted the task. "I knew what Uncle Earl was asking me to do couldn't be done unless I had total authority, and I knew that wouldn't be easy to get. I wondered how my Uncle Avis would react to the idea. I knew that my father had never encouraged me about coming into the family business. My dad had always had mixed emotions about that, primarily because of his fears about the future of the cowboy boot business. He was really proud of how well I was doing on my own in the belt business. So I figured he'd take a backseat on the proposition.

"As for my Uncle Avis, he and his son, Joe, my first cousin who also worked for the boot company, always seemed to have a lot of other things to do rather than tend to business. They were very active in fraternal lodge work and spent a great deal of time on those activities. I frankly didn't know how they would react to my coming in and taking over. But I kind of had the feeling that they wouldn't jump with joy over the prospect.

"So I told Uncle Earl that I didn't want to get into the middle of a family squabble, that I was used to running my own business and that I would be interested in the job only if I was assured of having complete control.

"He told me, 'That's what I'm asking you to do.' He said to me, 'Would you draw up the conditions under which you'd come in and take over management of the boot company?'

"I told him I'd give it my best shot."

Justin's best shot, in a letter he addressed to the board of directors of H. J. Justin & Sons, was short, sweet and to the point. He told them that he wanted absolute authority in running the company, that the only way they could change anything he was doing was by a unanimous vote of the board. He told them he wanted a salary of $25,000 a year. He didn't ask for any options to buy stock. He was simply going to be hired to be general manager of the boot company.

Justin showed the letter to Earl.

"He loved it," Justin said. "He said to me, 'This is just great, John, Jr. Are you sure you want to do this?'

"I said, 'Under these terms, I'll do it. I'll come over here and give it the best I've got.'

"And he said, 'I'll get the board together. Will you present this to the board?'

"I said, 'Yes, with your backing.'

"He said, 'I'll back you 100 percent.'"

Several days later, Earl called John, Jr., to notify him that the board would convene in a special meeting to hear his proposal. The site of the meeting was Youngblood's Fried Chicken, a restaurant on Hemphill Street, not far from the boot factory.

"They had a little room off to one side of the main dining area," John, Jr., recounted. "Uncle Earl told me they had reserved the little room for the board meeting. So I went out there. When I arrived, I found Uncle Avis was already there. He had brought his son, Joe. This surprised me because Joe was not a board member and the meeting had been called for board members only. My father was there and Uncle Earl and Bert Fisch. We sat down, ordered some chicken and enjoyed the meal.

"Uncle Earl was serving as the chairman of the board then and he opened the meeting after we'd finished eating. He was very factual. He said, 'I think we've got to have some new blood in here. I want you to know that I've gone to John, Jr., and he has presented a proposition to me that I think is great and which I think we should accept. I'm going to ask him to read it to you.'"

Justin doesn't recall whether or not he handed out copies of his letter before he began reading it. But he does remember taking a sip of iced tea just prior to beginning his presentation. "I started reading the letter," he said, "and as I looked up for a moment, I could see dissatisfaction on my cousin Joe's face. Uncle Avis didn't look too happy, either.

"I had my points numbered and I read them off one by one. As soon as I finished, Uncle Avis started objecting. 'I don't know why we need this. We've got a good thing going. I don't know why we need anybody else in here.'

"They got into a big rhubarb about it, just as I had feared. I listened to it for a while, then I got up from my chair and said to Uncle Earl, 'I appreciate your asking me, but this is what I told you I didn't want to get into. Thank you and goodnight.'

"And I walked out of the room."

Justin still remembers the shocked looks on the faces of the men in the room as he stalked out of the chamber. The next day, Earl came to see John, Jr., at the belt company. "He was just crushed," Justin said. "But I told him my decision was irrevocable. So the deal fell through. I figured my chances of ever running the boot company had now evaporated."

Justin spoke candidly about his uncle who had sabotaged his proposal. "My Uncle Avis could be the sweetest, nicest guy in the world one minute, but the next minute he could be livid with anger. He was very hot-tempered. He could also be extremely negative at times, especially in his dealings with his fellow board members. He would periodically vote against whatever my father and Uncle Earl or Bert Fisch wanted to do. If they wanted to buy some new equipment, he'd be against buying it. If they wanted to make a new style of boot, he'd say it wasn't needed or wouldn't sell. He'd frequently get very emotional and say, 'I want to get out of here. Buy my stock. This place is killing me. It's absolutely killing me.' And he was right. It really was killing him."

After these outbursts, the other members of the board would see about raising the money to buy Avis' stock. But when they told him they were prepared to buy him out, he'd have done a complete flip-flop and accuse them of trying to force him out of the company. As fate would have it, however, Avis had one more change of heart in his system. Shortly after the ill-fated special board meeting, John, Jr., received a telephone call from Earl.

"Avis is extremely upset," Earl said. "He wants to sell his stock. Are you interested?"

"Yes, I am."

"Then I'd get down here right away."

"I'll be right there."

With that, Justin headed for the boot company. It was a short drive from the Justin Belt Company on the south end of downtown Fort Worth to the sprawling red brick boot factory at Hemphill and Daggett, and John, Jr., wasted no time getting there.

"Uncle Avis ran the shipping room then," Justin recalled. "He was responsible for taking the boots and sending them to the dealers. So I went into the shipping room and found him there sitting at his roll-top desk.

"I said, 'I understand you want to sell your stock.'

"And he said, 'I sure do. Do you know anybody that wants to buy it? This business is killing me. Everything is wrong.'

"I said, 'Do you really want to sell it?'

"He said, 'Yeah.'

"I asked him, 'How much do you want for it?'

"He gave me a figure of $150 per share."

John, Jr., knew that Avis was the owner of approximately 340 shares of Justin stock, making him the single largest stockholder in H. J. Justin & Sons. The next two largest shareholders were Earl Justin with 320 shares and John Justin, Sr., with 183 shares. At the time, John, Jr., owned 104 shares of Justin stock, which included eighty shares he had bought from his mother in 1947. The $150-per-share price would give the transaction a value of approximately $50,000.

"Buying Avis' stock wouldn't give me control of the company," Justin said, "but with the shares that I knew would vote with me from Uncle Earl and my father, we'd have a majority."

Raising the $50,000 was the key.

"That was a potful of money for me," Justin confided. Fortunately, he had an ace in the hole. When his Uncle Earl had approached him about coming into the boot company, Justin had discussed the situation with Huck Newberry, who was now his loan officer at the Fort Worth National Bank. Newberry had been impressed with his youthful customer's business acumen and, more importantly, his promptness in repaying loans on schedule. "Huck had always been very nice to me," John, Jr., said. "He had told me, 'Anytime you get a chance to buy any more Justin stock, I'll back you.'"

Buoyed by Newberry's promise, Justin responded to Avis' price quote: "If you really want to sell your stock," he said, "I'll take it."

"When do you want to do it?" Avis asked.

"There's no time like the present," Justin replied. "If we're going to do it, let's get on with it."

At this point, Avis mentioned that his wife, Leta, owned a few shares of Justin stock. "Do you want to buy it?" he asked.

"Sure, if she wants to sell it."

John, Jr., stood at Avis' desk as his uncle telephoned his wife. "Leta," he heard Avis say, "John, Jr., is gonna buy my stock in the company. Do you want to sell your stock with it?"

Aunt Leta's answer was a firm, "No."

This seemed to upset Uncle Avis because he said, "You ought to sell your stock, too. We need to get out of here. This place is killing me. Nothing's going right. It's just too much for me."

But he failed to convince her. She still said, "No."

Shrugging his shoulders, Avis hung up the telephone and told John, Jr., "I'll go down to the vault and get my stock certificates. I'll meet you back at Blanche's desk in a few minutes." Blanche was Blanche Lotspeich, the company's credit manager at the time.

John, Jr., walked back to her desk while Avis headed for the vault. "I said to her, 'Miss Blanche, Uncle Avis is going to sell me his stock.' And she asked me, 'Are you sure you want to buy it?' I told her, 'Yes, I'm sure. He says the business is killing him.'"

In a few minutes Avis returned, his hands full of stock certificates which he handed to Miss Lotspeich. "Add these up," Avis instructed her. She began running a tape on her adding machine while Avis began signing the backs of the stock certificates. When she finished, Miss Lotspeich reported that the stock certificates totaled 339.5 shares. She then multiplied the number of shares by $150. The total came to $50,925. She so informed John, Jr. Taking a check out of his pocket, John, Jr., wrote in the figure, signed it and handed the check to Avis.

"Miss Blanche then handed me the stock certificates and said, 'It's your stock,'" Justin recounted.

Justin now turned to Avis and extended his hand. "We shook hands and I said to him, 'Thank you, Uncle Avis.'

"And he said, 'I really appreciate this. This thing has been really killing me. . . .'"

Justin said, "Thank you," one more time. Then he walked over to his father's office to break the news to him. John, Sr., was working at his desk when John, Jr., entered his office. He greeted his son warmly and asked how things were going at the belt company. "What brings you to the factory in the middle of the day?" he asked.

John, Jr.'s reply to his question nearly knocked him out of his chair. "I've just bought out Uncle Avis."

"You what?"

"I've just bought Avis' stock. He's now out of the picture and I'm planning to take over the management of the boot company under the same terms that I proposed earlier. I hope you'll give me your support. I'm ready to go."

John, Sr., came around his desk and embraced his son. "We need you," he told him.

Justin knew there would be some strong repercussions to the news from some of the shareholders, especially his Aunt Enid Justin, whose Nocona Boot Company was now one of H. J. Justin & Sons' principal competitors. "I told my dad, 'All hell is gonna break loose when Aunt Enid finds out. She's not gonna like it.' My dad knew what I was talking about. Avis had been Enid's grapevine into the Justin Boot Company operations. She'd come down to Fort Worth and visit with him or he'd go up to Nocona to visit with her and he'd tell her everything that was going on, what every customer was doing, where we were getting the leather, what every customer was paying, what we were doing new. So I knew that the news about my buying Avis out was not going to be received with favor by my aunt."

John, Sr., was not inclined to disagree with John, Jr.'s assessment of the situation. He had long been perturbed over Avis' serving as a conduit of inside information about the boot company to their sister. But when he had complained to Avis about it, Avis' reaction had been to shrug his shoulders and deny he was giving away any really significant information.

After securing his father's blessings on his stock purchase, John, Jr., called Huck Newberry. "I just wrote a check to my Uncle Avis for $50 thousand," he told him.

"Fine," Newberry responded. "It's covered."

Justin asked Newberry about collateral. Newberry said the Justin stock certificates would suffice. "I'm going to leave town for a few days," Justin told the banker. "I want to be away from my office when the manure hits the fan."

"It can wait until you get back," Newberry told him. "Have a good time."

Justin went home, threw a few things into a bag and took off for Galveston. Each day he checked in with Dorothy Morell, who confirmed what he had suspected. Aunt Enid was, as John, Jr.' had predicted, beside herself over the news.

"She wanted me to sell Uncle Avis' stock back to him," Justin said. Uncle Avis' wife wanted me to sell back the stock. But Uncle Earl's daughters, Maureen and Ruth, told me, 'If you do that, it'll kill our daddy.'"

John, Jr., assured them they had nothing to worry about. He had no intention of selling back the stock. After Earl Justin's death in 1952, John, Jr., bought his 320-share interest in H. J. Justin & Sons, plus a small number of shares owned by Earl's family. This effectively gave him personal control of the company.

On November 3, 1950, John Justin, Jr., was officially named vice president and general manager of H. J. Justin & Sons, Inc. The little boy who had once told his grandmother that his life's ambition was to run the boot company founded by his grandfather had finally achieved his goal. Now he faced the task of turning the struggling enterprise around.

ten

Young man in a hurry

If there was any doubt that there was a young man in a hurry at the controls of H. J. Justin & Sons, it was quickly dispelled. The thirty-three-year-old new vice president and general manager hurtled into his new responsibilities like a tornado roaring across the Red River into Nocona.

"I was impatient," Justin conceded. "Instead of doing it gradually and slowly, I wanted to do it all at one time. I was putting in new styles and doing things that had to be done, and it all cost a lot of money. And we were not capitalized that well. We didn't have much money. We skated on thin ice for a long time.

"Fortunately, Huck Newberry believed in me. He'd loan me the money. Once or twice we overextended ourselves, borrowed more money than we should have borrowed, stretched ourselves pretty thin. If we'd had some mishap or something, we'd probably have been in real trouble financially. But it had to be done and the quicker we did it, the better. So we kept going, making more boots, making more profitable boots, getting a better place in the boot industry.

"By that time, some of our competitors had gotten ahead of us, making more boots, making more popular boots, doing a better job than we were doing. So we were really playing catch-up, and that's a pretty tough way to play.

"When I got in there," Justin recounted, "I knew that if we were going to turn things around, we were going to have to do it in cowboy boots. It was just not going to be in shoes. People just didn't think of us as shoe people. You build your reputation on what you do best. And we'd built our reputation on our boots. But my father and my uncles were so convinced that the boot business was dying that they had begun concentrating on the shoe business.

"They were making a straight-last shoe, which is a shoe for old people. It's always made with soft leather. They had bought the equipment to make the straight-last shoes—the dies, patterns and lasts—from a company in Beloit, Wisconsin, that had gone out of business. So they started making these straight-last shoes. They were made out of two grades of leather, a high-grade kangaroo and lower-priced kidskin, a cheaper shoe. Both leathers were very soft and very easy on your feet, very comfortable—an old man's kind of shoe.

"Then they decided to go into dress shoes and compete against Florsheim and Walkover. They put in some additional equipment to make wing tips and square tips and things like that. These were excellent shoes, but they just didn't have any style.

"The first thing I did after taking over was to make a study of our cost figures. I was shocked to learn that we were losing $1.25 on every pair of shoes we sold. You didn't have to be a Harvard MBA to figure out that we just couldn't keep on doing that. They were making money in the boot business, but they were shoveling it all over to make those shoes.

"I talked to my dad about our doing away with shoe production," Justin continued, "but he remained adamant. He said, 'Oh, no, we can't do that. Shoes are our future.'"

Shortly after that conversation, Justin decided there was no longer any time for further equivocation. It was now or never. "One of the problems in those days," he recounted, "was that we had to lay off people during slow periods. They'd work two or three days a week. It was hard to keep your good people, your well-trained guys under those circumstances. So I was always looking for something for them to do in order to keep them on the payroll."

Late on a Friday afternoon during a slow period, Justin called a crew of his best workers together and informed them he had a job for them in the plant the next morning. He told them he wanted them at the plant at five o'clock ready to go to work on a special project. When the men arrived, they found that Justin had tied white ribbons on all of the machines involved in shoe production. Then, arming the men with crowbars and other similar type implements, he turned them loose on the beribboned machinery.

Shaking his head as he recalled the scene, Justin said, "My dad was always an early riser and he'd always go to the post office to get the mail and then come to the factory. He did this every day including Saturdays, and when he came into the building on the way to his office on this particular Saturday morning, he heard this infernal racket in the plant. He came running back there and when he saw what was happening, he just went berserk.

"He began yelling, 'What in the blankety-blank is going on?'

"I told him, 'I'm getting rid of the shoe equipment. We're going to stop making shoes.'

"I was scared to death he was going to have a stroke. He began yelling at the workmen, 'Put that stuff back, put it right back where it was.'

"But before I'd taken the job as general manager, I'd made it clear that I was going to have the final word, that I was going to do what I wanted to do. Very calmly, I explained this to my dad. I finally quieted him down and got him out of the factory and up to his office. I sat him down at his desk, and I explained to him what was going on and why I was doing it. He was still in complete disagreement, but he finally settled down and accepted the inevitable.

"So, as of that day, in early 1951, we quit making shoes. We sold the shoes we had on hand, got rid of them every way we could. We still continued to get orders that dribbled in, but they didn't amount to much. We had all these little dealers out in West Texas who bought our shoes, and they'd call in an order, and we'd have to run down to the bus station and put them on the bus to ship them out there. The whole order usually was, maybe, one pair.

"We also did away with cavalry boots, English riding boots, and all of the various boot lines other than cowboy boots," Justin added. "After closing down those lines, we had $1 million worth of old forms and dies and equipment that we had to get rid of as best as we could for the best price that we could. A lot of it was so obsolete, we had to sell it for scrap."

Another problem was the company's conservative styling. "My father and uncles had always made a very conservative boot," Justin disclosed. "They sold a lot of their boots to ranchers and sheepherders, line riders and fence riders, real live, honest-to-goodness cowboys, not pickup cowboys who drove pickups around their properties. Their principal product was a round-toed boot.

"They had made some little changes over the years to modernize and upgrade their products, but when the demand began for pointed-toe boots, they resisted it. I remember my dad saying, 'Why would anyone want a boot with a pointed toe? What's he gonna do with a pointed toe?'

"Then there was the matter of colors. Their whole deal, like Henry Ford's Model T, was that you could have boots in any color you wanted so long as it was black. We were still selling boots, good boots, and there were some people that really loved that kind of boot. But we weren't getting anywhere with people who wanted a more up-to-date product."

"We had excellent salesmen," John, Jr., emphasized. "They were eager and they tried hard, but they were simply outgunned as far as their merchandise was concerned. Two of our top salesmen, Bill Justin, who lived in Abilene and worked West Texas, and Howard Shaneyfelt, who lived in Houston and had South Texas, really helped to educate me. They both had worked in the factory before going on the road, so they really knew boots.

"They'd come into Fort Worth and we'd get together in a hotel room. They'd have some competitors' boots with them and they'd show me what our competitors were making. Sometimes we'd stay up all night just talking about boots . . . what's selling here, what's selling there, what's good and what's bad . . . learning more about the industry. We had the ability to make any kind of boots we wanted. It was just a matter of styling and giving people what they wanted."

Justin also was convinced the company had to change the way it was perceived by its dealers. He felt the dealers had the company categorized as a purveyor of old-fashioned boots; but if you wanted something fancy, you had to go elsewhere. To try to dispel this image and learn what the dealers wanted, Justin began spending a great deal of his time on the road.

"Around Fort Worth, there were a number of dealers that I knew and could talk to, but I wanted to know what was going on in Arizona, Southwest Texas, East Texas, Oklahoma, Kansas and Colorado and in other places around the country," Justin said. "Sometimes I'd ride with the salesman and sometimes I'd get into my car by myself and go out on my own. Before going out on a trip, I'd make up a list of dealers I wanted to see. If it wasn't too good a dealer, I'd plan to come in and see him at coffee time in the morning and I'd buy him a cup of coffee and we'd talk. If it was a pretty good dealer, I'd try to drop in around noon and take him to lunch. And if it was a real good dealer, I'd try to get in at the end of the day so that I could take him to dinner, get acquainted with him over a good steak. This allowed me to find out what the dealers wanted, what their customers wanted, what their problems were."

Justin also got a taste of what it was like to try to resuscitate moribund dealer relationships. "I was down in Kerrville one time," he recounted.

"There was a guy who had a big dry goods store there. My cousin, Bill Justin, who was the salesman in that territory, told me there was no point in going in to see the owner. 'This guy still has some of our boots that he bought thirty years ago,' Bill said. 'They're old-fashioned and discolored from sitting in the sun in the window and he's still got them marked up to full price.'

"So I went in and checked out the boots," Justin continued. "They looked terrible. They were short tops, out of fashion in every respect. I kind of argued a little with the proprietor, figuring I didn't have a lot to lose there. Finally, he said to me, 'If these were your boots what would you do with them?'

"I said, 'I'd get rid of them and get some new boots in here.' Then I added, 'You're asking $40 for a pair of these old boots. What you need to do is put them out front on Saturday and put up a sign that says, 'Your Choice—$25!' Then the next Saturday, I'd go to $20 and the next Saturday to $10. After that, if there are any left, I'd just give them away.'

"That made the guy so mad, he nearly threw me out of the store," Justin said with a laugh. "But, you know, he did what I suggested. He got rid of those old boots and still got his money out of them because he hadn't paid that much for them to begin with. And, after that, he began stocking some of our new boots and got to be a pretty good customer."

As quickly as he could, Justin began adding an assortment of new boots to the product line. "I never will forget, I bought some glove leather, soft leather, in yellow and a chartreuse green and bilious red and a terrible blue, and I started making boots in every combination you could think of. I made solids and I made them with different tops, and I made some with kind of a half wing tip on them. I made a green foot and a red top with a yellow wing tip. I cringe a little now when I think about it, but at the time those colored boots sold, and they got us out of that rut of people think-ing of us as merely making a good, heavy boot for working on the ranch but not anything that you'd wear around town."

Justin recalled running into a cowboy in Cheyenne, years later, who was still wearing a pair of those multicolored boots. "It embarrassed me," he revealed. "I just turned around and walked away," he said. "I didn't even want to look at them. But the boots sold and some people thought they were the greatest thing in the world. So we began to put more styling into our boots and, of course, got into the exotic leathers and colors. My father just couldn't believe you could sell those colors. He thought people were crazy to buy any of that."

As part of the new emphasis on styling, Justin decided to produce a boot with a sharply pointed toe. Again his father voiced his objections, but John, Jr., now had the bit in his teeth. Producing the pointed-toe boot, however, posed some severe problems in the factory. "The only way you could make pointed-toe boots in those days was by hand," Justin explained. "Our competitors like Tony Lama had plants on the Mexican border where they employed lots of hand workers very inexpensively. We did it the same way, but it was very expensive and the cost was eating us up.

"I worked on it and developed a way to make a real sharp pointed toe using a molded plastic toe and got a patent on it. This kind of updated us because everything else we were making was stuff that we'd been selling for the past twenty or thirty years."

Another major problem was that the factory and machinery were in dire need of updating. The electrical wiring was obsolete, the lighting eye-strainingly inadequate. Perhaps worst of all was the lack of any kind of a system, no matter how primitive, for airing out the premises during the torrid Texas summers.

"We used to buy salt tablets by the gallon for the plant employees to combat the heat," Justin remembered. "They opened the plant at six-thirty in the morning during the summer months to permit the employees to work during the cool part of the day. They closed at four-thirty, but when they closed, they closed all the windows for security reasons. So there was no way for the place to cool off. I remember walking into the plant early in the morning and being met by a blast of hot air like it was coming out of a blast furnace.

"They'd open the windows when the plant opened to try to get a little morning air in. But then the sun would begin to pour in and it would get hotter and hotter and hotter and the girls working on the machines would begin taking those salt tablets as if they were candy.

"After I came into the company, I wanted to put in air-conditioning, but it was too expensive. But the plant had these big old dormer windows set in the roof. So one of the first things I did was install some large exhaust fans in the windows. Then I had the windows fixed so that we could secure them at night. This permitted us to leave them partially open when we closed the plant. I put a timer on the fans so that they would come on at two o'clock in the morning and draw in all that nice, cool early morning air and push out all the hot air that had accumulated during the heat of the day. By the time people came to work, it'd be nice and cool in the plant."

As for the lighting, it was about as primitive as it could get. "The plant had these huge one thousand-watt bulbs," Justin recounted. "In one place you'd be blinded by the glare from the bulbs and in other parts of the plant you could hardly see. So the machine operators in the poorly lighted areas would jerry-rig some lighting for themselves. They'd measure out a length of electrical cord and hang it from an overhead pipe. Then they'd attach a one hundred-watt bulb and a metal shade to one end of the cord and plug the other end into the nearest available socket. Of course, somebody else would then do the same thing, plugging into the same socket using a double or a triple plug because there weren't that many outlets available. We didn't have the wiring to handle such loads, so fuses were continually blowing out. I was really afraid that we'd have an electrical fire and burn up the whole shebang."

Providing the power was a line shaft located in the rear of the factory that was turned by a large electric motor. The shaft had pulleys along its length to which belts that ran the individual machines could be attached. The machine operator used a long stick to place the belt on the pulley to provide the power for his machine. The problem was the system was inefficient. For example, on a Saturday, if you had just one machine working, you still had to run that big motor to operate your single pulley. Justin removed the line shaft as soon as he could and replaced it with individual motors on the machines.

Office procedures had also fallen behind the times, Justin found. "Nothing was modernized," he asserted. "The stock system was out of date, the billing system was out of date."

Eddie Kelly, who went to work in the Justin plant as a piece worker in 1949 and retired in 1991 as a fashion coordinator for the Justin Boot Company, described her initial impression of the factory. "It was just like any other sweatshop of that era. There were no fans. Your lighting consisted of a lightbulb with a metal shade around it hanging above your machine. It was very dark, very dismal. It had wooden floors, the chairs were nearly impossible to sit on, and there was a lot of irritability because of the people being hot, being uncomfortable. Like any old building there was no insulation. In the wintertime, you would freeze. In the summer, you sweltered. The working conditions were just not very good."

Eddie's first job was working on a machine folding leather pieces called quarters on the shoe production line. "I started out at sixty-five cents an hour," she reported, "which was a pretty good salary in those days. They were making a lot of shoes at the time. I would apply the cement to the quarters and then fold the edges so that they could put the lining to it around the tops of the quarters. I did that for about two or three months. One thing I'll always remember. I was doing piecework and I hadn't been on the job for more than two weeks when I made my piecework quota. All of the management, from the top to the bottom, came down and congratulated me. It just seemed like such a nice thing for them to do. But that was typical of the Justin family. They used to come into the plant and talk with us. They really communicated with all their employees. They knew them well. They knew their wives and their husbands and their children. The company was small enough to do that."

When an employee whose job was casing boots fell and broke her ankle, Eddie volunteered to take on the boot-casing chores in addition to her regular duties. "So I began doing both jobs without any problem," she related. "Then the little lady who was stamping the sizes into the boots decided that she didn't want to work anymore. I told my boss, 'If someone can do the cementing on the quarters, I think I can handle all three jobs.' He told me to give it a try. It took some night hours, but I did it. And soon it got to where I was moving around so much helping people out that Howard Shaneyfelt, the plant manager, made a supervisor out of me."

Ms. Kelly said the Justin employees, who numbered about a hundred at the time, took John, Jr.'s ascension to power pretty much in stride. "The people respected him for what he had accomplished in his belt company. Those who doubted him at first were won over when he began putting in all the changes in the plant. They really got on his side when he stopped laying off plant workers during slack periods. He felt that when business was slow, you should build up the inventory for the fall when you do have orders. He tried to keep everybody working. There was no more feast or famine."

John, Jr., became a frequent visitor to the plant after he took over as general manager. "Everybody knew when he came by," Ms. Kelly reported, "especially the young girls. He was very good-looking. He looked like a movie star.

"He got very involved in modernizing the equipment. He talked to the employees about changes they would like to see made. He was the kind of person that people would open up to. He listened."

The first new equipment Justin installed was a turning machine on which the boots are turned right-side out after the front and back portions have been sewn together from the inside. "The turning machine they were using was really obsolete," Eddie recounted. "So John, Jr., figured out a way they could turn the boots with an air cylinder. You'd stuff the boot into a pipe and turn it right-side out. This speeded up production a lot.

"At that time," she continued, "the amount of time it took to make a pair of boots was determined by Mother Nature. In many operations, the leather had to be wet, then shaped and then it had to dry. If there was a lot of rain or a lot of humidity in the air, it could take two to three weeks for the leather to dry, and the boots just sat there waiting to be finished. So John, Jr., had them put a large drying unit up on the roof. It was heat-controlled and you had air flowing through, so the boots could dry much more quickly. He installed a chain device that brought the boots up and then down again. You could dry a pair of boots in a matter of hours."

Ms. Kelly laughingly recalled an incident that made her a bona fide heroine with her fellow factory employees. "It was shortly after John, Jr., joined the company. One day he was in the plant with his father and his Uncle Earl. They were standing by the water fountain. I was just standing around surveying the plant, seeing what to do next, when one of the operators suggested that I take a chair over to them. She wanted them to see the kind of chairs we were having to sit on while we were working. They were cane-bottom chairs with the bottoms falling out. We used to bring our own pillows to stuff the chairs with so that we could sit on them.

"So I took the pillow stuffing out of my chair and took it over to where John, Jr., and the others were standing and I said, 'If you-all are going to stand around here and talk, don't you want a chair to sit on?' It was a chair all right, but with not much of a sitting area.

"John, Jr., asked me whose chair it was and I told him it was mine. He smiled and told me he'd see what he could do about getting me a new one."

Several weeks later, plant employees entering the factory one morning were greeted with the sight of brand new chairs at every work station requiring a seated operation.

"He really does care about people," Eddie said.

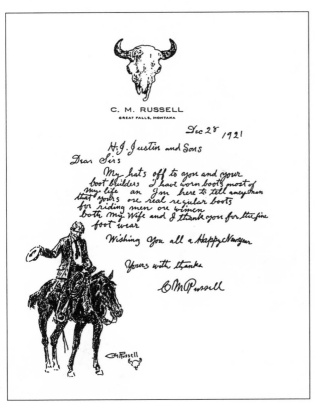

A 1921 greeting from Charles M.
Russell of Great Falls, Montana.

A 1930s design on the left, the 1919
Charles Russell boot on the right.

Military boot and field boot, 1920-1940.

This special 1920 boot has silver conchos and was worth $150 at the time.

The Lake Street Justin Factory, Fort Worth.

116

Earl Justin, John Justin, Sr., and Sam Justin (left to right).

Justin boots and shoes were exhibited in Texas, New Mexico, Louisiana and Oklahoma on a display truck with expandable sides and a top that could be raised.

The inside of the Justin display truck, with racks for boots.

Expert fancy stitcher Vane Justin stitched special designs for many movie stars and other celebrities.

The Justin Boot Company on the corner of Hemphill and Daggett in Fort Worth.

Boots designed for Paul Whiteman in 1936, the year of the Texas Centennial.

President J. S. (John) Justin pinns a deep red rose on Oscar Travis, a birthday tradition in the Justin factory.

Specially made boots, 1940.

A 1940s photo of John, Earl and Sam Justin around a portrait of H. J. Justin.

122

John Justin, Sr., presents an award to Jack Hamilton, who was the first to reach
$100,000 in sales in one year. This was in the era when Justin produced shoes as well
as boots, as can be seen by the pairs on display.

eleven

The corralling of a playboy

The job that John Justin, Jr., had once dreamed of holding was turning into a nightmare. Each evening, after the culmination of another frustrating day, Justin found himself wondering if he had bitten off more than he really wanted to chew. The task of revamping the moribund family business had quickly turned into a quagmire of aggravation and exasperation. To young Justin, it soon became manifestly apparent that his early confrontation with his father over the dismantling of the shoemaking line was a harbinger of things to come.

"He was having all kinds of problems over everything he wanted to do," Dorothy Morell recalled. "There were lots of arguments, not only over getting changes made but in getting them made to his satisfaction, especially in the manufacturing end. Plus he was trying to make changes in the office, too. He was fighting a pretty hard battle with everybody. I really ached for him at times."

Dorothy remembers seeing Justin return to his office from a confrontation in the boot plant with his face "blood red" in anger and exasperation. "He'd go into his office and slam the door shut. I knew that was the time to leave him alone and let him calm down. In a few minutes he'd be back to his normal self. But then it would happen again a few days later. He was running into opposition around every corner."

What was happening was not what Justin had bargained for when he had taken the job. True, he had a management contract that vested him with full power to run the company as he saw fit. But the other members of the management team, namely his father, his Uncle Earl and Bert Fisch, apparently were dedicated to testing his resolve.

By the early part of 1951, only months after his accession to the position of general manager, John, Jr., was facing almost daily disagreements with his colleagues, particularly Fisch, who had been with the company since before the move to Fort Worth.

Over the years, Fisch had won the confidence of the Justin brothers, who deferred to his expertise in merchandising and styling.

By the time John, Jr., appeared on the scene, Fisch was wielding the most individual clout in deciding what products went into the Justin inventory. It was a position Fisch was not about to relinquish lightly, particularly to a newcomer he felt didn't know beans about the boot business. Fisch was a determined adversary, Justin quickly discovered.

"Everybody in the company knew that Bert could be extremely hard-headed when it came to making changes that he didn't agree with," Justin noted. "He was an excellent motivator of salesmen. He wrote every salesman a letter every week, pointing out, for example, 'I see that you called on so-and-so. Did you show him such-and-such?' They were great letters. But he was totally inflexible. He was going to do things his way or not at all."

Fisch had happily welcomed John, Jr., into the fold because he felt his seniority would give him an edge over the youthful newcomer. "He wanted me to come in and buy out Uncle Avis because he thought he would now be able to do whatever he wanted to do," Justin said. "In the past, he had had to contend with Uncle Avis' regular questioning of his policies."

Unfortunately, Fisch soon found that John, Jr., with his ideas about updating and restyling the product line, was even more of a problem than Avis had ever been. Justin's argument was that the company had to modernize in order to survive. To Fisch, what Justin proposed bordered on heresy and represented disaster. He wanted to continue making the kind of boots the company had always made.

"From what I had learned talking with our customers and salespeople, I was convinced that it was absolutely essential for us to revamp our product line," John, Jr., said. "Getting acceptance of my ideas was another matter. It wasn't easy. It was like pulling teeth. I found myself arguing with Fisch about everything I wanted to do."

It was only a matter of time before things finally reached an impasse. "We were holding a meeting in the sample room to go over ideas for the new line," Justin recounted. "Bert and I submitted our ideas about what samples we should have made up to ship out to the salesmen. Needless to say, our suggestions were miles apart. Bert didn't like any of mine and I didn't like any of his. Bert tried to convince me to defer to his better judgment. He said, 'John, your boots won't sell.' He wouldn't give up trying to sell me on the products he wanted to have made."

Justin felt strongly that Fisch's ideas were simply a rehash of what had caused the boot company to fall behind its competitors in the marketplace. "We had a pretty big argument," Justin recalled. "But Bert remained adamant. Finally, I told him that there was no point in any further discussion. I said to him, 'Bert, I appreciate your point of view, but it's my decision to make and I'm making it now.'"

With that, Justin terminated the meeting and headed for the factory floor, where he turned over his sketches and specifications for the sample boots to the production manager. The next day Justin left Fort Worth for a trip to visit dealers in Texas, Oklahoma and New Mexico. A shock awaited him upon his return.

"The first thing I did after getting back was go down to the factory to see how my samples were coming along," Justin related. "I couldn't believe what I was seeing when I got there. The samples being made were not the ones I had turned over to the production manager, but the ones that Bert Fisch had originally proposed. I don't know when I'd ever been angrier in my life."

The irate Justin lost no time finding out what was going on. From the production manager, he learned that Fisch had countermanded his orders on the samples. Justin couldn't believe what he was hearing. He headed upstairs and stormed into Fisch's office.

"What's going on?" he demanded. "Why aren't they making up the boots I ordered?"

"I told them not to," Fisch admitted. "Believe me, John, I did it for the company. The boots you ordered are not going to sell. One of these days you'll thank me for what I did."

Justin paused as he relived the moment. "What you've got to understand," he said, "is that I had been perfectly happy running my belt company. I was making good money and I was having a good time. I really didn't need the aggravation the job at the boot company was bringing me. I looked at Fisch and suddenly I wasn't angry any more. I knew what I was going to do and I could hardly wait to do it."

Without saying another word, Justin turned around and strode out of Fisch's office. Earl's office was nearby. Justin walked in and, without any preliminaries, informed him he was quitting. Earl couldn't believe his ears.

"What do you mean?" he asked.

"Exactly what I said. I'm quitting my job."

"Why? What happened?"

John, Jr., told him about the boot samples, how he was fed up with having to fight a war over every move he made. He told Earl that the job simply wasn't worth the aggravation it was causing him.

"I don't need it," he said. "I don't want it. You guys can go back to running things the way you've always done."

With that, he left the premises and headed for the belt company. He had hardly gotten to his office before the telephone rang. Earl was on the line.

"John," he said. "I've got some news for you. Your father and I just met with Bert Fisch and he's decided to retire. We want you to come back and keep on running the company."

Several days later, a letter from Earl Justin, chairman of the board, was mailed to the members of the H. J. Justin & Sons sales force announcing with regret the retirement of Bert Fisch, praising the importance of the salesmen and calling for increased two-way communications between management and the sales force. The message marked the beginning of a major overhaul of sales force practices and procedures that John, Jr., felt was long overdue.

"Most of all," he emphasized, "it was a process of getting the salesmen to change their ingrained habits—and it wasn't easy. For example, salesmen always said they couldn't work in December because the merchants were getting ready for Christmas and didn't have the time to talk to them. Then they said they couldn't work in January because the merchants didn't want them in their stores while they were doing inventory. Then in March and April they were getting ready for their income tax returns. They always had an excuse for not working.

"This was killing us in the factory because when the salesmen weren't selling, there were no orders to fill and there was nothing to do in the plant. It was feast or famine in those days. At times, we'd have lots and lots of orders and we'd work night and day to fill them. At other times, when the orders dried up, there was nothing to do in the plant and people would be laid off. Employees would borrow money to live on from my father and pay him back when they were recalled. We had lots of spring orders and lots of fall orders, but not too many orders in between."

In December 1951, Justin called all the salesmen to Fort Worth for a special meeting. He minced no words in his opening remarks. "I've always believed in working twelve months a year," he told the assemblage. "I believe this business of not being able to call on your customers at certain times of the year is a cop-out, a bunch of bull."

He then outlined a new daily reporting program for the sales force. Beginning with the first working day in January 1952, every salesman would be required to send Justin a Western Union night letter informing him which customers he had called on that day and how much merchandise he had sold. The first day after the program went into effect, Justin received a night letter from every salesman but one.

Surprisingly, everybody had sold something. The next morning he again got night letters from everyone but the same salesman. What made the situation all the more interesting was the fact that this salesman, who had the Houston territory, one of the company's most lucrative sales areas, was Bert Fisch's son-in-law.

Justin placed a long-distance call to the salesman in Houston. "I haven't gotten your night letters," he told him. "I haven't sent any in," the salesman answered. "I think the whole thing is a bunch of foolishness. I don't want to bother my customers when they don't want to see me."

"We've been over all that," Justin informed him. "You know what the program is. I expect you and every other salesman to adhere to it."

There was a momentary silence on the line, then the response, "Maybe you'd like me to send in my samples?"

Justin got in the last word. "Okay."

As part of the effort to solve the feast-or-famine problem, Justin came up with another innovation. "I got the idea of having some fancy reorder cards made up which were then inserted in the box whenever we shipped some merchandise to a retail customer. So when a dealer received a pair of boots from us, he could send in the reorder card to replace the pair of boots he had just sold. Sometimes the merchant ordered more than one pair, maybe half a dozen. It helped get us over the hump that we had to get over. We just couldn't go on working day and night one week and doing nothing the next week."

The innovations caught on. Business picked up. By late summer of 1952, sales which had been dipping sharply since 1948 were back on a pace to exceed the $1 million mark. "A million dollars in sales was really something in the quality cowboy boot business in those days," John, Jr., added.

Justin's principal competitors in its price range were Tony Lama and

Nocona. "Both of them gave us a hard time," Justin acknowledged. "Lama had developed the pointed toe while we were still making the old sheep-herder-type boots and they had been eating our lunch."

The giant in the low-price field was the Acme Boot Company, with headquarters in Tennessee. "Acme made a cheap boot that sold for $18.50, and they sold a lot of kids' boots for $4 and $5," Justin reported. "Our boots retailed for $37.50 and up."

But Justin sales began moving up as the restyled products began hitting the marketplace. For John, Jr., it was an affirmation of what he had been fighting for since joining the company. For his father and for his Uncle Earl, it was a validation of their decision about Bert Fisch.

This made the death of Earl Justin on August 22, 1952, at the age of sixty-two, all the more painful for John, Jr. "I was sitting in my office one morning in late July," Justin related, "when Uncle Earl came in and said to me, 'John, Jr., I feel dizzy.' We took him to the doctor who put him through a series of tests that found he had a brain tumor. He died three weeks later after undergoing surgery.

"He was a fine guy," Justin said. "He understood that there were better ways to do things. He wanted to do things better than they'd done them in Nocona."

On September 17, 1952, John Justin, Sr., was elected chairman of the board of H. J. Justin & Sons, Inc., and John Justin, Jr., was elected president.

For the thirty-five-year-old Justin, things couldn't have been rosier. Among his friends in Fort Worth's social set, Justin had developed a rep-utation as a man about town. But his renown as one of the city's most eli-gible bachelors, with a penchant for dating beautiful women, soon extend-ed well beyond his hometown when his name began appearing in gossip columns from New York to Hollywood linked with that of Dorothy Shay, a popular chanteuse of the era who billed herself as "The Park Avenue Hillbilly." Justin met her at a party in Fort Worth, where she had enter-tained, and he squired her around town for several days afterwards, then visited her in California. The word in the tabloids was that they were planning to "tie the knot," as one columnist put it.

The fact that there wasn't an ounce of truth to the rumors didn't mat-ter. The handsome boot baron with a name synonymous with western lore was good copy for the tabloids and other gossip sheets of the era. So it wasn't surprising when the New York Daily News asked this writer, then a young Star-Telegram reporter, to do a feature on Justin for its Sunday rotogravure section. What the News' Sunday editor had in mind was something that would titillate the readers of the nation's leading tabloid newspaper.

I had written several other feature stories for the *New York Daily News*, as its Fort Worth correspondent. I had never met John Justin, Jr., but I called him for an appointment, to which he readily agreed. We met in his office at the Justin plant. I walked into the office and was greeted by a tall, smiling young man with a movie star's good looks, clad in a suit that looked as if it had been made to order. He was wearing, I was surprised to note, a pair of ankle-high jodhpurs instead of cowboy boots. Justin was perfectly agreeable to being interviewed for a New York tabloid newspaper, even after I emphasized that my assignment was to write about him as a playboy, not as a successful entrepreneur who had just been elected to membership in the Young Presidents Organization, a prestigious body composed of individuals aged thirty-five or less who headed businesses with at least one million in annual sales.

Justin and I spent the better part of an hour together in a conversation that probed into his active social life, his involvement with Dorothy Shay, and how his current Fort Worth girlfriend, an American Airlines stewardess, figured into the equation.

"When the right woman comes along, I'll know it," he declared. "Until then," he added, "I'm having too much fun and I'm much too busy to think about settling down."

The article on Justin appeared on November 2, 1952. The headline declared, "You'll get a boot out of this, girls—Here's a Texas millionaire neither old, married nor smelling of cattle or oil."

A photograph of a smiling Justin having a drink with the airline stewardess accompanied the article, as did a photo of Dorothy Shay clad in a sequined, low-cut gown. What Justin had no way of knowing when the article came out was that his bachelorhood and his playboy lifestyle were about to come to a screeching halt. He was about to be landed by a pretty girl he met at a chance encounter at a debutante ball in November 1952. Six weeks later, on New Year's Eve, he popped the question. He and Jane Chilton Scott, a beautiful blonde, recently widowed and the mother of two small children, were married on January 31, 1953, at the Hemphill Presbyterian Church in Fort Worth.

Jane recalled the whirlwind sequence of events during an interview at the Justins' town house on Fort Worth's West Side. "I had been a widow a short time," she began. "My husband, Clyde Scott, died a very untimely death as a young man of thirty-four with a malignancy. We had been married thirteen years. My brother-in-law, John B. Collier III, who had married my sister, Mabel Lea, kept telling me about a most attractive man he wanted me to meet. The man was John Justin, Jr. He and John B. were longtime friends.

"John B. didn't give up. He just kept on talking about how John Justin was the nicest, best-looking man. Then I went to the Steeplechase Ball with John B. and Mabel Lea. It was the first Steeplechase I attended after Clyde died. It was held in the old River Crest Country Club, which had that wonderful curving staircase. And as we came into the clubhouse, I looked up at the head of the stairs and I saw this very attractive man standing there. I always thought that John should have given me those stairs as a memento of the evening when the club was rebuilt after it burned.

"I asked John B. if he knew who the man at the head of the stairs was, and he said, 'That's John Justin, the one I've been telling you about. In fact, I asked him to go to the Texas-TCU football game with us tomorrow afternoon, but he said he had something else he had to do.'

"We began walking up the staircase, and as I slithered by where John was standing, I said, 'Oh, I'm so sorry you can't go tomorrow.'

And he said, 'Well, I don't know where we were going, but I'm sure sorry, too.'"

Jane and John had their first date the following Saturday night. "We went to the Keystone Room at the Texas Hotel," Jane recalled. "John B. and Mabel Lea went with us. They said that after about ten minutes, John and I had just cut them out of all the conversation. So they took off early and left us alone."

Justin proposed to Jane while they were driving to her hometown of Marlin to spend New Year's Eve with her family. Jane acknowledged that things moved at an unusually speedy pace. "The way I would justify what happened," she said, "is that I think, as you get older, you know more about what you want. John was thirty-six and I was thirty-four. I knew that I wanted John and he wanted me. The marriage has lasted more than forty-one years, which is a lot longer than some people thought it would last.

"Several of my friends told me I was making a big mistake to marry John. One of the men I was dating at the time told me that the marriage would never last. John, of course, had a reputation as a man about town. Even my family sort of worried about it, because John had a reputation for being a playboy."

Jane recalled that John always felt they were fated to marry. "One of his favorite sayings is that I was born in Marlin, a hundred miles south of Fort Worth, and he was born in Nocona, a hundred miles north of Fort Worth, so it was natural that we should meet in Fort Worth and get married. That may be stretching it a little bit, but that's the way John likes to tell it."

Jane's father, a banker, died when she was eight years old, leaving her mother with four small children to raise. Jane graduated from Marlin High School and enrolled at Texas Christian University, where she met her first husband. They had two adopted children, Mary and David. Mary was six and David nine when their mother married John Justin, Jr.

"I don't think John had been around children of any age until we were married," Jane confided. "So I didn't know how he'd react when they acted up. We hadn't been married too long, when one night David came into our bedroom, where John and I were sleeping. David had been chewing on a little toy animal and had gotten it sort of wet and he threw the little animal and hit John right in the face. When John accepted that without losing his cool, I knew things were going to work out. He has been so great to the children. He adopted them shortly after we were married and they've been proud to be Justins ever since."

When the Justins were honored in May 1985 with the prestigious Golden Deeds Award by the Exchange Club of Fort Worth as Fort Worth's Outstanding Citizens of the Year, one of the speakers, former Fort Worth Mayor Bayard H. Friedman, noted that Mary and David weren't quite certain that "John was a keeper and around to stay" after he joined the family.

"But perhaps they became a real family," Friedman continued, "during a vacation they spent together in Colorado that summer. They were en route in John's golden Buick convertible and had stopped for the night at the Melody Motel in Raton, New Mexico. As John was packing the car the next morning, Jane admonished the kids to stay close by. When the car was packed, however, they were nowhere to be seen. Jane, of course, was worried and John went off looking for them. Finally, he spied two tiny objects heading up into the mountains far off in the distance. He went after them and brought them back. With the children safely ensconced in the car, John took off without saying a further word.

"Several miles later, he turned off the main highway to a side road and stopped the car in an isolated spot. He ordered the children out of the car and began taking off his heavy western belt. 'You disobeyed your mother,' he informed them, 'and caused her a great deal of worry by roaming off after she expressly told you to stay close to the car. Now I'm going to teach you a lesson.' He marched them to the rear of the car and told them to bend over and grasp the rear bumper for support. He began swinging his belt ominously.

"'If you cry, I'll keep on whipping you until you stop,' he warned. Jane remained in the car, afraid to look. The sound of John's belt descending with great force was enough to shake her, even though it was the belt striking the rear bumper, not the children's rear ends. But the sound was enough to shake the kids, as well. Tears welled up in Mary's eyes, but she turned and said to Justin, 'I'm not crying.'

"There were no more discipline problems in the Justin household. The kids accepted John as their dad. It has been a close and abiding relationship ever since."

twelve

"You're my bootmaker"— Ronald Reagan

One of the shocking things that Jane Justin learned about her husband after their marriage was that he didn't wear cowboy boots. "People don't believe me when I tell them that John didn't own a pair of boots when we got married," she asserted. "He thought the real cowboys would think he was trying to 'out-cowboy' them. I told him, 'John, here you're the president of the world's leading cowboy boot company and you don't wear boots.' I finally convinced him he had to start wearing his own products."

For Justin, the change in footwear became a lifetime commitment. He's been a walking advertisement for Justin Boots ever since. "I warn people when I give them a pair of boots," he said with a grin, "that they'll grow on you . . . that they're habit-forming. I tell them that if they don't want to become addicted, they'd better not wear them.

"That's why," he added, "there are a bunch of investment bankers on Wall Street who wear cowboy boots to the office every day with their three-piece Brooks Brothers suits. They didn't listen to my warning."

Ronald Reagan and Lyndon B. Johnson, poles apart politically, were both inveterate cowboy boot wearers and shared a mutual loyalty to Justin boots. While he was still on the lecture circuit, before his ascension to the White House, Reagan came to Fort Worth to make a speech to the Sales and Marketing Executives Club. Justin, a past president of the organization, was introduced to Reagan at a reception after his talk.

When Reagan heard his name, he informed Justin: "You're my bootmaker. I've got lots of your boots at my ranch. I've even worn them in some of my pictures."

As for Johnson, he had a closet full of Justin boots at his ranch on the Pedernales River, and he frequently wore his cowboy boots while working in the Oval Office.

Speaking of LBJ reminded Justin of an incident that told something about the awesome power of the presidency. "I had gone out of town on a sales trip," Justin related. "No one, including my wife or my secretary, knew where I was. I'd met one of our salesmen in Phoenix and asked him where he wanted me to go to meet some of our dealers. He said he wanted to go to Tucson first."

Justin and the salesman checked into a motel in Tucson. The next morning, while they were visiting with one of their dealers in his store, John was told he was wanted on the telephone. It was the female proprietor of the motel where he was staying. "Mr. Justin, there's a call for you," the woman informed him and gave him the telephone number the caller had left. It had a Washington, D. C., area code.

Justin dialed the number.

"Mr. Justin," a voice at the other end of the line said, "please stand by for the president." A moment later, Lyndon B. Johnson came on the line.

"He wanted to order another pair of boots," Justin reported. Later, Justin asked one of LBJ's aides how in tarnation they had been able to track him down in an out-of-the-way Tucson motel. "We have ways," was the somewhat chilling reply.

Jane Justin had become a cowboy boot wearer years before she married John. Her sister, Pauline, lived on a ranch near Cotulla south of San Antonio, and Jane and her first husband visited there frequently. "They were having a big rodeo down there," she recalled, "and we were invited to attend. I wanted some really spectacular boots to wear, so I went down to the Justin Boot Company. I didn't know anyone there and the person I got to help me was Mr. Justin, John's father.

"He didn't believe in all these colors I was talking about. I wanted two pair of boots, one yellow with orange on it and the other with two or three shades of blue. Mr. Justin said, 'We just don't make anything like that.' So I went out to the North Side and Leddy made me the two pairs of boots in the colors I wanted. This was, of course, long before I met John. The boots became a bone of contention after we got married. I found out right quick that I was going to have to get rid of them. Fortunately, by then John had brought in a lot of new colors, so I was able to have the boots duplicated."

Shortly after taking over the Justin presidency, John, Jr., decided it would be good for business to associate the company more closely with the Professional Rodeo Cowboy Association. So he began hitting the professional rodeo circuit, which was expanding rapidly across the country. After he and Jane were married, she began accompanying him on these junkets.

"When I got into the boot business," Justin said, "I didn't know many cowboys. I hadn't been to any rodeos other than the Fort Worth stock show. Then, after I took over at the boot company, I thought, 'If I'm going to be in this business, I've got to know cowboys. So I began going to rodeos.'"

One of his and Jane's more memorable trips was to Cheyenne, Wyoming, to attend the Frontier Days Rodeo, Justin recalled. "I wore what I thought was a cowboy hat and I went out and bought a western suit," he related. "I guess I kind of looked like a dude. I hadn't been used to wearing western clothes. But I still wanted to meet some cowboys. So I asked some people where all the cowboys went at night after the rodeo, and they said it was a nightspot called the 120 Club, which was located on a highway on the outskirts of town. I said to Jane, 'Let's go to the 120 Club.'"

The Justins found the neon-lighted nightspot after a short drive, parked their car and walked inside to be greeted by a country-western record blaring out of a juke box and the sight of a packed dance floor. Justin decided to check his new hat, and when he checked it, the hat check girl asked him if he wanted to take a chance on a punchboard. It was $1 a chance.

He said, "Sure," and gave her a dollar bill. Justin took one punch at the punchboard and hit the jackpot—$100 in chits, which had to be taken out in trade. "Those were the days when you could get a beer for a quarter and a steak for $2," Justin related, "and I had all these chits. So we went in and sat down at a table and ordered drinks. There was a couple sitting at the next table, Tater and Jo Decker. Tater was a big rodeo star at the time, and we got to talking to them. They're still our very good friends. Then some other people came in and I tried to spend the $100 in chits making as many new acquaintances as I could. And I did.

"Finally, I'd had about all the entertainment I could stand. So had Jane. We'd met all these rodeo people. Anyway, I paid the bill, tipped the waitress, and we started to leave."

Then Justin remembered that he'd checked his new hat. So he retrieved it from the hatcheck girl, giving her a $1 tip. Justin now found that he still had a $1 chit left. So he said to the girl, "Give me one more punch at that punchboard." He punched and won another $100 worth of chits. His first thought was that his constitution couldn't handle another $100 worth of chits. About that time, Casey Tibbs walked into the club.

"Casey was then at the height of his glory as a rodeo star," Justin recalled. "I just barely knew him. Anyway, I said to him, 'Casey, what are you gonna do tonight?'

"And he said, 'Well, I've come out here to try and have some fun.'

"And I said, 'Well, then, have some fun on me,' and I gave him the $100 worth of chits."

During the evening the Justins had met a number of people, rodeo cowboys and their spouses, all of whom would be coming to Fort Worth for the stock show rodeo in January 1954. Jane said to John, "Why don't we have a little supper for them during the rodeo?"

Neither she nor John realized it at the time, but they were inaugurating an event that would become a Fort Worth stock show tradition. As John recalled it, Jane had no idea how many people she'd invited. But they all came. "Of course, we had plenty of liquid refreshments and Jane had some brisket cooked up, and everybody had a ball. The next year we had it again. We had it for about thirty years after that. It finally got so big, we couldn't handle it anymore."

Jane recalled, "At first, some people thought we were doing it for advertising and public relations and were hesitant about coming. But they got over that when they found out there was nothing commercial about it. I did all of the cooking for about the first six years. We had about sixty guests that first year. The next year we doubled the number of guests. The last year that we had it at our house on North Bailey, we served about 850 people. Walter Jetton was the caterer.

"They cooked everything at our place. They brought in their big baking trucks. We put up thirteen tents that night in our backyard, but the people were all over the house, too. I remember going through the laundry room on my way into the house and seeing Mrs. Busch of the Anheuser-Busch brewing family from St. Louis sitting on the top of the washing machine eating supper. There she sat elegantly dining on Walter Jetton's barbecue."

Jane recalled one of the parties, when she received a telephone call from a neighbor, Jinx Anthony, who informed her that Jane's daughter, Mary, who was then about eight, was sitting on the curb in front of the house asking all of the guests, as they arrived, what brand of boots they were wearing.

"John had indoctrinated Mary and David so much about Justin, that there was no boot like Justin, that they thought everybody should wear Justin boots and nothing else," Jane explained. "After John bought Tony Lama, we still hadn't convinced David that it was all right to have Tony Lama boots in the house. One day, David found an empty Tony Lama box in his closet, and he confronted us with the box and said, 'What's this doing in my closet.'"

When the annual rodeo dinner finally outgrew the Justins' home, it was moved to larger surroundings, first at a hotel and then, finally, to a sprawling site in a warehouse area near the stock show grounds, where it was held under a mammoth tent.

"But it was never as much fun after we moved it away from the house," Jane confessed. She retained a poignant recollection of the first year following the final party.

"On the day the party would have been held, we got so blue, we fixed ourselves drinks and drove down to the place where we'd had the party the year before. We were just sitting there, drinking our drinks, when here came this good-looking, shiny pickup with two young boys and two really cute girls. They seemed to be looking for something, and John said to me, 'They're looking for the party. Those cowboys have invited those girls out for a big evening. Now they're going to have to foot the bill themselves.'

"We finally left, and we were driving down 7th Street when we stopped at a traffic light. And here came that shiny pickup with the two couples. They pulled up beside us. They didn't know who we were, of course. John said to them, 'Are you looking for something?'

"'Yeah,' one of the boys answered. 'We're looking for the Justin party.'

"And John said, 'We're not having it this year.' We've always been sorry we didn't say, 'Why don't you all come over and have a drink with us.'"

The rodeo parties enabled the Justins to develop lasting friendships with a number of rodeo stars, world champions like Jim Shoulders, Harry Tompkins and Casey Tibbs, all members of the National Cowboy Hall of Fame. Jane has a special memory of the night Tibbs dedicated a ride to her at the Fort Worth stock show rodeo.

"There was this one bucking horse, Baby Doll, who was very flamboyant. She would go in circles and then begin jumping. She would jump straight up and come down real hard. Not many riders could take those jumps and hard landings. To promote interest in the event, Verne Elliott, the producer, said he would give $50 to anyone who could ride the horse.

"The next thing I know is that Cy Taillon, the announcer, comes on the microphone and says, 'Casey Tibbs is going to ride Baby Doll. He agreed to do this if he could dedicate the ride to Jane Justin.'

"So here comes Casey. He's wearing his heliotrope chaps and heliotrope hat for which he's famous. He starts out of the gate. The horse circles one time and jumps. He circles another time and jumps. And when Casey gets right in front of our box, just as the horse hits the highest peak, he jumps off Baby Doll, lands smoothly and bows to me.

"John said to me, 'I'll never be able to live with you again.'"

The trip to Cheyenne, which led to the inauguration of the rodeo dinner parties, also launched Justin on another series of equine-related odysseys. Jane remembered how it all began.

"We were in the country club in Cheyenne, when about eight or ten of these real good-looking, middle-aged men walked into the dining room where we were waiting to have lunch. It turned out they all were members of the Roundup Riders of the Rockies. They had just finished the ride and had taken the train from Denver to Cheyenne to take in the rodeo. They asked us to have lunch with them, which we did. At lunch one of the men asked John, 'Justin, do you ride a horse?'

"John said, 'Oh, a little bit.'

"And the man said, 'We have this horseback ride in the Rockies every summer, and we'd sure like for you to go with us.' They sent John a membership form and he asked me, 'What should I do?' And I said, 'Go on and do it.' I knew it would be good for his business."

The only trouble was that Justin, the bearer of one of the most famous names in the West and the president of the world's foremost cowboy boot manufacturing firm, had never ridden a horse.

"Fortunately," Jane continued, "someone told John about Walker Cheney." Cheney, a well-known Fort Worth businessman, was also a great horseman. He took Justin out to a ranch near Fort Worth and gave him a crash course in the rudiments of riding. But one thing Cheney forgot to warn his protégé about before he embarked on the horseback ride was to check the cinch on his saddle before mounting up. It was an old prank played on tenderfoot riders to loosen the cinch. John stepped into the stirrup and fell flat on his back.

Justin never forgot how sore he was after his first full day in the saddle. "On the morning of the second day," he recounted, "I was so sore, I was afraid I wouldn't be able to get up on the horse. If someone had come by in a pickup truck, I'd have given him anything he asked to get me out of there."

Justin, however, managed to clamber into the saddle. He was riding along in silent agony, when someone rode up beside him and said, "Justin, you're sore, aren't you?"

John replied honestly, "I'm about to die. Even my eyeballs are hurting." The rider then told him, "We're gonna stop for lunch by this river. It has a lot of boulders in it and the water is very cold. You get in that water and roll around on those boulders in that cold water."

Justin followed the man's advice. When the lunch stop came, he gingerly dismounted, limped over to the river, immersed himself in the icy water and rolled around on the boulders that dotted the stream. "Then I got back up on my horse," Justin said, "and all of the soreness was gone. I've never gotten sore from riding a horse since then."

That was the first of thirty-five annual rides Justin made with Roundup Riders of the Rockies. "We'd ride for a week in the mountains," he recalled. "I enjoyed that. It did a lot for me, because I wasn't that much acquainted with horses. I learned to ride a horse and how to take care of a horse, to doctor a sick horse, and do the things you have to do when you go into the mountains for a week with a horse. If I hadn't done that, I wouldn't have felt comfortable riding in the grand entry at the rodeo in Fort Worth."

Jane enjoyed telling another story of John's initial ride with the Roundup Riders. "They call the first-year riders, the first-timers, colts," she related. "They had to play all sorts of games, like running horseback with an egg in a spoon. Then they had this game they played with these little calves, which were as feisty as they could be. John and the other colts had to take a ribbon and tie it on the tail of one of the calves. This was up in Estes Park, where the air is very rarified because of the altitude. John chased and chased this little calf, but he couldn't catch him. The little calf just ran him all over the place. I tell you, John was embarrassed, in addition to being exhausted. But he really did love that ride."

Having an energetic, photogenic and public relations-conscious chief executive at the helm of H. J. Justin & Sons began to pay off in national publicity, including a syndicated column by Inez Robb that appeared in newspapers across the country on May 20, 1954:

Podner, everything, just everything, is bigger in Texas, including the feet of its cowboys. And I'm the li'l ol' visitor who can tell you why a cowboy's feet are bigger now than they used to be in the good, old days when he spent his life ridin' and ropin' on the hurricane deck of a horse. His feet are bigger, podner, from pressing the starter of his air-conditioned car and from walkin' around city streets, trying to find a place to park so's he can go into a picture show to see the latest Hollywood horse opera.

I have all of this on the authority of a family that has been making boots for Texas cowpokes for three generations. What Colt is to the revolver and Stetson to the hat, Justin of Fort Worth is to the cowboy boot. When the first Justin started making boots for Texas cowmen in the 'Eighties,' many a wrangler wore a boot size to shame Cinderella, a dainty 4 1/2 or 5. That was an average foot. By the time the second Justin came into the business at the turn of the century, the most popular sizes were 6's and 7's. And now John Justin, Jr., president of the company and grandson of the founder, says a cowboy's hoof has expanded just like all the rest of Texas. The most popular sizes today are 9's and 9 1/2's.

"In the old days, the only time a cowboy used his feet was to climb into the stirrup," Mr. Justin explained. "Now he patrols the fences in a jeep or a helicopter. And pressing down on the starter and the brakes have kinda' splayed out his feet, as well as walking around town trying to find a place to park." To accommodate the walkin' cowboy, the Justin firm has lowered the heel of the regulation cowboy boot by three-quarters of an inch. Compared with regular shoes, this heel still looks like an Adler elevator. But, and to tell the truth, the walkin' heel is now more popular than the old sloping spoke heel that once distinguished all cowboy boots. However, whatever the Justins have whittled off the heel, they have added to the top of their boots.

Boots are getting higher by the minute, a return to the old 'stove-pipe' boots that the first Justin once made. These new fourteen-inch boots come just below the bend in the knee and fit like paper on the wall. I kind of hate to reveal this next ugly fact, podner, but cowboys, real live cowboys, are now ordering nylon mesh boots for summer wear at $75 per throw. And that ain't all. They've got crepe soles!

The Justins are never surprised when a cowhand comes in and orders a custom-made pair of boots at from $75 to $250 per pair, depending on the amount of hand work required. At the moment, the Justin firm is engaged in designing the most expensive pair of boots in its history, a pair to celebrate the firm's Diamond Jubilee, or seventy-fifth anniversary, this year. The boots will be diamond-studded, and not with li'l, ol' chip diamonds either. A diamond sunburst in each boot will radiate from a ten-carat stone.

However, the Justins have made jewel-studded boots in the past, too. And boots with toes and heels of hand-chased silver are not unusual. This old Texas firm figures the reason so many cowboys hanker to die with their boots on is because the boots cost so much that the boys are afraid to take 'em off.

The year that H. J. Justin & Sons celebrated its diamond anniversary was also the year that Jack Carey began his career as a $1.25-an-hour jack-of-all-trades in the company's shipping department. Forty years later, from his vantage point as warehouse manager of the Justin Boot Company, overseeing an operation that stores as many as a million pairs of boots at one time and ships as many as a hundred thousand pairs in a week from a huge, modern warehouse, Carey reflected on the changes he had seen and experienced over the past four decades since he was hired on September 27, 1954.

"My first job was filling orders, pulling boots, in the plant," Carey recounted. "At the time, I made the third person in the shipping department. There were only two others working there."

The shipping department at that time was on the second floor, where the sample room is now located, Carey remembered. "We had wooden shelves and the floor looked as if somebody had hot-topped it. We would come in at six-thirty in the morning and ship out all our boots, and then the rest of the day we'd spend tearing out the shelves so that we could put in the new shelves. We'd do that until midnight. We filled orders by hand then. We'd climb up on those old wooden shelves to get a pair of boots and sometimes the shelves would break and we'd take a fall. There was no air-conditioning," he continued. "In fact, it got so hot during the summer that the tar on the roof would melt and sometimes drip through the ceiling. People in this building sometimes say, 'It's warm in here,' and I tell them, 'You don't know what warm is.'"

A photograph of the old shipping department hangs on a wall of the huge warehouse that Carey now oversees. He shook his head as he studied the photograph. Then he pointed to the rickety shelves on which he once climbed to pull out a pair of boots to fill an order. "We've come a long way from that," he observed. "Now we have forklifts and high-rises that go up twenty-seven feet. In the old days," Carey continued, "we stocked the boots on the shelves by hand. Today the location of the boots is all done by bar code computers that show where the boots are, how many there are, when they were put in place, and how long it took to do the job. Before the computers came in, we had to do it all by memory. We had to remember which boots were stored where. And we used to have to pick them by hand.

"We ship during the day and stock at night. It's a two-shift operation, so we work sixteen hours a day, from quarter to seven in the morning until midnight. There are about sixty people working here now. During the busy season in the fall, in October and November, there'll be as many as a hundred people working in the warehouse."

Justin was shipping around five thousand pairs of boots a week when he began working there, Carey recollected. Today, the company will ship twenty thousand pairs in a single day during the height of the fall busy season. As Carey spoke, a skid with twelve dozen pairs of children's boots passed by. All were size 2 1/2D. The boxes were stacked to a height that stretched nearly all the way to the thirty-foot-high ceiling.

"The reason the children want these boots is that they are exactly like mama's and daddy's boots," Carey observed.

Carey is convinced that the changes John Justin, Jr., instituted — new colors, new styles, new leathers—saved the company. "John, Jr., had already taken over when I got there," he recalled. "He was president of the company, but his dad was still there. I worked really close with John, Sr. The company was quite a bit smaller and John, Sr., even though he had the title of chairman of the board, would work orders and pick up the mail. He was active in the company until he passed away.

"But the company changed a lot after John, Jr., took over. If it wasn't for John, Jr., we wouldn't have made it. We'd have probably withered away like so many others."

He enjoyed relating an incident that occurred in the shipping department before it was moved to the new warehouse.

"One day we were way behind in our shipping and John, Jr., got word of what was happening. So he came into the department and asked me if there was anything he could do to help. I told him, 'Well, we could use some more hands pulling orders.' So he rolled up his sleeves and stepped right in with the rest of us. He pulled orders until around midnight when we finally got caught up. All night long, people kept waiting for him to make a mistake, pull the wrong pair of boots. But he never did."

thirteen

Family feud

On the morning of April 5, 1954, an envelope bearing the return address of the Nocona Boot Company caught John Justin, Jr.'s eye as he leafed through the mail. The envelope also proclaimed in large type, "Nocona, Boot Capital of the World." On the letterhead was a statement, "Nocona, the better boot." Enid Justin knew exactly how to get under her nephew's skin.

The letter declared:

> Gentlemen, as an original shareholder of H. J. Justin & Sons, may I ask that you please send me a detailed audit report of the company for the last four years, giving detailed expense accounts, salaries, etc.
>
> Thanking you in advance for a very early and favorable reply, I am (Miss) Enid Justin, President, Nocona Boot Company."

John, Jr.'s, reply, dated April 6, 1954, was less formal in its salutation. "Dear Auntie," it began:

> Thank you for your letter of April 5, 1954. I am glad to note your interest in the progress of H. J. Justin & Sons, Inc., particularly since you are operating a competing business. As a stockholder, we would of course be happy for you to inspect, or for your authorized representative to inspect, our records during business hours. I regret that you have not attended the annual stockholders meetings for the last several years, and hope that you will be able to attend the next annual meeting.

With every good wish, I am

Sincerely yours,
John S. Justin, Jr.,
President

The Justin annual meeting to which John, Jr., had referred had become a vehicle for Miss Enid to harass her nephew in absentia. "While I was try-ing to do everything I could to get the company going after I took over, she was giving me nothing but trouble because she was a competitor," John, Jr., said. "She wouldn't come to the annual meetings, but she had this lawyer in Wichita Falls who would come to the meeting representing her.

"All of my aunts and all these other people who owned stock would be there, and this lawyer would try to stir things up.

He'd say, 'I understand you're paying your rent out of company funds.'
"And I'd say, 'No.'
"And he'd say, 'Can you prove that?'
"I remember one time, he said, 'I understand you have a personal insur-ance policy made out to your wife and it's being paid for by the company.'
"I protested, 'But that's not true.' My poor aunts, who didn't under-stand business, would kind of look around at each other and wonder if I really was doing something underhanded."

Among other allegations made by Miss Enid's attorney at the annual meetings was that John, Jr., charged personal alcoholic beverage purchas-es to the company, an assertion that offended his nondrinking aunts. "I would look over at my aunts, who had never taken a drink in their lives, and they would be absolutely horrified," Justin recalled.

The continuing harassment from his aunt's attorney finally drove Justin to considering how to give Miss Enid a taste of her own medicine. "I thought about it a great deal," he acknowledged, "and I came to the con-clusion that if I owned some stock in the Nocona Boot Company, it would make a big difference in equalizing things."

Through his cousin, Bill Justin, John, Jr., was able to secure a partial list of Nocona shareholders. He then began contacting individuals on the list to see if they were interested in selling any of their stock. One of the shareholders he contacted was a woman who lived in Saint Jo, a small town only a few miles from Nocona. The woman agreed to see John, Jr. "I hadn't told her specifically what I wanted to see her about, other than it was about the Nocona Boot Company stock she owned," John, Jr., said. "So I drove up to Saint Jo to see this woman. I was kind of walking on eggs, not really knowing how things were going to go. I went into the house and told her husband why I was there. And he said to me, 'You're just trying to make trouble,' and he threw me out of the house."

Justin finally was able to buy some Nocona stock from a woman in Vernon who had inherited ten shares from her father. "I asked her what the stock was worth and she gave me a figure, and I said that was fine with me," Justin recalled. "She got the stock certificates and endorsed them and I gave her a check. Then she asked me if I'd be interested in buying her brother's stock. He had inherited nine shares.

"He lived in Nocona. So she called him in Nocona and said, 'John Justin, Jr., is buying Nocona Boot Company stock. Would you like to sell him yours?' And she quoted him the price I'd paid her.

"He said, 'Sure, I'm not getting anything out of it.'

"So she put me on the phone and I talked to him and he said he'd meet me at the Citizen's Bank in Nocona. When I got to the bank, there he was with stock certificates in his hand. He signed the certificates and I wrote him a check."

Justin drove back to Fort Worth feeling pretty good. He now owned nineteen shares of Nocona Boot Company stock out of only 400 total shares outstanding. He was a long way from exercising any control, but at least he had his foot in the door. He pondered what to do next.

"It was now my stock, but it was not on the corporate books," he explained. "I was really apprehensive about going up to Nocona to get the stock registered in my name because I knew my aunt would be so furious that she might tear up the certificates and claim they never existed. I held the stock a good while. I debated what to do. I wanted somebody with me when I finally decided to go up there, so I took my attorney, Sproesser Wynn, along."

John, Jr., made a date to see his Aunt Enid in Nocona without telling her the real purpose behind the visit. He and Wynn, a distinguished-looking gentleman and a highly successful corporate attorney in Fort Worth, drove up to Nocona in Justin's car. They arrived at the Nocona Boot Company and were promptly ushered into Miss Enid's office.

Justin had the certificates representing the nineteen shares of Nocona Boot Company stock folded in his inside coat pocket. Aunt Enid greeted the Fort Worth visitors warmly. She could be charming when she met someone who she thought was important and she had heard of Wynn and was properly impressed. She told Wynn about all the things she'd done and he told her about all the things he'd done, while Justin sat there sweating, wondering what he was supposed to do.

Finally, Justin recalls, he said "Auntie, I've got this stock that I've bought in the Nocona Boot Company that I'd like to get transferred,' and I reached into my coat pocket and brought out the certificates. Aunt Enid just went white. She looked at me in disbelief. I could hear her thinking, 'This can't be happening.' I handed her the certificates and she looked at each of them. She said, 'Oh, you've bought so-and-so's shares.'"

Justin said, "That's right."

She hesitated and Justin could tell that she was wondering, "What do I do now?" Then she said, "I'll get the stock book," and she left the office. She returned, but her hands were empty.

"I'm so sorry," she said, "but I've only got one certificate left in the stock book. So I can't transfer these certificates. Just leave them with me and I'll mail them back to you."

Unfazed, John, Jr., responded, "Auntie, I just need one certificate. You can just transfer all the nineteen shares on one certificate."

Miss Enid's face turned as white as the handkerchief she clutched in her hand. She again left the room. When she returned, she was carrying the stock book.

"Sure enough," Justin recounted, "there was only one certificate left in it. I know she was thinking, 'Is there anything I can do to keep from doing this?' But Sproesser was sitting there and there was nothing she could really do but comply with my request. So she made out the certificate and signed it. Then she got out the corporate seal and sealed it. I took the certificate, folded it and put it back in my pocket."

When John arrived home, Jane met him at the door with the news that Aunt Enid had been trying to reach him for the past hour or so. "She's called six or seven times already. She wants you to call her the minute that you get in." Justin didn't want to call her back, he admitted, but he knew he had to. She answered the phone on the first ring and began sweet-talking him:

"Now John, Jr., you don't really want that stock. This is a small company. We're just up here in Nocona on our own. The stock won't do you any good. I'll make you a good proposition. I'll pay you what you paid for it if you sell it back to me."

Of course, wild horses couldn't have gotten that stock away from him, Justin admitted. He said, "I'm sorry, Auntie, but I'm going to keep the stock. I think it's a good investment."

Miss Enid now changed her tactics.

"She started getting pushy and towards the end she got half-threatening, although I couldn't see what she could do about it," Justin said. "I finally got off the phone. She called me two or three more times a day over the next few days. But I just sat on my position and she finally stopped calling."

Miss Enid, however, was not quite ready to fold her hand. She had one more ace up her sleeve, a legal ploy that she unveiled in a letter to her shareholders. The contents of the letter stunned Justin.

"I couldn't believe what I was reading," he revealed. The letter said that Nocona stock could no longer be sold to anyone other than to Enid Justin or to the Nocona Boot Company. Stockholders were advised that they had to send in their stock certificates to the company so that a legend could be stamped on each certificate stating, 'This stock can only be sold to Enid Justin or to the Nocona Boot Company.'

The edict was not retroactive, so it did not affect the nineteen shares of Nocona stock Justin had previously purchased. "Her lawyer in Wichita Falls had told her there was no way she could do that," Justin said. "But he did tell her that she could place a time limit on having the legend affixed to the stock certificates.

"The letter to shareholders," Justin related, "clearly stated that if you didn't send in your stock for the legend to be stamped on it within a certain number of days, I think it was sixty days, the stock would be voided. So you either had to send your stock in to be stamped with the legend or it would become worthless. That's when we got into the act with a lawsuit."

The suit, which was filed by John Justin, Jr., against Enid Justin and the Nocona Boot Company, maintained that it was "improper and illegal" to place such a restriction on the sale of the company's stock. The trial was held in the picturesque Montague County Courthouse. Justin was represented by Atwood McDonald, one of Sproesser Wynn's law partners and an outstanding trial lawyer. Presiding was Judge Louis Holland, a highly respected jurist.

"Atwood presented our case and the lawyer from Wichita Falls presented Aunt Enid's case. It was really no contest. Judge Holland found in my favor and ordered Aunt Enid to take the legends off the Nocona Boot Company stock certificates."

The ruling infuriated Miss Enid. If looks could kill, Judge Holland would have never made it out of the courtroom alive. But after making his ruling, Holland was not quite through. He now turned to McDonald and said, "Counselor, your client is entitled to damages. In what amount was he damaged?"

McDonald asked Holland for permission to confer with his client before responding. Recalling the moment, Justin said, "I should have spoken up right then and given Atwood a figure like $150,000, but I didn't. I just told Atwood to forget the damages."

Before leaving the courtroom, John, Jr., attempted to speak with his aunt, but she turned her head away. And she continued to be a thorn in his side as a tough competitor with a flair for self-promotion. "She was really good at getting publicity for herself and her company," John, Jr., conceded.

She was also extremely adept at playing up the "woman's angle" years before the feminist movement became a force, working assiduously to enhance her self-proclaimed image as the "Queen of the Boot Industry." But most of all Miss Enid galled her nephew by advertising the Nocona Boot Company as the "world's biggest producer of quality Western boots," a claim H. J. Justin & Sons considered applicable only to itself.

Although Nocona Boot Company never approached Justin in size, it was enjoying sales of over $7 million annually and was employing more than three hundred workers in a modern building on U.S. Highway 82, at the eastern edge of the city, when Miss Enid observed her eightieth birthday and her company's fiftieth anniversary in 1975. Any suggestion that Miss Enid would ever consider selling her company, especially to a buyer bearing the Justin name, would have been met with total disbelief. Yet, six years later, the unthinkable did transpire with the sale by Miss Enid of her beloved business to the firm headed by her nephew and longtime adversary.

The chain of events leading up to the acquisition of the Nocona Boot Company by Justin Industries in 1981 actually began in 1954, when Joe Justin, Avis Justin's son and an officer of H. J. Justin & Sons, walked into John, Jr.'s office one morning and announced that he was leaving the company.

"He pitched a letter of resignation on my desk," John, Jr., recalled. "To say I was surprised would be putting it mildly. Joe, who was my first cousin, had been working for the company ever since he was old enough to go to work. Even though he and I hadn't exactly hit it off and he had opposed my coming into the company, he had remained on the job after I had bought out his father.

"When he told me he was resigning, I asked him, 'What are you gonna do, Joe?'

"And he said, 'I'm going to work for Aunt Enid.'

"That really took me by surprise. I said, 'Joe, that's fine, but you know it's going to be a tough row to hoe. Do you think you can do it?' I knew that Joe knew that working for Aunt Enid wouldn't be any picnic. She had a justly earned reputation for being hard to work for."

Joe replied, "I know it's gonna be tough, but I know I can do it."

Still not quite convinced that his cousin was doing the right thing, John, Jr., accorded him another twenty-four hours to rethink the situation.

"I'm going to leave your letter on my desk overnight," he told Joe. "If it's still on my desk in the morning, I'll accept it."

The next morning, the letter was still on Justin's desk when he arrived at his office. Shortly thereafter, Joe Justin was named vice president and sales manager of the Nocona Boot Company. It wasn't long before serious problems arose between Aunt Enid and Joe, including shouting matches overheard by employees.

"Things finally got so bad between them," John, Jr., said, "that she even had a peace bond taken out against him. He had been at her home one day and they'd gotten into a heated argument. He was so mad when he left the house that he slammed the door behind him with such force that it shattered the glass in a window."

Joe's tenure as vice president and sales manager lasted until 1957, when he resigned and moved to Wichita Falls to go into the steel business. He remained in Wichita Falls until July 1, 1974, when he rejoined the Nocona Boot Company as vice president and general manager. But the relationship between Aunt Enid and Joe continued to be strained.

"The straw that finally broke the camel's back took place in 1980, when Joe began trying to find a buyer for the Nocona Boot Company," John, Jr., reported. "Joe brought a representative of one of the big eastern shoe companies up to Nocona to take a look at the company. When Aunt Enid found out about it, she was irate. She thought that Joe was trying to sell the company behind her back. That's when she called me up and informed me that she wanted to sell the Nocona Boot Company. She asked if I was interested in buying her out."

Justin told her, "You bet."

By now, the Nocona Boot Company, which was turning out more than 1,250 pairs of boots per day and earning in excess of $1 million annually, was an attractive acquisition prospect.

Dee J. Kelly, partner in the Kelly, Hart & Hallman law firm and general counsel of Justin Industries, Inc., was John, Jr.'s lawyer for the purchase.

"I was fortunate to have Dee Kelly as my lawyer," Justin asserted. "Dee is the kind of guy you want on your side in a legal contest. He's a tenacious litigator." Kelly's legal talents soon were needed.

Negotiations began on working out an agreement between Enid Justin and John Justin, Jr., in which she would grant Justin Industries an option to buy her shares in the Nocona Boot Company, with Kelly representing Justin and William M. (Bill) Brown, a Fort Worth attorney, representing Miss Enid.

Then a snag arose that threatened to destroy the budding deal. It was the discovery of the existence of an agreement between Enid Justin and Joe Justin which stipulated that her stock in the Nocona Boot Company would go to Joe and never to John Justin.

"Joe had gotten Aunt Enid to sign the agreement to assure that he would wind up with control of the Nocona Boot Company," John, Jr., added. "However, in studying the document, we found that the last paragraph contained an escape clause. It stated that the agreement could be revoked by Aunt Enid by simply writing Joe a letter to that effect."

Bill Brown dictated a letter for Miss Enid to sign and deliver to Joe Justin. "That really threw the fat into the fire," John, Jr., recounted. "Joe was furious. He always thought he was going to get the company. In fact, he eventually got a bunch of Justin Industries stock when Aunt Enid died that she left to him in her will. Unfortunately for him, he sold the stock when it was at a low point."

Joe Justin tried his best to dissuade Miss Enid from revoking the contract, but failed. "She really seemed thrilled over the deal we made," John, Jr., said. "I remember getting telephone calls from her every day, sometimes two or three a day, before the final papers on the co-option agreement were signed. She wanted to know when the deal was going to be completed. I kept explaining to her that the paperwork took time."

After the signing of the co-option agreement, John, Jr., took off on a trail ride in the Rockies. "I was gone for about a week," he recounted. "When I returned, I telephoned my aunt. The minute she answered the telephone, I knew that something had gone wrong.

"I said, 'How are you, Auntie Enid?'

"Her first words were, 'What do you want?' She didn't sound very friendly.

"I told her I wanted to come up to Nocona to see her about working out some details involving the acquisition.

"And she said, 'I've changed my mind.'"

What had happened, Justin related, was that Miss Enid had received a letter from Joe Justin's wife, Pat, imploring her not to sell the company to Justin Industries. "It was a long letter, a real sob story, in which Pat told Aunt Enid how much she hated to see her sell the company and how much she hoped that she would change her mind," John, Jr., related. "And she reminded Aunt Enid of everything that was good about Joe and brought up everything she could that was bad about me."

The letter apparently had the desired effect. Aunt Enid now decided she didn't want to go through with the deal. Dee Kelly explained, "She'd given John Justin an option to buy her shares and then changed her mind after she made peace with Joe Justin. She and Joe Justin now filed a suit in Montague County to enforce the contract they had made for Joe to get Miss Enid's stock. Their suit really didn't attack the option agreement between John Justin and Miss Enid giving Justin Industries an option to buy her stock. So we filed a suit in Fort Worth to uphold the option contract."

As part of the legal maneuvering, Kelly also filed several motions in Montague County for continuances, which were turned down by the judge there. He then filed a motion with the Court of Appeals in Fort Worth to enjoin the suit in Montague County. "As a result of that," he related, "the Court of Appeals issued a writ prohibiting the case in Montague County from going forward until a verdict on the option contract suit in Fort Worth could be returned.

"We won our case in Fort Worth and we won in the Court of Appeals," Kelly added. "We got a summary judgment in the trial court in Fort Worth and we didn't have to go to trial in Montague County."

Kelly chuckled. "I remember personally going up to Montague County and handing that writ of prohibition from the Court of Appeals to that judge up there. I'll never forget that."

John, Jr., had an amusing recollection concerning the Montague County jurist. It involved an encounter that occurred before one of the hearings in the county courthouse on one of Kelly's motions for a continuance. "I had just walked into the courtroom with Dee," Justin recalled with a wide grin, "when the judge beckoned to me. I walked over to see what he wanted and he took me by the arm out into the hall. And he said to me, 'John, you ought to withdraw this case and get it out of my court. You know that Miss Enid is my wife's best friend and that there's no way that I can find in your favor.'"

Unabashed, Justin said to the judge, "Your Honor, you go right ahead and do what you have to do and I'll do what I have to do."

Recalling the incident, Kelly added, "John, of course, told me what the judge had said. Fortunately, we didn't have to go to trial in Montague County."

Following the trial in Fort Worth, Enid Justin had no further legal recourse and was forced to go through with the agreement she had made with John, Jr. The Nocona Boot Company was formally merged into Justin Industries on June 12, 1981, in an exchange of stock involving a total of 358,000 shares of Justin common stock, which gave the transaction a value of $8,950,000. Nocona Boot Company became an integral part of Justin Industries and a significant contributor to its growth.

John Justin, Jr., who had retained his ownership of his Nocona Boot Company shares over the years, was a participant in the stock swap. "I got a bunch of Justin Industries stock in exchange for those nineteen shares of Nocona stock I had acquired back in the early 1950s," he reported.

fourteen

The birth of the Roper

The Diamond Anniversary year of 1954 provided Justin with an opportunity to place his personal imprimatur on a new cowboy boot, the Justin Roper, which turned out to be one of the most popular products of all time. The Roper came into being as the result of a request by rodeo calf-ropers for a boot more suitable to the event than the stereotypical high-heeled product.

"In the late forties and early fifties," John, Jr., explained, "the rodeo calf-ropers wore baseball caps and tennis shoes in the arena. The cap wouldn't get in the way of the rope and the tennis shoes allowed them to jump off the horse and run real fast to catch the calf and throw and tie it in the fastest time possible.

"But," he continued, "the Rodeo Cowboys Association felt that it wasn't very good for the professional rodeo image for cowboys to compete wearing baseball caps and tennis shoes. So they issued a ruling that all rodeo contestants had to wear cowboy attire that included a western hat and cowboy boots. This was when some of the old-time calf-ropers came to see me and said, 'John, we don't really need that high heel on our boots. Can you make us something different?'"

While experimenting with various designs, Justin recalled a flat-heeled boot called the Wellington that the company had once made. "I tried to adapt the Wellington pattern for a cowboy boot with a flat heel, but I couldn't make it work," he related. He was getting frustrated, until he happened to think of an old military last called the 9315 that had been used to make boots for the army and for ROTC cadet officers at Texas A&M University.

"It was as fine-fitting a last as there ever was," John, Jr., said. "So I began working with the 9315 last. It didn't work at first. It didn't fit good, it didn't feel good. But after many, many trials, we finally developed the pattern for what we called our Roper. It featured a flat heel, just like a shoe heel, and we made it on the 9315 last. We put it into our inventory and it just went great. A lot of people began wearing it. And the rodeo calf-ropers loved it."

Even after its initial success, the Roper almost became a victim of the cowboy-western craze that hit the country in the 1960s. "When the craze began," John, Jr., explained, "people began demanding fancy hides like ostrich, alligator and snakeskins. We didn't have the capacity then to produce all of these exotic boots, plus the Roper. The Roper was a comparatively inexpensive boot, while the exotic boots with the fancy leathers were very expensive. Since we made more money on the more expensive boots, we kept on making them and cut the Roper out.

"But people kept on asking for them. So several years later, when we needed some more business and had the capacity, we put the Roper back into production. And it's just gone great. Today it represents a large portion of our sales."

The Roper was also instrumental in the development of another highly successful boot—the Justin Lacer. "Back in the Nocona days," John, Jr., said, "we made a lot of lace-up boots for the oilfield workers. We made what we called an eight-inch Driller. This was a big, wide-toed boot. Around the oil rigs, they liked a boot that you could pull up tight around your ankles. Now there was a shoe made in Oregon or Washington called the White's Packer that a lot of the lumberjacks wore. It laced up real tight and had a kind of an unusual-shaped heel on it.

"Well, some years ago, J. T. Dickinson, now the president of Justin Industries, was in Reno visiting one of our boot dealers who asked him, 'Is there any way you can make a Roper that would lace up like a Packer? A lot of those working cowboys up in northern California would like that.'

"So when J. T. got back to Fort Worth, he told the people in the plant about the dealer in Reno who had asked him about designing a lace-up Roper. They got on it right away. They found an old eight-inch Driller pattern and put it on the Roper last and made up a boot in the Reno dealer's size and shipped it to him."

The dealer in Reno loved the new product. No sooner had the boots arrived, than he was on the phone to the plant in Fort Worth asking, "Can you make me 500 pair?" As soon as the five hundred-pair shipment arrived, the dealer called back with another order. "So, without any fanfare or drum-beating, the thing spread like wildfire," Justin continued. "Now even women wear them and love them. We make them in most every color you can think of. There's a woman out in the Big Bend country who runs a museum there. She's about ninety years old. She wears them and she thinks they're just the greatest thing.

"They were so popular that for a long time we were way behind in filling Lacer orders. And they keep on doing just great. In fact, we now have two factories in Missouri that make nothing but Ropers and Lacers. We've even taken them into our Diamond J line, which is our less expensive line. They're not leather-lined the way our more expensive boots are. And they have a leather top and vamp. But they're still good boots, better than anyone else makes in that price range."

A feature story in USA Today noted that country-western singers George Strait and Garth Brooks wear the high-topped, lace-up boots.

Justin's innovative thinking showed itself in other product developments, among which was a new specialty line of college boots that made their initial appearance in the 1950s. The boots came about as a result of John, Jr.'s desire to show his allegiance to the TCU Horned Frogs while attending their football games. He designed a special pair of boots for himself in the TCU colors—purple and white—with the likeness of a horned frog inlaid on the front. After proudly showing off his new boots at a TCU home game, Justin soon found himself deluged with requests from other Frog fans for a similar pair. Pretty soon, after the media began publicizing the boots, requests began coming in from boosters at other colleges.

Justin's next step was to make up a pair of boots featuring the colors and the mascots of each of the teams on the 1954 TCU schedule for display the week of the game in each of the cities where the games were played. Boots were initially produced for the Arkansas Razorbacks, Southern Methodist Mustangs, Texas Longhorns, Baylor Bears, Texas A&M Aggies, Rice Owls, Texas Tech Red Raiders, Oklahoma Sooners, Kansas Jayhawks and Michigan State Spartans.

The college boots were naturals for media attention and excited so much interest that a number of Justin retailers across the country requested them for displays at rodeos and other civic events.

Justin's diamond anniversary year was historic for another reason. It was the year that three pairs of Fort Worth-made Justin boots traveled faster than any cowboy boots had been known to travel before. The boots were worn by three aerial cowboys from the United States Navy when their Texas-built F7U-3 Cutlasses broke the sound barrier at the National Air Show in Dayton, Ohio.

The boots had been presented to the pilots, Commander G. W. (Red) Brooks and Lieutenants Billy Phillips and Jack Christiansen, at the Justin plant in Fort Worth the day before they flew the Cutlasses from the Chance Vought Aircraft Corporation plant in Grand Prairie, where they were built, to Dayton.

Meantime, Justin continued to make news during its diamond anniversary year. On May 4, 1954, *Look* magazine featured a photograph of a pair of Justin boots belonging to Governor Dan Thornton of Colorado; they were decorated with the head of a champion Hereford bull. "While women are experimenting with fancy playshoes, men haven't hesitated to show their liking for cowboy boots and have helped one firm build up its business to eight thousand pairs a day," the *Look* article declared. "Governor Dan Thornton of Colorado wears cowboy boots for everything except golf—presidential inaugurations included. His latest pair, custom-made by Justin's, is imprinted with the likeness of his prize Hereford bull, TT Triumphant."

Thornton had been the recipient of considerable publicity after the presidential election of 1952 by wearing cowboy boots to the black tie inaugural ball of his close friend and golfing partner, Dwight D. Eisenhower. Ike and his wife Mamie were already the owners of matched pairs of made-to-order Justin boots presented to them by the famed Fort Worth wildcatter Sid W. Richardson. Richardson's gift to the Eisenhowers was chronicled in an article about Justin's individualized "Personality Boots" that appeared in *Western Horseman* magazine in 1954.

The publicity continued with the publication in November 1954 of a photograph in *American Shoemaking* magazine of Admiral Arthur D. Radford, chairman of the Joint Chiefs of Staff, receiving a pair of specially-made, "four-star" cowboy boots from John Justin, Jr., in Dallas after adressing the Dallas Council on World Affairs.

Then there was a letter postmarked Los Angeles and dated September 13, 1956, which brought John, Jr., the following tidings:

> "I am delighted with the boots which you so kindly sent to me. They will get a good working-out this weekend, as we are spending a few days with friends at their ranch in northern California. Thank you so much from both Robert and myself."

The letter was signed, "Jane Russell."

On January 12, 1955, H. J. Justin & Sons purchased the controlling interest in the Justin Leather Goods Company. The purchase was made through a $100,000 loan from the Massachusetts Mutual Life Insurance Company, to be paid back monthly over a period of ten years. "By combining some of the functions of these companies, economies can be affected that should put both companies in a more competitive position," Justin said in announcing the deal.

The year 1955 was marked by an upswing in sales and a return to profitability, spearheaded by the introduction of a number of new styles as part of a long-range plan to place greater emphasis on styling. The new strategy continued to pay dividends, as sales rose and net income increased. In 1956 and 1957 sales soared to an all-time high.

In late 1957, the company launched a carefully-researched marketing, sales promotion and advertising program featuring renewed emphasis on service to dealers by the sales force; the implementation of a new "Our Dealer is King" policy aimed at retailers; and a consumer advertising campaign tapped in on the Old West nostalgia then sweeping the nation.

"We felt what we had been saying in our advertising was pretty prosaic," John, Jr., noted. "We wanted to come up with something different that would have greater sales appeal." What resulted was an approach featuring photographs or drawings of cowboys in authentic western settings.

One of the first ads showed a cowboy rolling a cigarette while hunkered down alongside his horse out on the range. Another featured a cowboy leaning over a campfire, intently stirring something in a large pot. The copy read: "Some things are a tradition in the West—Like Son-of-a-Gun Stew; Like Justin Boots." A third ad showed two cowpokes sitting on a corral fence, with the copy stating, "A Westerner likes a break after a long hard day. A Westerner more often than not wears Justin Boots."

The ads hit home with a gratifying impact and evoked a surprising number of congratulatory letters, many from people in the North and East, where Justin was opening new markets. Although about seventy-five per cent of sales volume still came from Texas, Oklahoma, New Mexico, Arizona, California, Colorado, Wyoming and Oregon, the company now had true national distribution.

Dealer catalogs, dealer mailings, retailer mailing aids and customer statement inserts also reflected the new approach, showing cowboys and Justin Boots color photographs of cattle-country scenes. The campaign attracted the attention of *Sales Management* magazine, which sent writer Mary Pirie to Fort Worth to interview Justin officials. Her article, which appeared in the magazine's December 1958 issue, credited the new "softer sell" advertising campaign and the implementation of the "Dealer is King" program for retailers with sparking a strong upswing in sales.

She quoted sales manager Jack Harrell about other successful innovations. "We try to persuade each retailer that he's much more than just another name on our books," Harrell was quoted. "Nowadays, each new Justin dealer receives a personal letter of welcome signed by President John Justin, Jr., or myself."

The article concluded: Not all shoe-repair men can mend fine boots in a way that preserves their fit, comfort and appearance, so Justin suggests its cowboy boots come home for repairs. Tagged to each pair of new Justin boots is a small booklet that tells the customer how to care for his boots and included a repair order form.

fifteen

Hizzoner, the mayor

In early 1959, John Justin, Jr., was the recipient of a telephone call from H. B. (Babe) Fuqua, inviting him to a meeting to be held in the board room of the Fort Worth National Bank. An invitation from Fuqua, whose name was synonymous with hard-headed business acumen and political clout, was an offer he couldn't refuse. A wealthy oilman who headed the Texas Pacific Coal & Oil Company and also served as board chairman of the Fort Worth National Bank, Fuqua had assumed the mantle of leadership in Fort Worth after the 1955 death of Amon G. Carter, the charismatic publisher of the *Star-Telegram*.

Fuqua was the dominant figure on the Fort Worth political scene, exercising his power through the powerful Fort Worth Citizen's Committee, an organization of leading downtown businessmen, merchants, bankers and lawyers that also was irreverently known throughout the city as the "Seventh Street Gang." The term "gang" was a misnomer, evoking images of machine-run enclaves like New York's Tammany Hall, Boss Hague's Jersey City or Tom Pendergast's Kansas City. The fact was that the members of the citizens' committee were a far cry from a pack of ward-heelers. Fuqua and his cohorts' primary motivation was assuring that the city was run in a manner that would insure its orderly growth and attract new business and industry to town.

The power of the citizen committee lay in its ability to raise campaign funds for its anointed candidates and to dry up the sources of money for opponents. Traditionally, an aspiring candidate for public office would make his way to Fuqua's office in the Fort Worth National Bank Building to ask for his political blessing. The plain-spoken Fuqua would lay it on the line—yes or no—never leaving the supplicant unsure of where he stood. Some of the rejected suitors took the bit in their teeth and ran anyway, usually to no avail. But with the advent of single-member districts, the power of the Seventh Street Gang evaporated. Its eventual demise was inevitable.

But it was still in its heyday when John, Jr., received his summons from Fuqua. A city council election was in the offing and Fuqua and his colleagues were trying to put together a strong slate of candidates. There was some concern over the general calibre of some of the candidates they had backed and elected in recent years.

"After Mr. Carter passed away, there was this void which Mr. Fuqua was trying to fill," Justin said. "Because Mr. Carter had been such a strong leader, the city officials were used to sitting at their phones waiting for him to call and tell them what to do next—and that's what was done. We really didn't have much city government. And we weren't getting much leadership from the city council."

At the meeting in the Fort Worth National's richly appointed board room, whose paneled walls were graced by a priceless collection of Frederick Remington and C. M. Russell paintings, Fuqua told Justin and the others in the room they were going to comprise the citizens' committee slate in the upcoming city council election.

"He asked us to run for city council, "Justin said. "He really didn't ask us. He told us. He said, 'If you don't have any reason not to, we expect you to run.' He really laid it on us. He sugared it up pretty good. He said, 'You won't have to do anything. All you've got to do is say you'll do it. We'll run the campaign. We'll finance it. We'll run the ads. We'll do everything.' He asked us to let him know our decision as soon as we could. So I went home to talk to Jane about it.

"Jane was very knowledgeable about the council because she had been attending council meetings regularly as part of her Junior League work. She had told me a number of times that the council was weak and needed an infusion of new blood. When I told her that the citizens' committee had asked me to run, she strongly recommended that I do it. So the next day, I told Mr. Fuqua that I'd run."

Jane recalled urging John to make the race. "John really didn't have to ask me because he knew that I'd be for it as a result of attending all of those council meetings. I'd come home from the meetings and tell John about all of the things that were going on. I don't think he really believed me when I told him how bad things were. But he knew how strongly I felt about it."

All nine members of the Fort Worth City Council were still being elect-ed at large in 1959, but each candidate ran for an individual place on the council. Justin was a candidate for Place 3. To become an official candi-date, he recounted, he had to go down to the city hall and sign his name in a book saying he was running for the city council, Place 3. He wound up with two opponents.

"One of the guys who ran against me had one arm," Justin recalled. "He was a pretty good old boy. He had all these tenant houses that he kept up for a landlord, and he'd go around every week to collect the rent. The other guy who ran against me worked for a used car lot on the North Side and slept in one of the cars every night. His job was to keep the cars clean."

One of the first things Justin learned about campaigning was that it would involve numerous public appearances. This was before television advertising replaced stump oratory on the political scene. "Some of the churches were pretty political in those days," he recollected, "and they'd have meetings on their premises and invite all of the candidates. Getting an invitation was like receiving a summons. The invitation would read, 'Mount Pisgah Baptist Church is having a meeting of all city council can-didates so that our membership can make up their minds who to vote for.'

"I was new to the game, and when I asked if I should go, I was told that I was expected to be there. The first meeting I went to, the preacher got up and made a thirty-minute speech about how he was going to limit each candidate to twenty minutes. I don't know how many of us were there, but if we'd all spoken for twenty minutes, we'd still be there. He took us in alphabetical order.

"My one-armed opponent got up and said that he had lost his arm while serving in the marines during the war. He said he was one of the guys that put the flag up on Iwo Jima. He made a pretty effective speech, 'I lost this arm defending you on Iwo Jima and now I'm running for the city council. . . .'

"Then I got up. I was kind of unaccustomed to that type thing. So I told them my name and what I did and that I loved Fort Worth and that was why I was interested in serving on the council.

"When they called on the other guy running against me, he jumped up on the rickety folding chair he'd been sitting on. I thought it was going to collapse beneath him. And he threw his arms up in the air and screamed a Tarzan yell, 'Ayeyyee, aye-yee, aye-yee.' I couldn't believe my eyes or my ears.

"The next night we went to another church and he did the same thing. I thought that, maybe, there was something missing here that I didn't know about, so I went up to him afterwards and said, 'That's a pretty good deal you've got going there.'

"And he said to me, I'll never forget it, 'Oh, John, I couldn't talk to these people. When I get up on my feet, I couldn't even tell them my name. But I guarantee you that they'll remember me on election day.'

"And they did remember him on election day. He got twenty-five per cent of the votes. The one-armed guy got nearly twenty-five percent. And I got a little over fifty percent, so I was elected without a runoff."

The citizens' committee was successful in electing its slate of candidates in the council election in April 1959, and at the first meeting of the new council later that month, Justin was selected as mayor pro tem by his new colleagues. Thomas A. McCann was reelected mayor by a unanimous vote. Two years later, however, with the 1961 city elections coming up again in April, dissension divided the council.

"There were things going on that some of us felt were not equitable for the city," Justin recalled. "The citizens' committee wanted me to run again, which I did."

This time Justin failed to draw an opponent and was reelected without opposition. Now he was approached by the citizens committee about succeeding McCann as mayor. This was before the city charter was amended to call for the mayor to be elected at-large rather than by the city council.

"They wanted me to allow my name to be put up for mayor. They thought I could get the five votes needed to beat Tom McCann, who they felt needed to be replaced. I knew the council would be divided. Tom was a very well-liked guy, a lot of people knew him, he'd been serving as mayor since 1957 and had been on the council since 1955. He also loved being mayor."

The citizens' committee's opposition to McCann stemmed from the belief that he was too lenient on real estate developers. Justin agreed that a more rigorous development policy was needed, and his views were shared by another city councilman, Gene Cagle, a radio station executive who was Justin's principal backer for mayor. On the other hand, there were other members of the council who were committed to supporting McCann's bid for reelection. The race appeared to be a toss-up as the newly elected council convened for its first meeting on Friday morning, April 21, 1961.

After Justin was elected, McCann told council members that he thought the best thing he could do in the interest of harmony was to leave the council. After finishing his statement, McCann walked down the middle of the council chamber, out the door and to the elevator. As the door closed, his last words heard by newspaper reporters were, "no comment."

Two things have remained vivid in Justin's memory of his election as mayor. One is McCann stomping out of the council chambers. The other is council member Thomas D. Thompson chomping angrily on a cigar. "I'll never forget the picture that ran in the *Fort Worth Press* the next day," Justin said. "Tommy Thompson blew a big smoke ring and the photographer caught me inside the smoke ring, like it was a picture frame around my neck."

It was not the most propitious time to become mayor, Justin soon discovered. "We had a lot of problems as a result of the rapid growth the city had undergone after the war," he recalled. "We had water problems. We had development problems. We had pie-crust streets all over town. I had a friend, Gordon Thompson, who bought a new home out in a new addition in the southwest part of town. The street got so bad at his house, and it had been installed only two or three years earlier, that he had to park his car two blocks from his house and walk home."

Justin recalled inspecting a new addition and having his boot heel go through the asphalt of a brand new street. "There wasn't even a half-inch of asphalt there," he said. "One of the main problems the city encountered was that developers received the specifications for putting in a proper street, but wouldn't comply with the specs. Since the city was so understaffed with inspectors, a developer would say, 'I've got to get this job done. Just give me the money and I'll put the streets in.' The city would give him the money to do the job, but they never inspected it properly."

On one occasion, Justin found himself inundated with complaints about the slowness of a construction project on Beach Street, a major thoroughfare in East Fort Worth. Every week, the city council heard reports that the contractor was working night and day to complete the job. But every week, the complaints kept coming in from residents of the area. Justin finally drove out to the site, unannounced, to check on the progress.

"Beach Street had sunflowers up over my head," he related. "They hadn't worked on it in months. The contractor was taking advantage of the city. He'd work a while on Beach Street, then move the equipment someplace else, then come back to it and work some more. No wonder the jobs weren't getting finished."

At the next council meeting, Justin had a bus waiting outside the city hall. When the contractor's representative reported that work on Beach Street was proceeding on schedule, Justin announced that he had arranged for a bus to take the members of the council for an immediate inspection of the site, much to the contractor's consternation. The project was completed shortly thereafter.

Under Justin's prodding, the council finally enacted ordinances placing more rigid restrictions and requirements on developers, an action which did nothing to enhance Justin's popularity with this influential group which up to then had enjoyed carte blanche at city hall.

Justin also found there were a number of other problems that lessened the joys of public service. One constant thorn in his side was the newspaper coverage of council activities. "I'd come home from an all-day council meeting," Justin recalled, "and Jane would greet me and begin telling me that she'd read about the meeting in the afternoon paper. She would start telling me what the stories had said about what happened at the meeting, and I couldn't believe what I was hearing. Finally, I'd tell her, 'That's not the same meeting I attended.'

"The newspapers would give reports on what we were doing that had little or no relationship to what had really occurred," Justin added.

Then there were the constant telephone calls from irate taxpayers. Friends had suggested, after his election, that he get an unlisted telephone number, Justin reported. His answer was, "If I have to have an unlisted number, I'll quit." He almost had to reconsider as the calls began to mount. One hot Saturday afternoon, Justin received a call from a female constituent complaining that there was an elephant's foot on her front porch. Justin checked into the matter and found that the remains of a deceased pachyderm from the Fort Worth Zoo had been discovered by some fun-loving teenagers who had dismembered it and distributed portions of its anatomy around the more affluent areas of the city. Justin was successful in getting city cleanup crews into action quickly.

Another call came well after midnight from an upset citizen who reported that his neighbors' dogs were running loose on his street and keeping him awake with their barking. Justin promised to send out the dogcatchers to corral the canines, but the caller refused to say where he lived for fear his neighbors would get mad at him. Justin finally pinned down the site by asking the complainant to describe his surroundings and nearby landmarks.

Justin's all-time favorite disgruntled citizen story, however, revolved around an individual who awoke him at four o'clock one morning to complain that his garbage hadn't been picked up on schedule. "I was careful to be very polite to the guy," Justin recounted. "I thanked him for calling the matter to my attention and promised that I would look into the problem promptly."

Several days later, Justin set his alarm clock for four in the morning and called the complainant back. "I asked him if his garbage problem had been taken care of. He said that it had and thanked me for the quick results. Then I told the guy that I hoped I hadn't disturbed him by calling him at such an early hour. He assured me that I hadn't. It turned out that he worked the swing shift and had just gotten home."

With the completion of his term as mayor in 1963, Justin decided not to run for reelection. "Serving as mayor," he declared, "was rewarding, but it also was just about the hardest work I've ever done. After four years on the council, two years as mayor pro tem and two years as mayor, I figured that was all the time that I could afford to give."

Jane added, "John always believed that you've got to give something to your government, not just criticize it. And he gave four years of his life. I had urged him to agree to run for mayor. Later, when we were in the middle of his term, I sometimes wished that I hadn't felt so strongly about it."

One of the highlights of Justin's tenure as mayor was a visit he made to Berlin with twenty-two other U. S. mayors in October 1961 during the height of the Cold War. While there, he paid an official call on Mayor Willy Brandt and visited the Cowboy Club of West Berlin, of which he was made an honorary member. The club met in a rustic log clubhouse that resembled a Hollywood western movie set, Justin remembered. But what really impressed him was the fact that each member was attired in full western regalia that had been individually concocted, including denim jeans, cowboy hats, six-shooters, and cowboy boots with spurs.

At the time of Justin's election to the Fort Worth City Council in 1959, he was already well along in planning the company's eightieth anniversary observance. The celebration was highlighted by a week-long open house in September, with employees donning western attire and serving refreshment to the visitors who flocked into the plant to see cowboy boots being made. The company called the event the "Justin Service Anniversary."

At the opening of the anniversary observance on September 14, 1959, John Justin, Sr., snipped a ribbon outside the front entrance to the plant, while several hundred employees and visitors overflowed into the street. After the ribbon-cutting, a man who had been part of the audience attempted to push his way through the crowd and into the building. Unable to do so because of the crowd, the man accosted John, Jr., and asked, "Is this the place where I can buy some boots?"

"It sure is," Justin assured him and ushered him inside.

The customer, as it turned out, was T. P. Kendrick, a rancher from nearby Burleson, south of Fort Worth. Justin fitted Kendrick with a pair of boots of his choice and then informed him that the boots were on the house.

John Justin, Sr., participated in the festivities even though he had suffered a stroke several months earlier. John, Jr., recalled the circumstances:

"Jane and I were playing golf with Dr. Bob Barker and his wife at River Crest," he related. "One of the golf shop employees came out on the course and caught up with us and told me that my father had suffered a stroke. We jumped into my car and drove out to Eagle Mountain Lake, where my parents lived. When we got there, we called an ambulance and got him to the hospital in Fort Worth.

"He never recovered from the stroke, but he got to where he could handle himself pretty well. I'd get him every Thursday and take him out to Colonial Country Club for lunch. He had his old friends out there and he would play gin rummy with them.

"Then, about six months later, he had another stroke. We took him to the hospital, but he never regained consciousness. They did everything they could, of course.

"Until he had his stroke, he came in to the plant every day. He came in real early and opened the mail, which he'd done since it had been a small place. He had a little bone-handled pocketknife that he kept as sharp as a razor. He'd slit those envelopes open and take the mail out, separate the orders from the checks, and get the day started before anyone else got there.

"There was a lot of hand-cutting still going on in the plant at that time, and he'd go down to the hand-cutter's block every day and sharpen that knife. You could shave with it. And, boy, he'd open those envelopes. . . ."

Eventually, John, Jr., purchased a letter-opening machine to cope with the flood of mail that poured into the office every day. By then, his dad had pretty well accepted the modern innovations that his son had installed. "As much as he loved his little pocketknife, he thought the let-ter-opening machine was great," John, Jr., said.

John, Sr., died on Tuesday, November 17, 1959. He was seventy-one. Funeral services were held the following day at the First Methodist Church. Burial was in Greenwood Cemetery. "The King of Western Boot Makers is Dead," a headline in the *Fort Worth Press* announced. The *Fort Worth Star-Telegram* called him "one of the most colorful men in the leather industry," then added this footnote: "He saw the rise of boot pro-duction from 15 pairs a week to 1,000 pairs a day."

sixteen

Bricks and boots

In the early spring of 1960, John Justin was in his office when his phone rang. Governor Price Daniel of Texas was on the line.

"John," the governor declared, "there's going to be a national governors' conference in Glacier Park, Montana, this summer. It's customary for governors to exchange gifts on behalf of their states at these meetings. Texas hasn't given a gift in a number of years. I'd like to rectify that this year." Then, pausing for effect, he added, "What could be better than a pair of Justin boots?"

Daniel informed Justin that he was planning to raise the funds to finance the purchase of the boots from private contributions. Justin told him he would be glad to cooperate by providing the boots at wholesale prices. Daniel would provide him with the shoe size of each of the governors.

"But I knew that wouldn't assure our getting a proper fit for a cowboy boot," Justin observed, "because shoe sizes do not necessarily match boot sizes. A shoe size of 10C might translate into a 9 1/2D or a 10 1/2B in a cowboy boot. This meant that we would have to set aside several pairs of boots for each governor to try on to assure the best possible fit."

Justin was determined that each governor would receive a pair of boots that fit him properly, because for a number of them it would be the first pair of cowboy boots they'd ever worn. Over the next few weeks, Daniel's staff provided Justin with the shoe sizes of each of the nation's governors. As the sizes came in, Justin had cowboy boots in the same approximate lengths and widths taken out of regular stock and packed for shipping. The day before the governors' conference began, a Lockheed Lodestar that Justin later learned had been furnished by Senator Lyndon B. Johnson, then the majority leader of the United States Senate, landed at Meacham Field in Fort Worth. Justin climbed aboard the aircraft. Earlier, two plant employees had departed for Glacier Park in a truck carrying about 125 pairs of Justin boots in a wide variety of sizes.

When he arrived at the hotel where the conference was to be held, Justin was provided with a large room where the governors could be fitted with their boots. As each governor checked in, he received a letter from Daniel informing him that a pair of Justin boots personally fitted by John Justin awaited him.

"Of course, the governors flocked into the fitting room," Justin recalled. "The whole thing turned out to be even better than I had hoped. With the possible exception of one or two, every governor got a perfect fit, which was a miracle. They were really impressed."

Price Daniel, a Democrat, had more than gubernatorial goodwill in mind when he made the boot presentations to his fellow governors, most of whom happened also to be Democrats. The Democratic National Convention in 1960 was scheduled to be held in Los Angeles immediately after the governors' conference adjourned, and Daniel's major assignment at the conference was to attempt to secure backing from the Democratic governors in attendance for Lyndon Johnson as the Democratic presidential nominee. Johnson and Senator John F. Kennedy of Massachusetts were the front-runners in a no-holds-barred battle for the nomination. Daniel was so busy politicking for LBJ at the conference, Justin recalled, that he even enlisted Justin's aid in reporting to Washington on how he was faring in his efforts to secure pledges of support from the various governors.

"They gave me a number in Washington to call," Justin related, "and when someone got on the line, I would give him a name and just say, 'yes' or 'no.' That was all."

The hotly contested presidential nomination, of course, was won by Kennedy, who then profferred the vice presidential nod to Johnson. After LBJ's ascension to the presidency following Kennedy's assassination, he frequently wore his Justin boots to White House functions and on his ranch on the Pedernales River. In the presidential election campaign of 1964, Johnson's opponent, Barry Goldwater of Arizona, also was a confirmed Justin boot wearer.

A poignant note was struck in Fort Worth on November 23, 1963, at a breakfast attended by President and Mrs. Kennedy just prior to their departure for Dallas. The last gift accepted by Jackie Kennedy on that fatal day was a custom-made pair of pink Justin boots that just happened to match the suit and pillbox hat she was wearing.

In the mid-1960s, Justin was involved in a presentation ceremony of a specially crafted pair of boots for Jayne Mansfield that still remains vividly etched in his memory. Justin grinned broadly as he relived the sweltering day in Houston when the buxom blonde movie star accepted her pair of specially made white Justin boots, emblazoned with a big pink heart, and promptly bent to the task of putting them on.

"My good friend, Eddie Chiles, who was then the chairman of the board of the Western Company of North America, had invited a large group of oil company presidents to a big party in Houston," Justin related. "Eddie always did things in a big way, and for this particular party he had lined up Jayne Mansfield as a special guest to assure a big attendance.

"Well, Eddie called me up and asked, 'Can you make me a pair of white boots with pink hearts on them? I want to present them to Jayne Mansfield at a party I'm giving in Houston.'

"I told him that I'd be happy to accommodate him. That's when he invited me to fly down to Houston with him to make the presentation. He said it would add a special touch to the proceedings to have me present the boots."

The task of designing the boots for Miss Mansfield fell to the company's chief custom designer, Rudolpho Pacheco, a true artist at creating a design and then putting it on leather. Pacheco had been the designer of the college boots, as well as boots for a number of celebrities.

On the day of the party, Justin and Chiles flew to Houston in the Western Company plane. The weather in Houston was normal for a summer afternoon—hot and humid. "I'll never forget how hot it was at Hobby Airport when we went out to meet Jayne Mansfield's plane," Justin recalled. "We stood in that broiling sun as they rolled one of those portable ramps up to the plane. People began disembarking, but there was no sign of Jayne Mansfield. It must have been about 120 degrees out there. Eddie and I were wearing coats and ties, and I was beginning to sweat into my boots. We were about to give up, when here she came.

"What an entrance she made. She was wearing a low-cut dress and dragging a sable coat behind her. The newspaper photographers and TV cameramen ate it up.

"Eddie had an air-conditioned limousine waiting. When we got inside, she said to Eddie, 'Mr. Chiles, what do you want me to do?' Eddie told her there was going to be a press conference at which I would present her with a pair of Justin boots. She smiled at me and said that would be just great.

"When we got to the room where the press conference was to take place, it was jammed with photographers. Eddie introduced me, and I said a few appropriate words. Then I presented Miss Mansfield with the boots.

"'They're so beautiful,' she gushed, 'I've just got to put them on, right now.' I could see the photographers readying their cameras.

"She sat down, took off one of her shoes, picked up one of the boots and started to pull it on. Now, remember, she was wearing this really low-cut dress. And when she leaned over to pull on the boot, well, the cameramen really went berserk. . . .

"That night, that's all there was on the TV news in Houston—Jayne Mansfield and her white Justin boots with pink hearts."

In 1967, Justin celebrated his fiftieth birthday. By any measurement of achievement, his cup was running over. He was the head of a successful business. He loved his job. He was happy in his marriage. There were no clouds on the horizon. Or so it seemed.

"I now owned the boot company," he noted. "I'd bought everybody out. It was mine. So was the belt company. I figured I really had it made."

Some eighteen months later, he wasn't so sure.

An acute attack of appendicitis in the fall of 1968 caused him to reapprise his situation. "It came right out of the blue one Sunday night," Justin recalled. "I started to get up out of a chair and the pain hit me. I began hurting so bad, I almost fainted."

Within minutes Justin was on his way to the hospital, where he underwent emergency surgery. "There were no difficulties afterwards," he said. "They took out my appendix and I had a normal recuperation. But when I got to thinking about what had happened, I was scared. I began thinking about what would happen to the company if something happened to me. Everything I had was tied up in the company. I didn't want Jane saddled with having to try to run it. I knew there'd be nothing but problems and headaches for her."

Justin's soul-searching led him to discuss his concerns with Sproesser Wynn, his attorney, whose law firm at the time was also serving as legal counsel to First Worth Corporation, a Fort Worth-based company that had been formed in August 1968 as an outgrowth of Acme Brick Company.

Acme was a pioneer Fort Worth firm whose origins dated back to 1891. Early in 1968, Acme had begun broadening its construction products base through the acquisition of manufacturing facilities in Texas, Arkansas, Kansas and Louisiana. It also owned Ceramic Cooling Tower Company, a producer of custom-designed installations for air-conditioning, water treatment and related water-processing applications. With the formation of First Worth Corporation, Acme Brick and Ceramic Cooling Tower had become wholly owned subsidiaries of First Worth.

Wynn now suggested to Justin that he consider a merger with First Worth Corporation as a solution to his concerns. The proposal struck a responsive chord with Justin.

"It sounded like a pretty good idea," he recounted. "First Worth had plans for a new stock issue that would pave the way for it to apply for a listing on the New York Stock Exchange. They were already preparing the application to the Securities and Exchange Commission for the stock offering.

"Going on the New York Stock Exchange would at least give my stock a value. It would mean I could sell some of it if I wanted to. The way things were at that time, my Justin stock had no fixed value because it wasn't being traded. If something happened to me, it would have to be evaluated by the Internal Revenue Service, and I knew that it would be valued pretty high because the company was a good money-maker even though all of the money was being put back into it. There would be a lot of taxes due. I was afraid that Jane might have to sell the business to pay the taxes."

Justin began negotiating the merger proposal with D. O. Tomlin, the president of First Worth Corporation. "Tomlin wanted to make a deal," Justin said. "He painted a pretty good picture for me of what they were planning to do. They had just bought Louisiana Concrete Products Company and they'd acquired another concrete products firm in Wichita, Kansas. They had some ambitious plans for expansion and diversification. It all sounded pretty good. So I agreed to making a deal."

The agreement which Justin and Tomlin hammered out called for the acquisition by First Worth Corporation of all the outstanding capital stock of H. J. Justin & Sons in exchange for 72,225 shares of First Worth Corporation stock. The Justin Leather Goods Company, which was owned by the boot company, also was included in the deal. First Worth Corporation also agreed to acquire all of the stock of the Justin Belt Company in exchange for 37,775 shares of First Worth stock. As part of the agreement, John Justin received a guarantee from Tomlin that if the price of First Worth Corporation stock was less than $23 per share three years after the effective date of the merger, Justin would receive additional First Worth stock to make up for the deficiency.

On the morning of November 22, 1968, the front page of the *Fort Worth Star-Telegram* featured a photograph of John Justin and D. O. Tomlin shaking hands before a backdrop of boots and bricks. The accompanying story by Harold Monroe, the newspaper's financial editor, declared:

> Two of Fort Worth's oldest manufacturing companies—perhaps the two very oldest—joined Thursday under the aegis of a three-month-old corporation that bids fair to become a conglomerate. Acme Brick, already a wholly-owned division of First Worth Corporation, and Justin Boot will become one. The announcement was made jointly by D. O. Tomlin, president of First Worth, and John Justin, president of the three Justin companies. . . .
>
> John Justin will remain actively in charge of all Justin operations, and additionally has become a director and member of the executive committee of First Worth.

The linking up of Acme Brick Company with H. J. Justin & Sons brought together two enterprises dating back to Texas' pioneer past. There was a similarity in the heritage of each company. Acme's founder, George Ellis Bennett, left his home in Ohio at the age of sixteen to seek his fortune. He came to Texas by way of Missouri, where he apprenticed himself to a wholesaler in St. Joseph. In 1874, he established his own mercantile business in Butler, Missouri. The business, however, went belly up during the depression of the mid-1870s.

Scraping together a few dollars, Bennett set off for Texas for a fresh start, arriving in Dallas about the same time that H. J. Justin was opening his boot shop in Spanish Fort. Bennett landed a job in Dallas as a salesman with McCormick Harvester Reaper, a farm implement company, and then became general manager of the Tompkins Implement Company.

Late into the nineteenth century, the brick industry was still in its infancy in Texas. But the demand for brick was mushrooming. Bennett kept an eye out for the ideal combination of clay or shale deposits, fuel supply, an adequate labor pool and transportation facilities. In 1890, he borrowed a railroad handcar and pumped westward from Fort Worth along the Texas and Pacific line. In Parker County, at Rock Creek, a tributary of the Brazos River, he extracted some clay samples which he sent to Chicago for testing. The samples were found to be suitable for brick-making.

The initial Acme Brick plant was built in Parker County on Rock Creek, a mile from its confluence with the Brazos River at Littlefield Bend, some two miles southwest of the present site of the city of Millsap. Texas' first brick plant, still in operation today, is known as Acme's Bennett Plant.

The first bricks, made of sandy clay, were utterly useless. But three months of experimentation brought forth bricks of superior grade. Full production of the first factory required fourteen workers and a stable of mules and horses. Shale was mined by blasting, then dried, ground and screened and molded into brick shape under enormous pressure. A cheap grade of coal found in the area was used in the firing of brick handset in updraft kilns.

From the outset, Acme had more orders than it could fill. Plant expansion began almost immediately and a company-owned town grew up around the brick works. Facing problems of energy sources and high prices early in the life of the company, Bennett bought his own coal mines.

Bennett died in 1907 while on a business trip to Galveston and was succeeded as president by his son, Walter F. Bennett, then just twenty years old. Young Bennett also inherited a number of problems, most of which were a result of the financial panic of 1907. Declining sales led to layoffs, which provoked workers' strikes. Bennett took an inventory, locked the plant office, left the keys with timekeeper J. E. Fender at the company store, determined to sell the plant.

A fire in Midland, Texas, changed everything. Almost completely destroyed, the city needed building materials desperately. The plant reopened almost instantly, its kiln fires were roaring in response to a huge order. Acme Brick was back in business and growing.

seventeen

A new name and a new chairman

It didn't take long for John Justin's initial euphoria over the First Worth merger to turn into disillusionment. The smile he had displayed at the press conference announcing the merger soon changed to a grimace. He began experiencing his first doubts over the alliance only a few hours after it was made public. That evening, all of the First Worth directors and their wives attended a dinner party at the Ridglea Country Club. Everyone was in an understandably effusive mood, but Justin found himself watching the overexuberance of Sproesser Wynn and Dee Tomlin with increasing distaste.

"My antenna began to work as I watched Sproesser and Tomlin going around the room bragging about how big the company was going to become and how much money everyone was going to make," Justin recounted. "They were saying, 'We're gonna be rich. . . . We're gonna build the biggest company in Texas. . . .'

"It sounded kind of juvenile to me. And besides, that wasn't my style. I always believed in letting results do the talking. Anyway, my wheels began turning that night."

Two days later, another event added to Justin's discomfiture. He was at his desk at the boot company when three men carrying clipboards and stopwatches appeared in his office. When he asked them what they wanted, they said, "We're from First Worth. We're here to do some time studies in your factory."

"Now the first thing I told Tomlin when we made our deal," Justin said, "was that I knew the boot business. I told him, 'You're in the brick business. I'll run the boot business. I don't want anyone messing with me at all. If you want to know anything, call me and I'll come over and tell you what you want to know, give you the facts and figures or whatever it is you need.'

"So, as you might expect, when those three guys showed up at my office with clipboards and stopwatches, it didn't set too well with me. I politely showed them the door and told them not to come back. Then I called Tomlin and I said, 'That was not our deal. I'm not going to have any interference with how I run my business and there's no use talking about it.'

"He said, 'I'm sorry. Those guys should have known better. They didn't understand the situation.'

"But that got me to worrying some more over what I had gotten myself into." Recalling his growing concern over the merger, Justin added, "I had thought at first that it was the best deal I ever made. But before long, I began thinking that it was the worst deal I ever made."

Lending further fuel to his apprehensions was an incident that took place after a board meeting in New Orleans. "They had invited the wives of the directors to fly down to New Orleans in the company plane, a Queen Air, with us," Justin reported. "So they packed us all on that Queen Air. As a pilot, I couldn't help being a little concerned because the Queen Air is not a big airplane and it was just full of people. Our first stop was Baton Rouge, where we inspected a Louisiana Concrete Products plant. Then we flew to New Orleans. When we landed, there was a fleet of stretch limousines waiting for us that took us to our hotel. Every director's room was real plush and had a present in it for the wives. Everything was really first class. That night we all had a fancy dinner together. I found myself wondering what it all was costing the company.

"The next morning we went to the Hibernia Bank for our directors' meeting. The Hibernia is a real old southern bank. The board room was huge, and the board room table was the biggest table I'd ever seen. It must have been sixty feet long or, maybe, longer. There were only six or seven of us, and we sat around one corner of the table and held our meeting."

After the meeting, as the group arrived at the airplane for the return flight to Fort Worth, Tomlin came up to Sproesser Wynn and Justin as they prepared to board the aircraft and said to Wynn, "Maybe you ought to bring John up to date on that new development."

"I wondered what he meant by that," Justin added. "I was a director and I was supposed to know everything that was going on. Anyway,

Sproesser took my arm and led me to a spot underneath one of the air-plane's wings and said, 'John, we have a little problem, but it doesn't real-ly amount to anything.' Then he informed me that the company had had to withdraw its public offering. He soft-soaped it real good. I didn't find out the rest of it until later. But that's when I began to really worry about what I had gotten myself into."

Calling off the public offering, of course, signaled the death knell for First Worth's hopes of getting a New York Stock Exchange listing. Without the offering, First Worth simply did not have enough stock outstanding and a sufficient number of shareholders to meet the NYSE's listing require-ments. In addition, First Worth had been planning to finance its ambitious expansion plans with the proceeds from the public offering. The offering was going to be the catalyst that would allow First Worth to do all of the things it had talked about to Justin, including expanding boot production. So Sproesser Wynn's news blew Justin's hopes out the window.

Justin later learned the details of what had torpedoed the public offer-ing. "First Worth had sent one of its attorneys to Washington to expedite the registration of the public offering with the Securities and Exchange Commission," he recounted. "He was supposed to hand-carry the regis-tration papers around to the proper people and get them signed. So the attorney was in Washington doing his expediting, and he was on the verge of getting the paperwork completed, when he received a call from Fort Worth at his hotel room in the middle of the night. The caller told him to be at the door of the SEC the first thing the next morning to retrieve the papers before they were signed. What had happened was that their audi-tor had discovered some problems with their financial statements. There was some bad laundry in the drawer and they couldn't go to the SEC with those numbers."

Justin recalled this period as the most onerous and depressing of his business career. "I was really troubled, really worried," he declared. "There were so many mystifying things happening, things coming to light, that I hadn't known about. I now realized I was out of the loop. Things simply weren't the way I had been led to believe. I knew that I needed legal advice on what to do, but here again I was in a bind."

Justin's attorney, Sproesser Wynn, was also First Worth's legal counsel and a member of the First Worth board. "I didn't know what to do next," Justin admitted. "I was badly in need of legal advice. I was really fright-ened that I had made a serious mistake that could cost me everything I'd worked for."

The magnitude of the despair he was suffering was noted by his family, friends and co-workers. "It finally got so bad," Justin recalled, "that I was having trouble functioning." He remembered once when he was walking from the Fort Worth National Bank downtown and was so overcome with emotion that he had to stop for fear of passing out.

"I was leaning against a 'No Parking' sign," Justin related, "when Howard Jennings walked up to me. He could tell that something was wrong and he said, 'John, what's the matter? Are you sick?' And I began to tell him about my problem."

After listening to Justin's tale of woe, Jennings, a Fort Worth oilman, told him that he knew a bright, aggressive young attorney named Dee Kelly who might just be the answer to his problem. Kelly, at that time, had an office in the Fort Worth National Bank Building. "Kelly is smart as a whip and he's as tenacious as a bulldog when he's handling a case," Jennings told Justin. "You ought to talk to him. Let's go over to his office and see him right now."

Justin chuckled as he recalled his initial meeting with the man who would become his legal counsel, confidante and close friend. "Dee's office was so small, there was barely room for his desk and chair and the two chairs Jennings and I occupied," Justin said. "But by just talking to him, I felt as if a load had been lifted off my back."

Recalling the incident, Kelly stated, "This was in 1969. I was practicing law alone at the time. I knew who John Justin was, of course, but I didn't know him personally.

"John was very upset over the way they had taken his company into First Worth. There were a number of problems with it. John thought they had misrepresented a lot of things about First Worth when he agreed to make the deal. And, of course, Sproesser Wynn was his lawyer, and Sproesser was also on the board of First Worth. So there were some very sensitive issues involved in the case."

Kelly's advice to Justin, after reviewing the situation, was for him to sue to nullify the merger agreement. "I was prepared to file suit to get the Justin Boot Company out of First Worth, get the boot company back for John," Kelly said.

At this point, J. Olcott (Ocie) Phillips, a partner of Sproesser Wynn's in the McDonald, Sanders, Wynn, Ginsburg, Phillips and Maddox law firm, approached Kelly with an offer from First Worth Corporation. "Ocie Phillips, who was now representing First Worth, played an important role in effecting the change in management," Kelly averred.

"He came to see me and said that First Worth was prepared to give the management of the company to John if he agreed to drop the lawsuit."

Kelly, however, still felt Justin had made a serious mistake getting involved with First Worth. "At that time, as I remember it," Kelly declared, "the Justin Boot Company was the only entity in First Worth Corporation that was making any money. I don't think Acme Brick was making any money in those days. I wasn't sure in my mind about First Worth, but I was confident that John had a great boot company. So I recommended to John that he take the boot company back and forget about First Worth.

"I thought that was the more conservative approach. But John had better judgment than I did about it. He declined my advice, and he accepted the offer to become president and chief executive officer of First Worth. After that, he went about appointing his own board, and I subsequently became the company's general counsel. It all turned out a whole lot better in the long run than I thought it would."

Ruminating on his decision to take over the First Worth managerial reins rather than follow Kelly's advice, Justin said: "I could have sued. Dee had advised me to do that. But when I got to checking on it, and after talking to Ocie Phillips, I found that if I sued and won, First Worth would have to appeal. They would have to appeal all the way to the Supreme Court, which would have meant years and years of litigation. Who knows how much money would have been spent and what would have happened in the meantime? The company would have been rudderless. And there was one other consideration, an important one. All of my net worth was tied up in First Worth stock. What would happen to it in the meantime?

"I gave it a lot of thought. I really suffered over it. And I finally decided that my best course was to take over management of the company and try to pull it out."

At a special meeting of the First Worth board, Justin reminded his fellow directors that he was the largest stockholder in the company and had more at stake in First Worth's future than anyone else in the room. He said he was going against the advice of his legal counsel, but that he was willing to remain in the fold and try to turn things around provided he had full management control, including restructuring the board.

"I laid it on the line," Justin said. "Most of the members of the board knew I was right. They were worried about the way things were going. So they fired Tomlin and named me to replace him. I'll never forget what happened after the vote. Tomlin got up and said he would see us all in court. But he never filed suit against us."

Justin's election as president and chief executive officer of First Worth Corporation was announced on December 23, 1969. The news release stated that Justin would take over active direction of First Worth, in addition to retaining his duties as president of the Justin Boot Company, the Justin Belt Company and the Justin Leathergoods Company.

The news release also contained an announcement of the election of three new directors: Bayard H. Friedman, who was then a senior vice president of the Fort Worth National Bank and a former mayor of Fort Worth; Howard W. Jennings, the independent oil operator who had brought Justin and Kelly together; and Richard C. Newkirk, a certified public accountant and industrialist who later was elected a Fort Worth city councilman.

Shortly afterwards, Justin completed his restructuring of the board with the election of Jerry L. Brownlee, a former Fort Worth city manager who was then a vice president of Kimbell, Inc., and Robert E. Glaze, a real estate investor.

The new board took over under totally inauspicious conditions. An article by Barry Cheshier, financial writer for the *Fort Worth Press*, gave this description of the situation:

> Some called the 1969 slump of First Worth Corporation a reversal, a business setback, a financial embarrassment. The euphemisms, while not flattering, failed to do justice to the actual situation. In reality, the slump more closely resembled a wounded bomber, its wings shot off, spiralling flames in its earthward plunge.

"John's timing couldn't have been worse," recalled Ed Stout, who was an Acme Brick Company division vice president in Little Rock at the time of the First Worth-Justin Boot merger. Stout, who has served as president of Acme Brick since 1973, related:

"The company began to fall on hard times in early 1969 brought about by a number of factors. Number one, Acme Brick had always been subject to the cycles in housing starts, and in 1969 housing starts dropped rather dramatically from the prior year. Also, a number of acquisitions had been made by First Worth. These were not brick operations, but concrete architectural panel, prestress and concrete block companies. We made all of these acquisitions, but we didn't seem to run them very well. The existing managements were mostly owner-entrepreneurs, and we did a poor job fitting them into our corporate structure. In addition, there was the fact we were strapped for cash. We had made a pretty substantial cash outlay because we purchased all of these companies for cash. The only company First Worth didn't pay cash for was Justin. John took stock at his own request.

"So here's John, the third generation of a family business that's been going for nearly a century. He's traded for stock that's going down the tube. I could understand how he felt."

As he assumed his new responsibilities, Justin harbored no illusions over the magnitude of the problems he was facing. "I knew once I had made my decision, there was no turning back," he recalled. "Of course, I didn't know anything about the brick business. It was kind of like when you can't swim and they throw you into the pool. You either swim or you drown. I had to learn the brick business."

He had to learn it in a hurry, as it turned out. "One of the first things that happened," Justin related, "was that Bill Darwin, who had replaced Tomlin as president of Acme Brick Company, decided he wanted to go into the brick business for himself. So he resigned. I didn't have anyone to run the brick business. So I took over as president of Acme Brick. Now I was running the brick business and the boot business, too.

"I was scared," he admitted. "Maybe scared is not the correct word. It was more like I knew I was facing a challenge, a real big challenge. I felt that I knew how to run a company and how to work with people, but the brick business was entirely new to me. I soon found out, however, that the brick business wasn't all that different from making boots.

"There are two or three things that make them alike. One, bricks and boots are both made from natural materials. They are not made out of plastic or metal that you have to cast. They are natural materials, and there are certain ways you handle natural materials like a leather or a hide. No two pieces of leather are ever exactly alike. They are always a little different. You have to cut them differently. And brick is the same way. It's made out of clay and each clay deposit is a little different."

Marketing brick, Justin found, was also not all that different from selling boots. "Both are sold by displaying them to customers," he noted. "People buy bricks and boots with their eyes. I can take you over to the Acme sales office, and you'll usually find a woman there who's been coming in for the last two or three days. What's she doing? She's trying to pick out brick for a new house she's building. She'll finally get her choices down to two brick that you and I couldn't tell the difference between with a magnifying glass. She'll look at one brick and then she'll look at the other and then she'll say, 'I like this one a little better. That one's a little too brown. I sure like the texture on this one.'

"Buying brick," Justin continued, "is a decision-making process that people agonize over. The architect studies it forever trying to pick out the exact texture and color that he wants. And it's the same with boots. People will go into a boot store where there are all these boots on display and they'll look at boots for an hour trying to pick out the pair they want. A customer will say, "This one's a little too brown' or 'I like this one's color stitch pattern.'

Justin began learning the brick business by visiting Acme plants in the Fort Worth area. "I'd put on some old clothes, drive out to a brick plant, introduce myself to a workman and say, 'Show me how you make a brick.' You'd be surprised how much information you can get that way. I learned how they mixed the clay and how they extruded it, all those kinds of things. It was a constant learning process."

One of the first things that Justin discovered, as he went out into the field, was that the Acme Brick plant in Denton, which was geared to supplying large quantities of brick for major construction projects, was having a major problem with quality control. "On large orders, where uniformity of color was essential, the bricks kept changing colors," Justin said. "It had gotten so bad that none of the salesmen wanted to sell Denton brick for fear of alienating their customers. The plant was right in the middle of the large Dallas-Fort Worth market, a perfect location.

"So I got the salesmen together and told them they had to start selling Denton brick. They said, 'We're not going to sell it until you make the brick consistent. We sell a big job and we get halfway through it and the brick starts changing color. Then we get grief from the customer.'"

Delving into the situation, Justin made a number of trips to Denton, where he received a variety of opinions as to what was causing the problem. "Finally," he recounted, "I talked to one of the people at the plant and I asked, 'What can we do to make these brick consistent?' And he said, 'You can't do it the way we're doing it. The way we're mining is terrible. We have to take into account that the clays up here, the undulating clays in the ground, are different. First you have some white-burning clay and then you run into some clay that's red-burning. The only way you can correct for that is to build what's called a layer-cake process.'"

Intrigued, Justin asked, "How do you do that?"

The answer was, "I'll need some equipment. I need a big front-end loader and a scraper, which is going to cost a lot of money. But if you'll give me that, I can do it."

"Fine," Justin said. "Go ahead."

The layer-cake process worked to perfection. Denton brick began selling. The salesmen were enthusiastic. The layer-cake process is still in use at the Denton plant.

Another confidence-builder for Justin was the fact that in the brick business he was dealing with a manufactured product. "Manufacturing," he observed, "was my first love and my long suit. It's what I like the most. I like to make things, to see things made. I've never been in a manufacturing plant that I didn't see something that I could bring back with me and improve something that we were doing in our plants. I don't care what kind of manufacturing it is. So long as you're producing something, taking raw materials and making a product that somebody wants, I'm intrigued by it.

"I soon knew enough about what I was doing that no one was going to be able to tell me, 'John, we can't do this' or 'We can't do that.' If someone told me, 'We can't do that,' I now could say, 'Yes, you can.'"

In the latter part of 1970, with the company's brick production at a virtual standstill as a result of the continued doldrums in the housing industry, Justin made a decision to begin building up inventory in anticipation of an economic turnaround. It was a decision that paid off handsomely the following year, when housing starts rebounded.

Ed Stout recalled the meeting at which Justin ordered the production go-ahead: "We were talking about our inventory levels and what kind of business expectations we had for the coming year. We discussed the economics of running a brick plant at various levels of capacity and how it is just as inexpensive to keep it operating at low level of capacity as it is to shut it down because the fixed costs will continue anyway.

"We also pointed out that our business had always been very cyclical and that, historically, except for the Great Depression, the down cycles usually lasted from eighteen to thirty months. Then there would be a year of buildup and then a year or two of high activity before the next down cycle began. We have records dating back to 1917 that show that to be pretty consistent. Some of us felt that the market had to turn around. It had been down for over a year and a half, pushing two years, and John made the decision.

"He said, 'Let's go forward, let's build some inventory, because if the market is going to turn around, we'll need the brick.'

"And it turned out, he was right. In 1970, we bottomed out the down cycle. In 1971, housing starts jumped to over two million, which at that time was a record high. We went into 1971 with our wagon loaded and were able to capitalize on a good year."

Sales rose and profits soared. On October 16, 1972, two significant events took place. John Justin, Jr., was elected chairman of the board and president, and the name of the company was officially changed to Justin Industries, Inc. The company's directors had recommended the name change after a survey indicated that the First Worth identity did not reflect the corporation's current trend of growth and diversification. To many people, First Worth sounded more like a bank holding company than a manufacturing enterprise, whereas Justin Industries would take advantage of an already well-established corporate entity.

A name synonymous with cowboy boots now also stood for bricks and concrete blocks.

eighteen
Boots carry bricks

The name change coincided with a new spirit of optimism that swept over the company, welcome as a breeze to a becalmed sailor. The first glad tidings came in the form of an early Christmas greeting to Justin Industries stockholders announcing a special year-end dividend of ten cents per share, payable December 30, 1972, to shareholders of record on December 18. Stockholders were further cheered by an announcement that the board of directors intended to resume regular quarterly cash dividend payments of five cents per share in the coming year.

Wall Street also responded favorably. Jessup & Lamont, a New York Stock Exchange member firm, issued a report in early December noting that Justin Industries had achieved "dramatic improvement" over the past three years under the new management headed by John S. Justin, Jr.

The report concluded, "Considering the modest valuation of the shares, purchase of the common shares is recommended."

By this time, John, Jr., was already scarred by clay-hauling problems he had inherited from the previous management. "They weren't operating people," he asserted, "and we paid the price for that. We had trouble with the clay we were shipping to the Denton plant from a pit near Dallas. Clay has to have elasticity in order to make brick. And the clay in this particular pit had lost its elasticity because of water seepage. Workers were loading the hopper cars with wet clay for shipment to the Denton plant. By the time the clay got to the plant, it had solidified. Workmen had to use crowbars to unload it."

Every day, it seemed to Justin as he recalled that era, there was a new problem. One of the most unusual occurred one Saturday morning when Justin was enjoying one of his infrequent days at home. "The phone rang," he related. "I answered it and heard a woman, apparently very distraught, screaming at me, 'Mr. Justin, you've got to do something. One of your trucks just crashed into my house.' I finally calmed her down and elicited the information that she was calling from Denton, where she lived right next to the brick plant.

"What had happened was that a truck had been loaded with brick on Friday at the Denton plant and had been left parked at the top of an incline. Somehow, the brake had failed, and the truck had rolled down the ramp and smashed into this woman's house. She was in the kitchen washing the breakfast dishes on Saturday morning when the truck broke in. The front of the truck was actually sitting in her kitchen right next to the sink where she was standing. Fortunately, no one was hurt. But we had to rebuild the house."

Justin also recalled with a grin a meeting of the board of directors that was held at the Denton plant after he had assumed the board chairmanship. "The directors had been after me to schedule a board meeting at one of the plants so they could see, firsthand, how brick was made," John, Jr., recalled. "So I gave them their wish."

Unfortunately, the date he chose for them to visit the Denton plant was in July. "Oh, it was hot," Justin related. "All of the directors were dressed in suits. We held the board meeting in an air-conditioned room. Then we went into the plant. There's nothing hotter than a brick plant in summer, with the kilns going full blast. They never asked to visit another brick plant."

On February 1, 1973, Justin Industries reported record sales and earnings for 1972, attributing a major portion of the gains to continuing strong demands for building materials experienced by Acme Brick, which ended the year with heavy backlogs. John, Jr., who had continued to hold the title of president of the Acme Brick Company, now turned over the title and the responsibility for the brick operations to Ed Stout, who had been serving as vice president for clay production since 1971. Stout's election as president of Acme was announced on February 14, 1973.

Referring to Stout as "Mr. Brick," Justin said that the Acme president "knows more about the brick business than anybody I know."

Justin recalled that in 1971, he was up to his eyebrows with production problems. So he brought Stout to Fort Worth. "I said, 'Ed, you're a brick salesman. I want to put you in charge of brick production.'"

"He said, 'I don't know anything about production.'"

"I said, 'Well, that's good. You can learn.'"

"So I put him in charge of production of the Acme Brick operation. It was a big job, with sixteen plants in several states, but he did it. He got into it and did a great job.

"So, two years later, I made him president."

The new Acme president faced an immediate problem caused by the Arabian oil embargo. With the exception of labor, natural gas was the largest cost component in brick manufacturing. Natural gas prices had escalated rapidly in the wake of the oil embargo, and gas producers, stuck with long-term contracts, suddenly had no gas available at the "old" prices. Acme addressed the supply dilemma by entering into oil and gas exploration. The strategy paid off with the discovery of substantial quantities of natural gas. In addition, Acme was able to reduce gas consumption by as much as two-thirds at some of its plants through the introduction of new, innovative production techniques. By 1978, even though gas prices had increased tenfold from preembargo levels, the fuel reduction programs enabled Acme to minimize price increases to its customers.

The importation into Texas of six hundred to seven hundred million sub-standard Mexican brick was another major problem for homebuilders and the brick industry during this period. Most of the imported brick did not meet building codes. In cooperation with builder groups, Acme developed and delivered consumer advertising messages about the imported brick problem. As a result of this cooperative effort, substandard brick imports shrank dramatically. Radio, television, print, direct mail, and billboard advertising were utilized to build brand identification and to promote increased use of Acme brick featuring the slogan, "Acme Brick—The Best Thing To Have Around Your House."

One homebuilder, after hearing Acme's message for three consecutive years, was heard to exclaim, "First I was asked to stop using Mexican brick. Then, Acme suggested that I use brick on all four sides. Now they want me to put brick in the gables, too!"

On June 20, 1973, Justin stepped out of its bricks-and-boots orbit with the acquisition of the Northland Press of Flagstaff, Arizona, a regional publishing company specializing in fine books on the history and art of the American West. Justin had met Paul Weaver, the president of the publishing house, some years earlier and asked him to continue as Northland president.

In buying Northland, Justin had the unique opportunity of indulging his love of western history, while bringing under his corporate umbrella a company that specialized in western art publications. Sitting in his office, he was surrounded on all sides by whispers of the American past . . . bronze sculptures of cowboys, majestic faces of Indian warriors, a bronze steer in a defining moment of courage. . . . Some of the art was bought by Justin from the once-struggling artists he helped succeed. For other pieces, he simply did some old-fashioned haggling. He found the bronze steer in an antique shop and bought it for $75 simply because it struck his fancy. He later learned it was an original by western artist C. A. Beil, and he has been offered large sums of money for the bit of Americana. He's not selling.

What actually transpired, Justin recounted, was that he and Jane, accompanied by Jim Shoulders, the world champion bull rider, and his wife Sharon, were browsing in a shop in Scottsdale when he spotted the bronze steer. "I asked the woman proprietor how much she wanted for it," Justin recalled, "and she told me $150. Well, that was a lot of money to me in those days, so I told her I'd think it over. Later on, I decided I really wanted it, so I asked Bill Powers, a Justin boot salesman who lived in Phoenix, to buy the steer for me. I gave him the $150 and asked him to deliver it to me next time he was in Fort Worth. I didn't want him to ship it for fear it would be broken.

"A few weeks later, Bill walked into my office carrying the steer. He'd held it on his lap on the airplane ride from Phoenix. He put down the steer on my desk and then pulled $75 out of his pocket and handed it to me.

"'I offered the woman $75 for the steer and she took it,' he explained."

At a Fort Worth Club luncheon announcing the Northland acquisition, Justin asserted to the audience of a hundred civic and business leaders and art patrons that the purchase was more than a self-indulgence brought about by his longstanding love affair with western history and art. "The figures had to be right for my directors to approve the acquisition, and Paul Weaver is a good friend and I have long admired what he's been doing," Justin stated.

Weaver responded that a major consideration in his agreeing to join Justin Industries was that he knew that "John truly shares my deep appreciation and love for our great western heritage and the need for its preservation."

Among the luncheon guests was Dr. Ben Green, a veterinarian turned author, whose books about the Old West had been published by the Northland Press. "He's a real maverick," Justin said as he introduced Green. "When we first talked about the merger, he candidly stated, 'I don't like it a bit.' But I assured him things would be the same."

Justin's relationship with Green blossomed into a close friendship that lasted until Green's death in 1974. "He would drop into my office unannounced, sit down on the sofa and spend the day," Justin said with a chuckle. "One day, he showed up at the front door of our house carrying a sack full of squabs. He presented the squabs to Jane and matter-of-factly informed her that he had invited himself and two other couples for dinner that evening.

"'I hear you're a good cook,' he said to Jane. Then he promptly gave her painstaking instructions on how to fix the squab and left. Jane, who hates squab, told me the squab would look uncooked and be unedible if she followed his instructions on how to prepare it. So I told her to ignore him and do it her own way. She cooked the squab to perfection and carried them into the dining room on a silver platter. But I'll never forget the look of Green's face. He could tell Jane hadn't followed his instructions."

Even after divesting himself of the Acme Brick presidency, Justin found himself still wearing too many hats as president of the Justin companies and as board chairman and president of Justin Industries. His decision was to go outside the company and bring in an executive with whom he had worked closely during his tenure as mayor of Fort Worth. The announcement of the appointment of Jerry L. Brownlee as president and chief operating officer of Justin Industries was made on November 13, 1973. Brownlee, who had served as Fort Worth city manager from 1963 to 1967, had resigned his position at city hall to become executive vice president of Kimbell, Inc., a large Fort Worth-based food company. Brownlee would serve as president of Justin Industries until 1982, when he was succeeded by Ernest Blank.

In another major personnel move that took place in June 1974, Justin gave up his hat as president of the boot, belt and leather goods operations to be succeeded by Bob Whisenant, a longtime Justin sales and marketing executive. Whisenant, who had joined H. J. Justin & Sons in 1956 as a sales trainee after graduating from the University of Texas at Austin, had been serving as vice president of sales and marketing since 1970.

Shortly before the end of the first quarter of 1974, Justin Industries was back in the news with the announcement it planned to acquire the Sanford Brick Corporation of Sanford, North Carolina, in a "multimillion dollar cash transaction." Sanford Brick, which was about one-third the size of Acme Brick, was the largest brick manufacturer in North Carolina. It marketed its products in North Carolina, Virginia, Washington, D. C., and other points along the Atlantic Seaboard, a lucrative construction market in which Justin Industries had no penetration.

Only a month after the Sanford acquisition, John Justin spoke of further Acme Brick expansion in appearances before securities analysts, stockbrokers and bankers in Oklahoma City and Tulsa. In Oklahoma City, he announced plans for a major new brick plant in the area that would employ 200 workers.

The next day, speaking in Tulsa, Justin reported that Acme Brick was actively considering expansion of its new Tulsa plant, which he termed "the finest brick plant in the United States." He noted that the Tulsa facility had an annual capacity of fifty million bricks, but added: "It is not big enough. We hope to expand it to fifty-eight million brick soon, and then we have plans to ultimately double its size."

Justin told the group gathered at the Tulsa Petroleum Club that the brick business was "looking up."

The skepticism that had greeted the Acme-Justin nuptials in the investment community lingered on, even in the face of evidence that there was a synergy at work in the marriage. In John Justin's mind, the benefits of the merger had been self-evident from the start.

"One of the main reasons I felt the merger was a good idea was that Acme is a cyclical business," he averred. "Acme's sales fluctuate with the homebuilding market. But the boot business is different. It's a lot more stable. The boot company does reasonably well even in periods of economic downturn. In good times, it makes a lot of money. So Justin and Acme made a good combination."

For some reason, though, Wall Street failed to grasp the picture. Justin remembered his frustrations in trying to break through the lack of understanding exhibited by most securities analysts, investment bankers and brokerage houses. "It took time to get them to listen to me, much less accept what I was trying to sell them."

Boots and bricks were turning out to be a good combination. The markets were big and growing bigger. To meet the challenge, Justin Industries, on December 15, 1976, announced the launching of a major expansion of its brick-making capabilities. In a press release, John Justin declared: "This expansion will give us from 125 million to 150 million more brick annually, which are needed to satisfy the growing demand for brick in the Southwest."

The announcement also quoted Acme President Ed Stout as reporting that twelve Acme plants would be expanded to provide the additional production and that "new techniques for firing brick and other advances in mechanization of brick manufacturing" would be incorporated as a part of the expansion program."

John Justin often compared running a brick company to playing a game of chess. "You've got to make your moves slowly and deliberately because they can make you or break you," he declared.

"In the brick business," he added, "you've got to have the product at the right place and at the right time and you've got to make the right kind of brick for the market you're going to serve. And it goes without saying that you have to make the brick reasonably priced. All this takes knowledge and good judgment, which Ed Stout, fortunately, has."

He told of the time, in the early 1980s, when Stout came into his office and said he wanted to build a new brick plant in San Felipe County to serve the Houston area. "Ed told me they'd found some good clay deposits down there that would support a new plant. I told him, 'Go ahead.'

"Well, it takes a couple of years to build a brick plant and when that plant came on there was an economic downturn and Houston was at the very bottom of the heap. Everybody thought I'd lost my mind. They asked me, 'Why did you build a fifteen million-dollar brick plant when the market has just cratered? What were you thinking about?'

"Well, when the turnaround came, as we anticipated it would, business really boomed. Houston led the nation in housing starts. We couldn't make enough brick to take care of the orders that came in. We nearly doubled the production and still couldn't meet the demand. And San Felipe became one of our most profitable plants."

Jon Bennett, a Justin vice president, remembered an incident when he was called on from a most unlikely source to expedite the delivery of brick to a homebuilder. "This was in the late 1970s," he recalled. "I'd just been through difficult contract negotiations with the union at the Denton plant, which was our flagship plant at the time. We'd had a pretty rough time agreeing on a contract. The union's business agent negotiator didn't like me very much because I was the 'bad guy,' and I felt the same way about him. So I was really surprised when several weeks after we'd gotten the contract signed, I received a telephone call from him.

"He said, 'I wonder if you can do me a favor?'

"That really took me aback, his asking me for a favor. As I said, the negotiations hadn't been very pleasant. But I answered, 'I'll be glad to try. What is it?'

"He said, 'Well, I'm building a new house out in Wise County and I'm not having any luck buying brick. I can't get any brick. They tell me I have to wait months to get any brick. I wonder if I can prevail on you to move me ahead in the line some way. I'm really in a bind. I've got the frame up on my new house, but there's no brick in sight.'

"I told him, 'Let me see what I can do.' So I looked into it. We were able to find him some brick. I remember that he wanted dark brown brick, which we managed to find."

Bennett grinned. "He did pay a premium price for the brick," he reported. Matching a customer's demand for color can often be a headache, Bennett revealed. "There's an old story in the brick business," he said. "A customer comes in and says, 'twenty-five years ago, my daddy built this house and now I want to add a wing on it and I want the same brick.'

"Well, we're now mining a half-mile away from where the clay for that original brick came from and we're using different kilns. It's gonna be tough. But we try, and usually we can make the match."

Acme has perfected some products that nobody else in the brick business can produce. For an example, an architect doing a shopping center in a northern city had seen a Perla light buff type of brick. He decided he wanted this uniform buff-colored material for his shopping center. The brick had to be shipped from Perla, Arkansas, to Philadelphia or Rahway, New Jersey.

Bennett told the story of a restaurant that was built in midtown Manhattan some years ago. "I forget the name of the restaurant," he said, "but it was very posh. The architect wanted to do a front facade with a Colonial-type brick made by Acme. He had either seen the brick in some Acme literature or he had seen the brick itself somewhere. It was a beautiful dark red tumbled brick. And that's what he wanted for the restaurant. It's a brick that, when it's formed, is conveyed up a ramp and then tumbled down the other side. This puts bruises and minor twists on it. Then it's fired and has those anomalies in it, which makes it look like it's been hand-thrown. So these carloads of brick went all the way from Texas to Manhattan—and probably passed 150 brick plants along the way."

On November 14, 1978, Justin found himself on the receiving end of a "roast" at Ridglea Country Club in Fort Worth, at which he was honored with the Humanitarian Award of Operation Orphans, Inc., in recognition of having donated thousands of boots to underprivileged youngsters. Operation Orphans was a program inaugurated by the Fort Worth Sportsmen's Club in which children from orphans' homes in Texas, New Mexico and Oklahoma were taken to a ranch on the Llano River near Mason, Texas, and taught the basics of hunting and camping.

After noticing that many of the participants lacked proper footwear, two of the organization's trustees, R. C. (Carl) Ledford and Ralph Middleton, contacted Justin and asked him if he would donate boots to the project. Justin readily agreed. Thus began what has been termed the largest boot giveaway in Texas. "They came to me and told me about these children, and I asked what I could do to help," Justin said. "Giving the boots was their suggestion, and I was glad to do it."

Left to right, The gentlemen: Jack Benny, Edward G. Robinson and Andy Devine. The ladies are unidentified, but all wear Justin boots.

Chet Louck (Lum) and Norris Goff (Abner) of the Lum & Abner radio show. Organist Sybil Chism is in the center.

Tex Williams, Gene Autry, Nudie, Roy Rogers, and Rex Allen at Nudie's of Hollywood western outfitters, early 1940s.

A 1950 photo of
John Justin, Jr., then
president of Justin
Belt Company.

Mrs. John Justin, Sr.,
with an employee of
Justin Belt Company,
1945.

Employees of Justin Belt Company. Mrs. John S. Justin, Sr., in back center, W. D. Barton in middle row center, and John Justin, Jr., in center dressed in military uniform.

John, Jr., and Jane at the Puyallup (Washington) Rodeo in 1954.

J. S. Justin, Jr., and J. S. Justin, Sr., stand before a painting of H. J. Justin (1959).

Jane and John Justin, Jr., with their children, Dave and Mary, at the Fort Worth Rodeo. The occasion was the Justin's fortieth wedding anniversary.

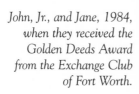

John, Jr., and Jane, 1984, when they received the Golden Deeds Award from the Exchange Club of Fort Worth.

nineteen

A hundred years of legendry

"When the Statue of Liberty was unveiled on October 28, 1886, my grandfather had been making boots for seven years." No one but John Justin, Jr,. could make that claim which began appearing in publications around the country in early 1979. It was the Justin Boot Company's way of letting people know that it was celebrating its hundredth birthday and that the third generation of Justins was firmly in the saddle.

The centennial observance was marked by a number of promotions, but the pièce de résistance was the introduction of the Justin Signature Edition Boots. Limited to a total of 1,000 pairs of men's boots and 250 women's, the antique brown ostrich boot featured an inlay of the map of Texas, with a rose-cut diamond set in a fourteen-carat gold star marking the location of Spanish Fort. Each pair of boots carried John Justin, Jr.'s personally enscribed signature, came encased in a commemorative box and was accompanied by a letter of congratulations from Justin.

The Signature Edition, even at $450 per pair, sold out almost as soon as it hit the marketplace. "We never dreamed there would be that kind of a demand," John, Jr., said. "We could have easily sold several thousand more pairs." Asked who got the first pair, Justin grinned and replied, "Well, the first pair just happened to be a strange size—11AAA—and that fit me."

"We could sell that pair," a Justin executive told Lloyd (Cissy) Stewart of the *Star-Telegram*, "but we haven't found anybody else who can wear John's boots."

The sellout of the Signature Edition prevented opera diva Beverly Sills from acquiring a pair of the coveted boots when she was in Fort Worth to sing at a Fort Worth Opera production. When the opera association approached John, Jr., about presenting Miss Sills with a pair of the centennial boots, he had to inform them that there were no more available. Miss Sills, however, did become the owner of a pair of boots trimmed with golden butterflies, which Justin presented to her as a memento of her Fort Worth appearance.

As part of the centennial observance, the company also conducted an old Justin boot roundup. The oldest pair of boots were proffered, complete with spurs, by Mrs. Lyle Simmelink from the state of Washington, whose father had bought them in 1911 from a Justin dealer. Two of the more unusual pairs of boots submitted were a ladies' knee-high, lace-up style that were made in Nocona in 1917 and a pair of military boots that were crafted in Fort Worth in 1927.

The high point of the centennial observance, however, came during the first week of May, when some sixty salesmen representing the boot, belt and leather goods operations of Justin Industries convened in Spanish Fort for their annual sales meeting. For three days, Spanish Fort lived again. The *Nocona News* described the event in its May 10, 1979, edition:

> H. J. Justin, Bootmaker, read the sign in front of a small board-and-batten building containing a workbench and some leather-working tools in 1879 in the town of Spanish Fort. H. J. Justin, Bootmaker, read another sign in front of a big tent in the same town 100 years later. . . . A replica of the front of H. J. Justin's first shop decorated the entrance to the large blue and white tent which was erected on the spot where H. J. Justin's first shop was located. The tent was necessary because there was no building in Spanish Fort to accommodate the sales meeting. Participants were bussed to the site each morning from a motel outside Nocona where they were housed.
>
> Normally dressed in suit and tie to ply their trade, the salesmen let it all hang out for the three days, dressing in the style of their great-granddads 100 years ago. Scruffy bluejeans, faded shirts, cowboy hats of every description predominated, and boots, boots, boots—of every style and color imaginable, and all Justins. . . .
>
> At the conclusion of the [annual awards ceremony] program, Bill Powers, a longtime boot company salesman, made a special presentation on behalf of all those present. Asking John, Jr., to join him at the podium, Powers presented Justin with the deed to the land on which they were standing—the

land on which H. J. Justin's first shop had stood. Not only did Justin receive the deed to the property, he also was handed a receipt testifying to the fact that the taxes had been paid on it for the next ten years.

"I've received a few awards in my time," Justin acknowledged, "but this one tops them all."

The hundredth anniversary sales meeting was not the first ever held at Spanish Fort. It was predated by one that took place in 1957, when Justin decided it would be appropriate for the sales personnel to relive a bit of company history.

"I thought it would be a good idea for the salesmen to see the place where the company started," Justin recalled. He also wanted to surprise them, so he kept their destination a secret.

"I just told them we were going to leave from in front of the Texas Hotel in downtown Fort Worth early in the morning and for them to dress in leisure clothes and bring an overnight bag." Justin had the bus driver take a circuitous route, which kept the passengers further in the dark about their destination.

"It finally got to where they were all asking me, 'John, where in the hell are we going?'" Justin recounted.

After what seemed an eternity, the bus arrived at its destination, a tree-covered area overlooking the Red River. The group disembarked in front of a narrow path through the trees. Justin took the lead, calling out, "Follow me, fellers." The path was so narrow, Justin recalled, that the men had to follow him in single file.

"We walked down this path until we reached a clearing," Justin related, "and there was barbecue king Walter Jetton waiting for us with a gigantic breakfast."

As the salesmen emerged from the path into the clearing where Jetton was cooking eggs, bacon and biscuits, he welcomed them with the words, "Come and get it."

The meal was served chuck wagon-style and eaten on wooden picnic tables set up near the river. Nearby was a large tent that had been erected to house the sales meeting. That night, cots were set up inside the tents for sleeping.

"I had told the guys we were going to rough it," Justin said. He didn't foresee how rough it was going to be.

"I had checked with the weather bureau before we left Fort Worth," Justin related, "and they told me there was a cold front coming in but that it wouldn't hit until after the meeting. Well, about three in the morning a wind came up and an arctic front moved in. It was just like someone had opened the door to an ice box. By the time we got up for breakfast, it was down to nearly freezing and dropping fast. No one was dressed for that kind of weather."

Stepping into the big tent for the sales meeting after breakfast was similar to entering a deep freeze. "Jetton had a lot of charcoal," Justin recalled, "so, in desperation, I had him put some burning charcoal in a tub inside the tent, hoping it would warm things up a little."

Unfortunately, the smoke from the burning charcoal soon filled the tent, enveloping the speakers. "It got so smoky inside that tent, we couldn't see one another," Justin recalled.

The Justin centennial coincided with a boom in western wear that was sweeping the country from Hollywood to Broadway. An article in the *Washington Post* on February 13, 1979, documented the rage:

> It's hardly what you would call a stampede, but the cowboy look is leaving its mark on Washington, as cowboy boots, ten-gallon hats, yoked shirts and hand-tooled belts are finding a home on a range of customers. . . .
>
> Westernwear, particularly jeans and flannel shirts, became widely accepted in the 1960s by a generation seeking inexpensive, non-establishment clothes. It was not long until jeans shops picked up the western theme and filled out their stock with other western accessories, especially the tooled, big-buckle belt, the yoked shirt and the cowboy hat.
>
> But nationwide, the fastest-moving fashion in western chic is the cowboy boot—with $200 million in business this year alone. And Washington is no exception to the national trend. Cowboy boot sales are really booming in New York, where Billy Martin, the former manager of the New York Yankees, opened a westernwear shop that was proving so successful that he was considering selling franchises.
>
> What's the appeal? Most wearers list comfort and the long-wearing quality of cowboy boots. But White House speechwriter Henrick Hertzberg asserted that he wore boots because they made him feel close to being a movie star. William Rossi, author of the book, *The Sex Life of the Foot & Shoe,* said that the appeal of cowboy boots was the fact they represent an image of aggressive male thrust, of hard toughness. But whether these boots are worn by psychosexually aggressive or passive men, the machismo or gladiator character of the boot itself feeds the undernourished sexual ego of the wearer.

Whether it was the result of Texas chic or Freudian machismo, Justin boot sales were on a roll. While in Denver to attend the 1979 style show of the Men's Apparel Club at the Merchandise Mart, John Justin reported that the cowboy boot business was better than ever—and that exotic leathers such as python, ostrich and anteater were the main reason. "The exotics," he told reporters covering the show, "are helping us break all sales records. From a volume standpoint, sales of boots to people who wear them to work or to relax in are running steady year after year. That includes the working ranchers and farmers, others who walk outdoors a lot and the people everywhere who like western garb. But in these days of leisure time and discretionary income, our sales records are being made by people who want to buy something exotic and stylish."

The fact was that the entire line of Justin boots was selling fast. The company was turning out some twenty-six hundred pairs a day, two thousand in Fort Worth and six hundred in El Paso. "We can hardly make enough boots to meet the demand," John Justin told Ellen Middlebrook, a *Houston Post* business writer, during a centennial year promotional appearance in that city.

"He wears cowboy boots all the time," Middlebrook wrote, "because it's easier than explaining to people why he doesn't."

One of the questions Justin was asked by Middlebrook was how long he expected the so-called cowboy boot "fad" to last. His answer was that he couldn't remember when the cowboy market was not steadily increasing.

There was no doubt that cowboy boots were the glamour boys of the Justin Industries' bricks and boots partnership. But it was the company's building materials division—primarily bricks—that was proving to be the cash cow. Building materials contributed seventy-one percent of the net sales and eighty-two percent of the profits racked up by Justin Industries in 1979, while the western and outdoor division—primarily boots—contributed twenty-one percent of the corporation's sales and fourteen percent of its profits.

But as a result of the western-chic phenomenon, western and outdoor sales nearly doubled in 1980 and rose again in 1981.

But problems lay ahead.

A year later, a deepening recession and the related decline in consumer spending brought on significant setbacks in the boot operation. Following two years of unprecedented demand for western wear, retail sales declined sharply during the second quarter of 1982, leaving many Justin customers overextended and with excessive inventory. The Justin Boot Company was caught unexpectedly by the rapid changes in demand as the second quarter started, causing it to record operating losses greater than Justin Industries as a whole. Nocona Boot Company faced similar problems, and Justin's El Paso plant was closed for an indefinite period and later sold.

To return the boot operations to profitability, Justin turned to J. T. Dickenson in November 1982. "J. T. had been with Justin Industries since 1974. Prior to that, he had been with General Dynamics in Fort Worth for a number of years. He was originally hired as general production manager in the boot factory and he did a good job there for several years. But there were some real problems that developed at the boot company for which he was not responsible. The people who were responsible needed someone to put the blame on—and they put it on J. T. So they let him go. But I felt he was too good a man to lose. So I transferred him to the brick operation as personnel manager of Acme Brick Company, where he did an excellent job.

"Meanwhile, problems were piling up at the boot company. Things finally got so bad that I had to step in and clean things out. In one day, I let the four or five top guys go. We began looking for someone to take over the boot operation. We looked and we looked. We looked in Nashville and up in New England and in all of the shoe centers, but we couldn't find anybody we felt could handle the job.

"Then one day, I was talking with Jon Bennett in my office and he called J. T. on the telephone to ask him to bring over a report we'd been discussing. J. T. was working for Bennett at Acme Brick. When he left my office after delivering the report, Jon turned to me and said, 'How about him?'

"And it was as if a thousand-watt light bulb had just lit up," Justin said. "I told Jon, 'J. T.'s the man we're looking for.' So I put J. T. back in his former job."

Dickenson did a magnificent job "rearranging and reorganizing" the boot operations, "doing what needed to be done," Justin said. In 1983, Dickenson was named president of the Justin Boot Company. He later was elected executive vice president of Justin Industries, and in December 1991 was promoted to president and chief operating officer of Justin Industries.

Dickenson, a tall, broad-shouldered native Texan who played football at Baylor University in the late 1940s, recalled his initial meeting with John Justin at the boot factory in 1974. "I didn't own a pair of boots and I had never worn a pair of Justin boots. The only boots I ever owned were Leddys. My father-in-law bought them for me. I'd even worn them in

Korea when I was serving there with the air force. So my first day on the job at Justin, I reported in and John looked at my wing-tip shoes and asked, 'What are those?' By that afternoon, I was wearing a pair of Justin boots and I haven't been out of them since. I don't even own a pair of shoes."

Dickenson was frank in describing his disillusionment over being relieved of his duties as general production manager of the boot company in 1979.

"It was very frustrating for me because production was my game," he said. "I felt like I had done a pretty good job." Dickenson's first order of business upon his return to the boot company in November 1982 was cleaning house of the deadwood that had accumulated. "We eliminated a lot of people," he said. "There was also a real attendance problem. One reason they had been hiring ten to twenty percent more people than they really needed was the fact that attendance was so bad. People were constantly missing work and coming in late. One of the first things I did was start an incentive program on attendance. We used the Justin outlet store as part of the awards. We'd give gift certificates to employees who had sixty days without any tardiness or absences. We'd give them 'X' number of dollars they could spend at the outlet store to buy boots, belts and leather goods.

"The program worked beautifully. There was just enough of an incentive to cut down tardiness and make attendance more stable. We reevaluated some of the jobs and started getting the wages up. As a result, our production cost per pair of boots went down because productivity increased, and we didn't need as many people in the plant."

Dickenson also found that boot company staffing had been "completely overdone," particularly in industrial engineers. "They were really overloaded with staff people," he said. "There must have been sixteen to eighteen industrial engineers on the payroll. And there were no good, clear lines of authority and responsibility. It was Parkinson's Law all over again—you have a staff that has a staff."

Worst of all, the boot operation was losing money. "We'd gone through this dip following the 'Urban Cowboy' boom," Dickenson recounted. "The 'Urban Cowboy' deal, of course, came from the movie with John Travolta. He got everybody's attention on boots and western wear. Everybody got in the act. Boot companies produced as many boots as they possibly could to take advantage of the situation. We had good years in 1979, '80 and '81, particularly '80 and '81.

"But there was also an overreaction to what was happening. Some huge inventory problems developed, particularly in the ladies' boot business, because ladies' fashions peak and then hit bottom very quickly. The ladies' boot business is especially fashion-oriented," Dickenson declared, "and that makes things very difficult. At the height of the boom in western wear, the Justin companies had jumped in and really overproduced some styles.

"In addition," Dickenson continued, "management had made some errors. What happened was they had contracted long-range for a lot of material, particularly exotic skins, signing one-year and two-year contracts. You can't do that in the boot business. You want to contract about six months ahead, at the outside, because leather prices fluctuate and the old supply-and-demand factor comes into play. As a result, we were hung out to dry on a lot of contracts."

One of the first things Dickenson did after taking over his old job was eliminate a number of the purchasing people who had made the long-term material contracts and begin re-negotiating the contracts.

Another immediate problem Dickenson had to address was the product line which had grown tremendously during the boom years. "We had to reduce the number of styles we were producing and do a better job of promoting the basic Justin products," he expounded. "During the 'Urban Cowboy' phenomenon, they were selling all of the exotic boots that they could make at premium prices. So they discontinued the Roper. One of the first things we did was take a look at the basic products that had made the company successful over the years, and what jumped out at us was the Roper. So we resurrected the Roper product line. We had no idea that it would be the huge success that it became—and still is.

"Then our design people came to me with red, green, white and navy ladies' lace-up Ropers. I said, 'You guys are nuts, absolutely nuts.' Well, the rest is history, as they say. The gals wear them with jeans, they wear them with denim skirts. Today, we're selling five hundred thousand pairs of ladies Roper pull-ons and Roper lace-ups a year, which is a tremendous percentage of our business."

Dickenson singled out Frank Scivetti, then vice president of footwear operations for Justin Industries, for his sales and marketing contributions to the resurrection of the Roper. "Frank joined the company in the middle of 1982," Dickenson said.

At about the same time the Roper lace-up was making its debut in 1985, Dickenson, Scivetti and Gary Liggett, who was then the boot company's chief financial officer, came up with the idea of duplicating the Roper in children's boots, Dickenson reported. "We thought, 'Wouldn't it be great if we could start kids out in Justin boots when they're three or four years old? If we do the right thing, we've got them for the rest of their lives as far as bootwear brand awareness is concerned.'

"At that time, Acme Boot Company had most of the kids' boot business. We decided to make a run at them. Some people in Leon, Mexico, had made some overtures about making boots for us. So we had them make duplicates of the Justin Roper in kids' boots that looked identical to mom's and dad's boots. They did a great job on the sample boots. So we contracted with them to make Roper boots for boys and girls.

"The first year we put the things out, in 1985-'86, we sold about seventy-five thousand pair. The next year, we almost doubled our sales and really hurt the Acme Boot Company kids' business. Our pricing was very competitive. We were a little higher-priced, but the quality was there. One of the things we insisted on when we began doing business in Mexico was to have our own quality control people go down there and set the thing up. We inspected all of the shipments. If they didn't meet our specifications, we wouldn't buy them. The incentive was, 'Do it right or you're not gonna get paid.'"

Dickenson grinned. "We call our kids' boots 'grandma and grandpa bait.' They see them in the stores, particularly at Christmas time, and they buy 'em for their grandkids."

In 1983, when Dickenson was named president of the boot company, he also took responsibility for the Nocona Boot Company. "The old management was trying to increase production to 1,800 pairs of boots a day in three plants," Dickenson recounted. "They had the original plant in Nocona and they had opened plants in Vernon and Gainesville. When I first went up there in '83 to look things over, I decided, number one, that we didn't need the three locations. The facility in Nocona was ample.

"The people running the company told me if we brought all the production back to Nocona, we were going to have to operate a second shift. I was told that we couldn't run a second shift in Nocona, that people there wouldn't work a second shift.

Well, we did it anyway, and much to everyone's surprise, therewere people actually volunteering for those second-shift jobs.

"We wound up doing exactly the same thing we had done before in Fort Worth. People's wages went up, production went up, and the number of people employed went down. It was the same old routine."

twenty

Prophet or true believer?

An article in *Forbes Magazine* on October 26, 1981, speculated whether John Justin was coming perilously close to betting his company. The article, written by Anne Bagamery, said that Justin was stockpiling bricks with four hundred million in inventory—worth $26 million at a time when money was costing twenty percent plus. Why? Because in the housing slump of 1974, Justin cut back production like everybody else and got caught short when housing starts in the company's Texas market area took off again. Mexican brick came in to grab fifty percent of the market in 1975.

"We never want to get caught like that again," Justin told the reporter. He didn't know whether housing would turn up early in 1982 as he expected. If it did, he would recoup the carrying costs of his brick inventories and then some. Philosophically, he told Bagamery, "It hurts me a lot less to bite a few bullets in bad times than to watch profits go out the window in good times."

Bricks, Justin might have added, don't disintegrate. They have a long shelf life. In the boot business, fashions change, colors change, so shelf life is a more critical issue.

Meanwhile, boots carried bricks again.

Justin would later admit that there were times when he felt he had gambled and lost. But throughout those trying times, he kept reiterating, "We'll never be able to make brick as cheaply as we're making it now."

But as burgeoning mortgage interest rates strangled new home construction in the second half of 1981, the short-term outlook for Justin Industries remained cloudy. If 1981 was bad, 1982 bordered on the disastrous, as the boot business went into a swoon and housing starts remained in the doldrums. Impacted by losses in its boot operations, Justin wound up 1982 with a net loss.

During 1982, brick production fell to approximately forty-five percent of capacity, as Justin sweated out the turnaround he was convinced was still around the corner. The turnaround came none to soon, heralded by a news release dated April 19, 1983, that trumpeted the news: "Justin Industries reported today that its Acme Brick and Featherlite Building Products subsidiaries led the way to recording profits of $465,000, or 12 cents per share, on sales of $56,096,000 for the first quarter of 1983."

Improving economic conditions and mild weather resulted in increased residential construction activity. Justin's stockpiling gamble had paid off just in the nick of time. The economy bounced back from recession, housing starts rose to 1.7 million, and Acme Brick Company enjoyed its largest-ever brick shipment year in 1983. The turnaround propelled Justin Industries back into the black.

John Justin, Jr., had long been active in promoting the western image and supporting rodeo-related activities. His efforts had been complemented by Jane's enthusiastic involvement, and in 1984 they were jointly honored as the Rodeo Historical Society's Man and Woman of the Year, the first time that a couple had been named honorees. It also marked the first time that a woman became the recipient of the prestigious award. The presentation took place at the National Cowboy Hall of Fame and Western Heritage Center in Oklahoma City during the National Finals Rodeo.

Also featured in the winter 1984 edition of the employee newsletter, *Justin Times'* was a photograph of movie cowboy legend Gene Autry being greeted by John Justin during a surprise visit to the Justin Boot Company in Fort Worth. Autry and his wife Jackie toured the plant and then headed for the showroom to look over the new Justin line.

They did not leave empty-handed.

"They each bought three or four pair of boots, including one or two pairs of exotics," Justin recalled.

Another celebrity who did not leave Fort Worth empty-handed was Bob Hope, who was the recipient of a pair of Justin boots personally presented by John Justin at a New Year's Eve party. Hope was so taken with his Justins that he sent John the following letter:

Dear John:

Took another good look at those boots you gave me on New Year's Eve. They are really beautiful, and I'm going to wear them in the Palm Springs parade on January 30, and I will be thinking of you every minute. It was very thoughtful of you to give me a gift like that, and you helped make my holiday season a great one. They're beautiful boots, and everybody who's seen them just gasps a little and I just say, Fort Worth, Texas—Justin's.

Thanks again, and have a great New Year.

Regards,
Bob

Justin recalled the New Year's Eve party at which Hope entertained. "Bob was really at his best. He had the crowd eating out of his hand, telling one joke after another. When the band began playing his theme song, 'Thanks for the Memory,' as a signoff, Bob stopped the music, saying 'I'm having too much fun to quit.' And he remained onstage for at least another forty-five minutes. Everyone loved it."

Justin especially remembered one of Hope's stories that brought down the house. He was driving on a rural road not far from Fort Worth, Hope said, when he spotted a three-legged chicken running alongside his automobile. "When I speeded up, the chicken kept up with me easily," Hope said. "Finally, the chicken zoomed out ahead of me and then turned onto a road leading to a farmhouse."

His curiosity now piqued, Hope followed the chicken up to the front door of the farmhouse, where the farmer stepped out to greet him. "Where'd you get that three-legged chicken?" Hope wanted to know.

"Well," the farmer drawled, "my wife and I and our son love drumsticks. And she has to kill two chickens in order for each of us to each have a drumstick. So I decided to breed three-legged chickens so that we'd only need one chicken."

"How does the three-legged chicken taste?" Hope asked.

"I don't know," replied the farmer, "we haven't been able to catch one yet."

Sales and profits soared in 1984. Contributing to the stellar performance was a record year for Acme Brick sales and earnings and a sharp increase in profitability by the footwear group. At the Justin Boot Company, new customer order control and customer information systems were developed and installed during the latter part of 1984 as part of a program to improve customer service operations.

Looking back on the installation of the customer order control and information systems, Justin said it would be difficult to overemphasize the importance of the move to the growth of the boot company. "We couldn't handle the business we have now if we didn't have that equipment," he declared. "We have a telephone bank, both incoming and outgoing, and we have one group of young women who take nothing but incoming calls from our customers.

"Each girl has a computer in front of her. The calls come in so regularly that the customers get to know the girls they're talking to and the girls get to know their customers, even though they've never seen each other.

"The customer will say, 'Betty, this is Joe,' and she'll say, 'Joe, how are you?' She immediately knows who he is. She then calls up his account on her computer screen and when he asks about the status of his order, she tells him."

Another group of young women works on an incentive basis calling customers, Justin reported. This is another major departure from the way things were done in the past. "In the old days," Justin said, "our salesmen might drive fifty to seventy-five miles to call on a customer. I remember when I was up in Montana one time making calls with one of our salesmen and he said, 'We're gonna have to get up real early tomorrow morning because I want to call on this guy.'

"It turned out the guy was located 180 miles from where we spent the night. It was a really out of the way little town. You had to drive up into the mountains, go off the main highway and climb some more, then double back, a 360-mile round-trip. There were two customers there and we probably got an order for fifteen or twenty pairs of boots. Today, it's just not economically feasible for the salesmen to do that with the price of gasoline what it is.

"So we now have this group of girls working the telephones. Each girl has a certain number of customers and she calls those customers on whatever schedule they want. If they want to be called once a week, that's what she does. If they want to be called every two weeks, they're called every two weeks. If a girl knows that ten o'clock in the morning is the best time to call a certain customer, she'll call him at ten o'clock.

"She'll say, 'Hi, Jim.'

"He'll say, 'Hi, Debbie.'

"She'll ask him what he needs and he'll tell her what he needs to replace his stock. He's been expecting her call and he has his order list in front of him. She puts the order right into the computer. When she's through putting in the order, she says:

"'By the way, Jim, we've got a new color Lacer we've just put in in olive green or pink or whatever it is. And it's really going big. You really ought to try it.'

"And he says, 'Oh, yeah, well send me a dozen pair then.'

"She sends him the dozen pair by punching the order into her computer. The beauty of the thing is, she does all that and then she might say: 'By the way, don't you need this or that?' And he'll say, 'Yeah, yeah, send me this or that.'

"They're on a first name basis, but they've never seen each other. They say, 'Goodbye,' and she hits a flick that goes straight to our computer and goes straight to our shipping department. If it's, say, ten o'clock in the morning, that order could very easily be shipped this afternoon. Two or three days later, the customer gets it. You just can't beat that kind of service."

When Justin visits customers on the road, one of the first things he usually hears from them is a greeting to their telephone order girl. They'll invariably say, "When you get back to Fort Worth, John, tell Debbie hello." Or Mollie. Or Suzie. Or Joan. When customers come to Fort Worth, the first thing they say is, "I want to see Mollie" or "I want to meet Debbie."

"We do an awful lot of business through those girls," Justin said.

In his letter to shareholders in the 1988 annual report, John Justin wrote:

"Justin Industries continues to be challenged by the weak Texas and southwestern economy that has affected the company's profitability in recent years. While we are optimistic and have begun to see some very encouraging signs, 1989 is being approached with caution, as the upcoming year appears to offer little from 1988 in terms of general levels of business activity. A more noticeable upturn in the company's earnings is probably another twelve to eighteen months away."

Justin, of course, had no way of knowing it at the time, but he would soon be faced with a challenge that threatened to cost him his company.

twenty-one

"John, have you lost your mind?"

On January 19, 1988, at the Ten-Gallon Gala Grand Opening of the Will Rogers Equestrian Center, Mayor Bob Bolen received a four-foot-by-two-foot cashier's check for $3,433,200 from an exuberant John Justin.

Bolen and Justin had something special to celebrate with the opening of the equestrian center, a $17.4-million, three-building complex on the city-owned grounds of the Southwestern Exposition and Livestock Show. A year earlier, it had appeared that the equestrian center was doomed. But that was before Justin, the stock show's board chairman, stuck his neck out and promised the city fathers that he would raise the $3.4 million necessary to complete the project. The remaining $14 million came from city bond money.

As Justin walked out of the city council chamber after making his pledge, W. R. Watt, Jr., stock show president and general manager, turned to him and said, "John, have you lost your mind?"

Justin's response was, "Bob, I probably have."

The presentation of the oversized check to Mayor Bolen by Justin highlighted the equestrian center grand opening ceremonies attended by two thousand western-garbed guests. "People simply can't believe what's been done in eleven months," said Justin. "They can't believe it because the old horse barns were leveled and this center started from nothing.

"We got donations from people who didn't even know what an equestrian center was," Justin said, standing near an arena in the center named for him. "It says a lot for this city and our western heritage."

The equestrian center is made up of three major buildings: the 215,000-square-foot Richardson/Bass Building, the 197,000-square-foot Burnett Building and an attached 761-space parking garage. The Richardson/Bass Building houses the John Justin Arena that seats approximately two thousand people. The Burnett Building contains steel stalls for horses and holding pens for cattle, as well as a veterinary clinic, wash stalls, fire station, photography area and dressing rooms. Combined, the two buildings contain about nine hundred horse stalls and ninety-seven cattle pens.

Recalling the events leading up to his pledge to provide the funding to save the project, Justin noted: "The equestrian center is a fabulous thing for Fort Worth. The city makes a lot of money out of it. It's booked every weekend.

"Bob Watt and I started working on the city council to put the equestrian center in a bond issue. It was badly needed. The old horse stalls were absolutely obsolete. They were vermin-ridden, everything was bad about them. We had to either do something or quit. We felt if something wasn't done, the stock show rodeo would start going downhill and eventually fade away.

"We worked with the city council members. They were in favor of doing something, but they also had a lot of other needs—water, sewers and streets, etc. We had no idea what the project would cost, but the council set aside $7 million for it. We knew that $7 million wouldn't even get us started.

"So we kept on going back and talking with them and we got them up to $8 million, then $9 million, and we finally got them up to $14 million, which would include the parking garage, and they agreed to put that amount in a bond issue they submitted to the voters in an election in 1986.

"We worked hard on promoting the bond issue. We got the stock show directors involved, worked our hearts out and helped get the bond issue passed. Then the stock show hired an architect to get the drawings done for a first-class installation. The city had the plans bid to find out what it would cost, and it turned out to be considerably more than the amount that had been in the bond issue. Instead of $14 million, it was going to cost more like $17 million or $18 million.

"The council just said, 'No way.'

"We talked to the council and they said, 'Leave the seats out or leave the roof off, or do something else, but $14 million is all we've got and that's all we can spend.'

"Finally, we reached the point where the contractor was going to remove his bid if the council didn't act on it. We talked to the council again at an early morning special session and they said, 'There's nothing we can do. Either you cut it to $14 million or we can't go.'

"Later that morning, Bob Watt and I attended the regular council meeting. Bob Bolen was the mayor, and he asked me if I wanted to say anything. I said, 'Yes, I do.' I went up to the microphone and gave them a real pitch on why we had to have the equestrian center, that it was absolutely necessary, and that if we started cutting the plans, it would wind up as a second-class deal.

"Bob Bolen then said, 'John, there's no way we can do it. We just don't have the money.'

"I don't know what caused me to speak up then and say what I did, stupidity, I guess. But I said, 'I'll raise the money.'

"Bob kind of jumped me and said, 'John, do you guarantee that you'll raise the extra money?'

"I said, 'I can't guarantee it, but I will guarantee that I'll give it my best effort.'

"Then the council voted nine to nothing to accept my offer and go ahead with the project," Justin grinned.

"Bob Watt and I walked out of the council chamber together, and that's when he asked me if I'd gone out of my mind."

Immediately after that, the fund-raising effort got under way. "We got busy raising the money," Justin recounted. "Bob Watt worked his heart out. He feels about the stock show as I do. It's his life. It was his father's life. It's his son Trey's life. We just knew we had to do it. We visited people. We did everything that we could do, and we raised the money. Even before the center was finished, we had the money in the bank.

"We got it built according to the original plans. If we had done anything else, it wouldn't have been proper. It's a wonderful facility and it's getting used more and more. Wherever I go all over the country, they talk about it, about what an outstanding horse facility and livestock facility we have here.

"One thing that Fort Worth has that makes it special is its western heritage. We've got wonderful museums. We've got wonderful parks. The zoo is just fabulous. We've got wonderful performing arts. And so many other things. Fort Worth is a fabulous place. But the one thing we have that nobody else has is our western heritage. It provides the background for everything else. Fort Worth is where the West begins. Its history is the West."

Bob Watt echoed Justin's recollections of the building of the equestrian center. "We were in a real jam on the project," Watt recalled. "For several years we had been trying to convince the city that we had to do something about our old horse facility that was really just a series of sheds that had been added onto over a long period of time. The horse stalls were very small and inadequate.

"We had tried to get the city's attention about the problem. What really got the city's attention was when the National Cutting Horse Association told the city that if it didn't do something about the horse facility, they were going to move their annual World Championship Futurity, one of the nation's premier horse events, to another locale. It's held here annually just before Christmas and brings something like $12 million into town. The wives would come with the horse owners and do their Christmas shopping while they were in Fort Worth."

Equestrian events, Watt explained, have always been an important part of the stock show. "The truth of the matter is," Watt avowed, "if we had not gotten the equestrian center built, the stock show might have gone out of business by now." He illustrated:

"Back in the 1950s," Watt reported, "there were four highly respected livestock shows in the entire country—in Chicago, Kansas City, Denver and Fort Worth. But they did not take care of their facilities and they went out of business in the '70s."

Perry R. Bass, patriarch of the wealthy Bass family in Fort Worth and chairman of the board of the Sid W. Richardson Foundation, described John Justin's pivotal role in bringing the center project to a successful conclusion. "John has devoted a lot of time and effort to the stock show over the years," Bass declared, mentioning the threat of losing the cutting horse futurity because of inadequate facilities.

"What had happened was that Las Vegas had come along and stolen the National Rodeo Finals away from Oklahoma City. And having lost it, Oklahoma City realized what a big drawing card the event had been, bringing a lot of people and money into town. So they began looking around to see what they could do to replace it.

"And they decided that they would try and take the National Cutting Horse Futurity away from Fort Worth and bring it to Oklahoma City. They felt Fort Worth was vulnerable because the community had never given one nickel to the futurity. The only prize money came from splitting the entry fees among the winners.

"And those old horse stalls out there at the stock show, I'm told, were in such a mess that horses were getting sick while stabled there. People were reluctant to bring their horses there, and when they did, they tried to get them out as quick as they could. So everything was kind of in a bad state of repair, facility-wise."

The new equestrian center, Bass said, has been "nice for the hotels restaurants and merchants. It's been a big thing, a growth facility for Fort Worth, and if it wasn't for John Justin working hard, beating the drums, and doing the thing as a civic enterprise, it wouldn't have happened. He's the kind of man who when he came and asked, it was hard to turn him down. He was the bellwether on that facility. The fact that his name is on the arena out there is highly deserved."

The center yielded a major plum in the fall of 1989 when the National Appaloosa Association moved its championship show from Oklahoma City to Fort Worth. The biggest event held annually at the Justin Arena is the World Junior Quarter Horse Show, with the Texas Classic, another major Quarter Horse show, running it a close second. Other prestigious competitions held there include the National Appaloosa Show, the National Paint Horse Show and several Arabian horse shows. During the stock show, some cattle shows are held in the Justin Arena, in addition to horse shows. However, with the completion of a new structure in January 1996, the Justin Arena will be utilized exclusively for horse shows. The new facility, the Charlie and Kit Moncrief Building, also will house cattle events during the year, primarily national junior breeding cattle shows. "The new Moncrief Building was an easy sell to the city council," Watt said, "because we built up so much credibility with the equestrian center.

"Of course," he added, "John was instrumental in getting the new building approved. It will cost $11 million. The stock show is paying for the new building completely. The city sold some revenue bonds to finance it, which we agreed to retire over a twenty-year period."

John Justin's involvement with the stock show had begun during his boyhood when he served as an usher at the show when it was still being held at the North Side Coliseum in the city's Stockyards Historic District. He was elected to the Fort Worth Fat Stock Show board in 1959 and was named chairman of the board in 1982 after the death of Amon G. Carter, Jr., the former publisher of the *Fort Worth Star-Telegram*.

"Mr. Justin was the logical choice to succeed Mr. Carter," Bob Watt said. "He had been on our executive committee for a number of years and was serving as vice chairman of the board. There is no one who supports our western heritage more and who does more to enhance it than he does. He is totally committed to our organization. I have never called him with a problem that he didn't always have time for. He has been there every time I needed help.

"We've had a lot of people who have been tremendous leaders for the show over the years," Bob Watt avowed. "But—and this is not to take away from anything these people have contributed—there is nobody who has done more for the show and provided greater leadership than John Justin has."

Justin recalled an incident during his tenure as vice chairman of the stock show board when Bob Watt's father, Billy Bob Watt, chewed him out for risking his neck in a wild horse scramble at the rodeo. "During the rodeo that year, a group of us that included Reg Kessler, the rodeo producer from Canada, and Jack Roddy, a great rodeo performer with whom I had become close friends, had partaken of Jack Daniels rather sumptuously," Justin related with a grin.

"We were talking about the rodeo, and someone said, 'What we ought to do is enter the wild horse race tomorrow night.'

"And we all agreed. So we entered."

Justin, whose rodeo appearances up to that time had consisted of riding in the Grand Entry, has never forgotten that night's performance. "There are three-man teams out in the arena. One man tries to hold the horse by a length of rope while a second guy tries to put a saddle on him. The third guy then has to climb into the saddle and ride him. My job was to hold onto the horse while Jack Roddy saddled him. His instructions were not to let go of the horse at any cost. Our third guy was a little guy, who was going to try and ride him.

"I had hold of this really mean horse who was trying his darnedest to kick and bite me, while Jack was trying to get the saddle on him. There I was, holding on for dear life, when I happened to look up and there was Mr. Watt standing at the railing overlooking the arena and yelling at me, 'John, John, what are you doing out there? You're gonna kill yourself. Let go of that damn horse and get out of there. Right now.'"

Watt, the colorful stock show ramrod, was used to having his orders obeyed. But not this time. Justin was not about to let go of the wild horse, figuring that where he was was probably the safest place he could be. "Finally," he said, "we got the horse saddled, and the third guy on our team even rode him across the finish line. We took first place and had a good time without breaking any bones."

Afterwards, Justin recounted, "Mr. Watt chewed me out and said, 'Don't you ever do that again.'

"But it was something I had to try once.

"Our rodeo, the world's oldest indoor rodeo, is a real rodeo," Justin emphasized. "In other cities, people go to rodeos to see the entertainers, the country-western stars who headline the show. And the audience thins out after the star's appearance. In Fort Worth, the rodeo cowboys are the stars."

There's an old rodeo cowboy saying that goes, "It's not a matter of if you get hurt, but when and how bad." It's a rare cowboy who cruises through an entire career free of injury. That's why rodeo contestants praise the Justin Sportsmedicine Program as the most beneficial sponsorship program in the Professional Rodeo Cowboys Association. It's as simple as the fact that when you're hurt, you have no shot at the big prize money.

The Justin Sportsmedicine Program made its debut at the 1980 National Finals Rodeo. When a cowboy gets hurt in the arena, Justin sports medicine specialists, known as "Justin Heelers," are immediately available to provide first aid or more comprehensive emergency assistance. "The cowboys love to see one of the massive, red Justin Sportsmedicine mobile units when they pull into a rodeo," Bob Watt said. The program has grown steadily over the years, from a ten-rodeo schedule in 1981 to 125 rodeos a year. It was conceived by John Justin, Jr., after years of watching injuries to contestants at rodeos across the country. The program was organized by sports physicians Don Andrews and J. Pat Evans.

"The Justin Sportsmedicine Program, in my mind, is the most important program in the PRCA," commented three-time world champion bull rider Tuff Hedeman. "There's no way we could do without it."

A related program inaugurated by the Justin Boot Company in 1989 is the Justin Cowboy Crisis Fund, which lends a financial hand to seriously injured rodeo performers and their families. Through 1995, more than $800,000 had been distributed to injured professional rodeo cowboys and cowgirls in need of financial assistance, said Don Andrews, program director.

John Justin's support of the stock show and his other contributions to the promotion of the city's western heritage were recognized on December 9, 1992, when he received the second annual Charles Goodnight Award. The award, named for the legendary nineteenth-century cattleman, is presented annually by the National Cutting Horse Association and the Fort Worth Star-Telegram to the person who has done the most to promote the western lifestyle in Fort Worth.

The ceremony at which Justin was honored coincided with the opening night of the Cutting Horse Association's World Championship Futurity in Fort Worth—the event that was saved from leaving Fort Worth by the construction of the Will Rogers Equestrian Center. Perry Bass, the initial recipient of the Charles Goodnight Award, made the presentation to Justin at a gala dinner at the Worthington Hotel.

"His boots are part of our tradition," Bass said. "The cowboy boots and the cowboy hats are the symbols of our West."

twenty-two

A takeover attempt is thwarted

Despite posting increased 1988 sales and earnings, interest in Justin Industries remained lukewarm on the stock market. At its March 27, 1989, price of $16 a share, the stock was trading at lower than its estimated liquidation value of $17.90 per share. Then began an unusual activity in Justin stock in the NASDAQ market.

"People noticed it," John Justin recounted, "and I began receiving telephone calls about it. One morning, I received a call from someone in Los Angeles who said, 'You know who's buying your stock, don't you?'

"I told him that I had no idea and I asked him, 'Do you?'

"And he said, 'Yeah, but I can't tell you.'"

By late September, the price of Justin Industries' stock had risen to 18 1/2. Then, in three consecutive days of high-volume trading November 8 through 10, the stock jumped from 21 3/4 to 24 5/8 with extraordinarily high sales of 349,700 shares on the third day. On each day, Justin Industries was listed among the NASDAQ volume percentage leaders in the *Wall Street Journal*.

The mystery over who was doing the buying was resolved on November 20, when a Kansas City investment group, Choctaw Securities LP, disclosed in a filing with the Securities and Exchange Commission that its members owned 348,550 shares of Justin Industries, or 6.6 percent of outstanding common shares. In its filing, Choctaw also said that other group members held an additional 21,900 shares. Perry Sutherland, a Choctaw representative and a member of the family that owns the Sutherland

Lumber chain of building supply stores, told Dow Jones News Service on November 20 that his group had had informal discussions with Justin Chairman John Justin, Jr., but that no proposals were exchanged and no agreements reached.

"Choctaw may make an offer to acquire the company, but has not yet decided to do so," Sutherland added.

In an interview with the *Star-Telegram* that appeared on November 22, John Justin asserted that he had no plans to sell the company. But he did confirm that he had met the previous Friday with members of the Choctaw group. Justin said the meeting was informal and the group did not make an offer to buy Justin Industries.

"If somebody offers me enough money, I guess most anything is for sale except my wife and children," Justin declared. "But the company is not for sale. We don't have any reason to sell the company. It's been doing very well lately."

A *Star-Telegram* interview with Justin also contained a quote from David Leibowitz, an analyst with American Securities in New York, who contended,

> What we have here is a case of a large investor perceiving hidden value in a stock that Wall Street may not be following as closely as it should, or valuing as high as it might. Clearly, Justin is a premier company in boots, and given its leadership positions in brick and concrete products, one could make a strong case for why it's worth more.

Looking back on that period, Justin recalled, "After they had to identify themselves as owning 6.6 percent of our stock, Sutherland called me and said he wanted to come see me. He came down. I showed him around, as I would any shareholder, and I took him to lunch. He was very upbeat, saying, 'We just think you've got a great company and we just want to be stockholders. We have no bad intentions, no designs on you.'

"So I told him, 'If you're sincere, if you're telling me the truth, you've made a good deal by buying our stock. You'll make some money. But if you're not telling the truth, if you really have designs on the company, you're wasting your time because I'm not going to give up.'

"And he said, 'No, we just want to invest in your company.'"

On February 8, 1990, Justin found out otherwise.

A filing with the SEC by the Sutherland group announced that it now owned 11.2 percent of Justin Industries' outstanding stock and wanted to acquire the company. "The group members have determined to seek to negotiate a mutually agreeable acquisition transaction with the company," the SEC filing declared.

The filing did not specify a purchase price, but Justin Industries' stock closed at $16.50 per share on February 8, up fifty cents. A story in the *Wall Street Journal* on February 9 listed Barry S. Rosenstein, a former associate of Asher Edelman, whom the *Journal* identified as a "corporate-takeover specialist," as a member of the Sutherland group. The *Journal* added,

> The group includes two limited partnerships formed to pursue the Justin Industries acquistion: Choctaw Securities Limited Partnership led by Perry Sutherland of Sutherland Lumber Company and Reatta Partners Limited Partnership comprising Messrs. Sutherland and Rosenstein.
>
> Mr. Rosenstein said the group has 'maintained a dialogue' with Justin Industries over the past few months. Chairman John Justin declined comment.

The first sign that Justin was not about to step away from a fight came in a proxy statement to stockholders dated February 21, 1990, in which Justin Industries reported it had signed John Justin, Jr., to a new five-year employment contract, effective December 1, 1989, and extending through November 1994. Under terms of the contract, Justin was to be paid not less than $385,000 annually. The proxy statement revealed that Justin's salary at the time was $410,000 a year, with a provision that it could go higher as the company's performance continued to improve.

The next step in the escalating melodrama was taken with the announcement by the Sutherland group that it had made a formal offer of $18.50 per share, or about $140.5 million, to acquire the Justin Industries shares it did not already own. Justin Industries had approximately 8.5 million shares outstanding, of which the Sutherland group now owned 954,775. The offer, which was made in a letter to John Justin, Jr., dated March 7, 1990, for the first time addressed the possibility of breaking up the company and selling it piecemeal.

"Our offer is proposed in only the friendliest manner and is negotiable in all respects, including price to the extent that you can demonstrate the existence of greater value," the letter from Perry Sutherland and Barry Rosenstein declared. The letter called the $18.50-per-share offer "fair and generous" and said it represented a seventy-six percent premium over the stock's price on June 12, 1989, the day the group said it began buying Justin stock. The letter added that the group was "confident" that it would be able to obtain financing for the transaction."

The Justin Industries board met on March 23 to consider the proposal. "The directors found the offer really nonexistent," John Justin declared, "because Sutherland and Rosenstein hadn't yet found the financing for it. They only said they were 'confident' they could get the money. The board discussed the letter at length, but declined to take any action on it."

The board also authorized John Justin to advise the Choctaw group that Justin Industries had no interest in any further discussions of a sale of all or part of the company. On March 28, Choctaw notified the SEC in a supplementary filing that it was "reviewing" its investment in Justin Industries and that its future transactions "may involve seeking to acquire control of the company through a negotiated or non-negotiated transaction, proxy contest, tender offer or otherwise."

The next thing, Justin recalled, was that Choctaw was demanding to see certain things like the company's long-range strategic plan, minutes of all board meetings over the last two years having to do with purchase offers for Justin Industries and a plant-by-plant breakdown of the profitability of Acme Brick. "We let them see some materials, such as stockholder lists and things like that," Justin said. "Then they'd ask for more. Our position was that they were not a group of normal investors, but corporate raiders who weren't entitled to the information."

In mid-July, Sutherland and Rosenstein disclosed in a new SEC filing that they had hired PaineWebber Inc., a New York investment banking firm, to advise them on making a possible hostile bid for control of Justin Industries. The group disclosed it had recently boosted its stake in Justin to 993,475 shares, or about 11.6 percent of the company's outstanding shares, and that its preliminary operating plan included the possibility of closing or selling several of Justin's businesses and consolidating some of the company's operations.

Some two weeks later, on August 2, a Choctaw filing with the SEC revealed that it had negotiated an agreement with an investment bank, Creditanstalt Bankverein of Vienna, Austria, for the financing of the takeover. However, a spokesman for the bank said that its lending officers had agreed only to seek approval from bank directors to provide the financing.

Wall Street reacted to the news with a yawn.

Justin Industries lost 37.5 cents to close at $15.50 in the day's trading on a lower than normal volume. On August 22 came an announcement from Justin Industries that triggered a far more voluble response: Justin was buying the Tony Lama Company, the noted El Paso bootmaker. The deal included the assumption by Justin Industries of Tony Lama debt, plus cash for Tony Lama stock.

John Justin recalled with a grin the reaction to the news from Perry Sutherland. "We'd been trying to buy Tony Lama for twenty years," Justin declared. "But when we bought them, it affected the Choctaw deal because we assumed that Lama debt. Sutherland was furious. He called me and said: 'Why in the hell would you buy Tony Lama?'

"I said, 'I did it because I think it was the best thing to do for this company.'

"He said, 'You just did it to ruin us.'

"I said, 'No, this was a separate deal.'"

J. T. Dickenson recalled Tony Lama as a competitive thorn in Justin's side during the 1980s. "They were Nocona's and Justin's main competitor," he said. "Tony Lama had already incurred some problems, but they were beating us to death as far back as 1982 to 1984. While we were shipping around seven hundred and fifty thousand pairs of boots a year in the Justin Boot Company, they were shipping close to a million pairs. But they started getting sloppy in their quality, and their management wasn't really doing their homework. Family members were running the company, and for whatever reason, their interest started to subside.

"So, about 1985 or '86, our sales lines crossed. We were gaining market share and they were losing it, and from that point on, through 1990 when we bought them, Tony Lama really went through some major problems."

Dickenson reported that Justin had looked at the possibility of buying Tony Lama as far back as the 1970s and again in 1987, but that nothing could be worked out. "They were still mighty proud of their company and they wanted a very inflated figure for their stock," Dickenson said. "We told them we were interested, but that we couldn't go for the price they were asking. But when the opportunity arose again, this time through an investment banking company, we were able to make a deal. We bought their stock and absorbed their debt."

Before John Justin agreed to finalize the deal, Dickenson related, "He said to me, 'I want to see the place before we actually say we're gonna buy it.' So we flew out to El Paso and went to the plant after dark one night. We met Louie Lama, one of the brothers, and a fellow named Tisdale, who was the vice president of production. And they took us around."

Dickenson said the plant was one of the "worst organized" he'd ever seen. "There was no production line, as such. It was just all over the place—zig-zag. They double-and triple-handled material. Louie couldn't even describe how the merchandise went through the plant. And neither could the vice president of production. It was one of those things where, instead of planning out a good, straight-line production flow, they'd gone in and set down machines where there was an open space. So we knew that there were a lot of ways that we could improve the efficiency of the plant and do it fairly rapidly. We also knew that we could improve their quality and customer service.

"The forecast I'd made to the board was that it would take eighteen months to turn the plant around," Dickenson revealed. "They did it, actually, in about sixteen months."

As for Perry Sutherland's reaction to the Tony Lama purchase, Dickenson said, "He called it, 'scorched earth,' because the Tony Lama debt we assumed was debt that Sutherland would have to absorb if he was successful in taking us over."

Barry Rosenstein later told Katherine Weisman of *Forbes Magazine* that before the Tony Lama purchase, he and Sutherland had been willing to pay up to $20 a share for Justin Industries and that they had been working on financing the purchase of 100 percent of the Justin stock. "But the Lama deal threw a monkey wrench into their financing plans," Miss Weisman wrote in *Forbes* on June 24, 1991. "Their bankers, worried about the increased debt load, would now lend them money for only seventy-one percent of the Justin shares. Raising the balance, around $50 million, was a problem for the young men."

The announcement of an $112 million offer for Justin Industries was made by Rosenstein and Sutherland on September 25, 1990. "There was a half-page ad in the *Wall Street Journal*," Justin recalled, "and, of course, the newspapers and radio and television newscasts were full of it. The tender offer was for $18 per share, but only for so much stock. If more than that came in, they would give you stock in a new corporation that would not pay dividends and in which you would not have a vote. Also, a substantial part of the payment for the stock would be in the form of junk bonds."

Justin also noted that Choctaw had lowered its bid from $18.50 per share to $18 because of the Tony Lama debt acquisition. "Our board had already turned down $18.50," he said. "It really wasn't a good deal for our shareholders."

At a meeting on October 9, the Justin Industries' board rejected the offer. The directors voted to fight the takeover and recommended to its shareholders that they not tender their stock because it was a bad deal.

The Justin board also cautioned shareholders that there was "a substantial likelihood" that the offer was not an all-cash deal and that they might receive only part of the money and another security to make up the remainder.

Meantime the Sutherland-Rosenstein forces were mounting a full-scale stock solicitation campaign. "They got the stockholders' list, set up a telephone bank and began contacting stockholders around the country," Justin reported.

"They even called me. A young woman called me from New York and read to me from a script. All of their callers were reading from a script. If you asked them a question, they couldn't answer it."

Justin said that his good friend, Jim Shoulders, the rodeo star, who owned a substantial amount of Justin Industries stock, received a call from the telephone bank. "They called him, and he told them, '$18 a share, that's great. I'll take it. Send me my money right now and I'll send you the stock.'

"They said, 'No, no, that's not the way it works. You've got to send the signed stock certificates up here first. . . .'

"Jim said, 'No way I'm sending you my stock certificates. You said $18 a share. You send me $18 a share, and I'll send you the shares.' He said he figured the longer he kept them on the phone, the less time they'd have to call someone else."

With Choctaw on the warpath, Justin's advisers began urging him to get on the telephone and begin contacting shareholders personally. "I hesitated at first," Justin said. "I really didn't want to do it. But everyone insisted that I get on the phone and talk to the shareholders."

The first person he talked to was a woman in a small Texas town who, with her husband, jointly owned some Justin stock. Justin dialed the number. The woman answered the phone. Justin identified himself and she said, 'Oh, Mr. Justin, how are you?' I said, 'I'm fine, thank you.' And I told her I was calling about the tender offer for the stock. I said, 'You know, these people are trying to take over the company and we don't think it's a good deal for the stockholders.'

"And she said, 'Don't you worry about us. My husband and I are for you 100 percent. We're not going to tender our stock. These other people called me. They don't know what they're talking about.'"

The next person Justin called was a woman in North Carolina. The conversation was virtually identical to the first call. That gave him confidence, Justin said. So he began calling all over the country, receiving the same positive response. He'd talk to the shareholders and they'd say, "Don't you worry about us." There was this woman in Tennessee who must have called Justin a half a dozen times and said, "They just called me again, and I told them to go jump in the creek." Every time they called her, she'd call Justin and tell him about it.

On November 21, the Sutherland-Rosenstein group said it owned 34.7 percent of Justin Industries' 8.6 million outstanding shares and was extending its $18-per-share tender offer for another month, to December 20. The announcement added that, through the original November 20 deadline, 1,959,791 shares of Justin Industries' stock had been tendered out of the six million outstanding shares the group did not already own.

John Justin responded to the announcement by questioning whether the Choctaw group actually controlled all of the shares it had acquired. "In no way do they control that stock yet," he asserted. Justin also contended that some shareholders believed the Choctaw proposal was an all-cash offer.

"It is not," he emphasized. "It is subject to numerous contingencies, the principal one being that it is subject to financing. Even if financing is obtained," he added, "there is a substantial likelihood that shareholders would not receive all cash for all their shares."

On December 17, three days before the expiration of the tender offer, the Sutherland-Rosenstein group again extended the deadline for its $18-per-share offer, this time to January 17, 1991. "We need to get more stock," Perry Sutherland said.

The additional stock, however, failed to materialize, and on January 17 Choctaw extended the life of the tender offer another two months, to March 15, 1991.

But time was running out for Sutherland and Rosenstein. "They never could get much stock," Justin recounted. "Most of the stockholders just never responded to the takeover effort. Finally, it got to where it was getting expensive for both of us, particularly on them. But we'd also spent a lot of money on legal fees. We won a suit in Judge David Belew's Federal District Court in Fort Worth and in the Court of Appeals."

Now came a critical development.

John Justin received a phone call from Peter Forman, a Chicago investor who owned a large block of Justin Industries' stock. Forman said he wanted to set up a meeting, which elicited an invitation from Justin to have dinner the next day in Fort Worth. Over dinner, Forman disclosed that he was interested in selling his Justin stock and that if he did, another major shareholder, Michael Steinhart of New York, would also sell his stock as a part of the deal.

"This was crucial," Justin related, "because I knew that Sutherland was counting on Forman and Steinhart to vote their stock with him. Without their shares, the ball game was over." This was when two wealthy Fort Worth residents, Ben Fortson, board chairman of the Fortson Oil Company, and Anne Marion, the daughter of the late Anne Burnett Tandy and the great-granddaughter of famed rancher Burk Burnett, stepped into the picture.

Fortson picked up the narrative. "Back in the early fall of 1990, I got a call from Dee Kelly. Dee talked a little bit about golf, then said, 'Ben, would you be interested in buying an interest in Justin Industries?'

"I'd been following what was in the newspapers about the battle that Justin was having with the Sutherland group from Kansas City. I told Dee that I wasn't really interested. Then I got to thinking and I called Dee back in about five minutes. I told him I was interested in hearing more about the situation.

"Dee said that the company was thinking about an offering of preferred stock convertible into common stock and would like to make a presentation to me. So a meeting was set up to be held in my office.

"I then called Anne Marion, who is the only partner I've ever had in business dealings. Anne is on our Kimbell Art Foundation board and I'm on the Burnett-Tandy Foundation board. My wife Kay and I have had a long, close relationship, family-wise, with Anne. She is a very astute business woman. So I called Anne and asked if she'd be interested in looking at the Justin situation. So we both attended the meeting in my office.

"As I said, the presentation was about a preferred stock offering convertible into Justin common stock at a strike price quite a bit above the market. About two or three days after the presentation, I called Dee and told him I wasn't interested in the proposal that was presented, but that I was interested in buying some Justin stock in the open market as a long-term investment."

On November 8, 1990, Fortson made his initial purchase of Justin stock, 14,250 shares at a price of 11 1/4. On December 28, he bought 7,000 shares at 13 1/4. And on January 3, 1991, he bought another 6,000 shares at 13 1/4. Anne Marion participated with Fortson in the purchases on a 50-50 basis.

Fortson then received another call from Dee Kelly, who informed him of John Justin's dinner meeting with Peter Forman. Kelly said, "Ben, there's a large block of stock out of Chicago that you may be able to buy."

He was talking about 387,200 shares.

Almost incredulously, Fortson asked: "You mean there's that big a block out there?"

Kelly said, "Yes, it's out there."

Fortson responded, "That's a key block. I'll get to work on it right away."

Fortson now began negotiating with Forman. "I told him that I wouldn't pay more than $14 a share," Fortson related. "The market price of the stock was around 12 1/2 or 13 at the time. I said fourteen was my top price. There was a lot of discussion back and forth, and we finally arrived on a strike price of $14." The purchase of the block of 387,200 shares, representing nearly five percent of the total Justin Industries stock outstanding, was completed on January 14, 1991, at a total cost of $13,892,100.

"That was critical," Fortson said, "and I was surprised that the stock was still out there. I couldn't believe that the Sutherland group hadn't picked up that block, because I think if they had picked it up, it would have tilted everything their way. With my buying it, it tilted things the other way."

As Justin recalled, "After Forman and Steinhart sold their stock, Sutherland and Rosenstein threw in the sponge."

Recalling the chain of events, Fortson revealed, "Anne Marion and I had already purchased 414,450 shares on a 50-50 basis. The purchase of the Sutherland group's stock would bring the total to 1,435,725 shares, making it a $20 million deal.

"When it turned into a $20 million deal, I called her up and asked her what she would really be comfortable with. And she said she would really be comfortable with around $6 million. And I said I'd be comfortable doing $11.5 million. So we were short about $2.5 million. So I called my good friend John Cox in Midland and talked to him about ten minutes. He asked me some questions about the company. Then he said, 'Count me in.'"

The formal announcement came on February 19, 1991, with the Sutherland-Rosenstein group declaring that it had dropped its takeover bid and had sold its stake in Justin Industries to the Fortson family interests, Anne Marion and John Cox. "Anne, John Cox and I didn't have any contractual agreement," Fortson reported. "I bought the stock and then I billed Anne for her shares and John Cox for his shares. We owned our shares individually. It wasn't any kind of partnership. But it was a venture we did together—a $20 million venture.

"All of us were long-term players," Fortson emphasized. "I looked at it as a good investment. I saw Justin Industries as an opportunity with a good upside potential. And it turned out to be a very nice investment. First, it was a good business decision," he declared. "Second, it was good for Justin Industries. Third, it was good for Fort Worth. I was glad to be a part of it."

Dee Kelly, who headed the takeover defense, was convinced from the beginning that Perry Sutherland had totally misjudged John Justin. "He came to see John, and John is always interested in what something's worth," Kelly observed. "If he's got something and you show some interest in buying it, he always cares about what you'd pay. John likes to know what things are worth. That doesn't mean he'll sell anything. I think that's what happened here.

"Sutherland came down, and John was nice to him, polite to him, as he always is to people. And Sutherland talked to John about buying the company. John asked him what he thought it was worth. John later told me Sutherland's figure wasn't close to being in the ballpark, but Sutherland somehow came away with the impression that, maybe, he could go ahead and force the issue with John. And he misjudged him. A lot of people misjudge John because he's such a nice, polite, gentlemanly man.

"Sutherland and his partners misjudged John Justin much to their regret. It cost them a lot of money. It cost us a lot of money, too. But the affair turned out favorably for Justin Industries because it called a lot of people's attention to an undervalued stock. The stock got a big run-up afterwards, just like John said it would."

As for the litigation in federal court in Fort Worth, Kelly explained, "They tried to force us to have a special stockholders' meeting to vote on their proposal prior to our annual meeting. And they didn't succeed. The case went to the Fifth Circuit Court on appeal, where they lost, after Judge Belew refused all their pleadings."

In a letter to John Justin dated February 25, 1991, U. S. District Judge David O. Belew, Jr., commented on Dee Kelly's handling of the litigation. "Now that the 'Justin matter' has been laid to rest, I wanted to drop you a note about your attorney, Dee J. Kelly," Belew wrote. "I've been at this law practice for over forty years and I have never seen such an advocate as Dee. Not only was your business interest at stake, but also your personal interest which Dee was protecting."

twenty-three

Honoring a man and his horse

Justin now knew the real meaning of riding tall in the saddle. He had just disposed of a pair of pesky takeover artists, whose combined ages didn't add up to his seventy-four years, and he was savoring every moment. Letters, telegrams and congratulatory phone calls poured in from across the country, many of them triggered by an article entitled "How to Skin Dealsters" that appeared in *Forbes Magazine* on June 24, 1991.

At the Justin Industries headquarters on West 7th Street in Fort Worth, euphoria reigned. "Everybody here is just delighted," Justin told a visitor to his office. "There seems to be a renewed spirit. When you have a company as old as we are and as close as we are, you hate the thought of someone new coming in and tearing everything up."

Asked if he felt any pressure now that he had convinced his shareholders that, in the long run, their stock was worth much more than $18 a share, Justin responded: "The only pressure I feel, is to run the business the way it ought to be run. The stock price will take care of itself. We've made some mistakes, but we own the Justin, Nocona and Tony Lama boot lines—the best names in the business. Combine that with the market strength and brand recognition of Acme Brick and we're in a very good position."

Wall Street was inclined to agree with his assessment. In early December 1991, Justin Industries stock began a steady upward climb after having languished between $10 and $14 per share for the prior year. By the end of the first quarter of 1992, it stood at $27—nine dollars per share above the price that Perry Sutherland and his Choctaw group had offered for the company. The stock split three-for-two in April 1992 and then two-for-one in May 1993.

Ben Fortson recalled the rebound. "Actually," he said, "the stock went down to around $10 a share after I bought it, and it stayed there for nearly a year. Then, all of a sudden, it began moving. It would move a point at a time, it seemed like. It was fun watching it go up. If you looked at my original cost of $14, and you figure in the two splits, I have a cost of $4.60 per share. And the stock went as high as $25 after the splits, which is $75 per share on the old stock. That was really a lot of fun."

John Justin added, "We knew the stock was worth more than $18 a share and that's what we told our stockholders. Choctaw sold out at $14 per share. They left a lot of money on the table. It couldn't have happened to a nicer bunch of guys."

Among the major factors behind the stock's resurgence, according to some analysts, was the appointment in 1991 of J.T. Dickenson as president of Justin Industries and Justin's heir apparent. Dickenson, sixty-one, had been serving as the company's executive vice president at the time of his promotion.

"I think it shows some continuity," Justin declared. "It shows we have depth to this company. I'm not as young as I used to be. I'm seventy-five. I wanted someone to be here to step in."

Augmenting the company's financial position at the end of the year was the sale of its Ceramic Cooling Tower subsidiary. Commenting on the sale, Justin said, "We expect that Justin Industries will henceforth be a more focused company in two primary business segments: building materials and footwear. There is solid growth potential in both."

Justin then added: "In the last half of 1991, we sold more boots and bricks than we ever have before. From where I sit, we are on a steady rise. We had a good January and a good February and we feel pretty good about 1992.

"Our problem is we don't blow our horn enough. This is a solid company. Our two principal businesses—Acme Brick and Justin Boots—are over a hundred years old. They have survived the storms, depressions and everything else and have grown steadily. This is a major corporation that builds industry-leading products with some of the most sophisticated technology in our business."

Most of all, Justin emphasized, Acme was a money-maker—in both good times and bad. "When we first got into the brick business, people always said we would lose money in bad times and make money in good times," Justin related. "I have always said that we would structure Acme so we could make a little money even in bad times. For the most part, it has worked the way we planned it."

On December 16, 1992, the *Dallas Morning News* devoted a major part of its business section to a report on how country-western and other cultural trends influenced the Justin product line. The story by Jim Mitchell began:

> The summer hit movie *Pure Country* featured Grammy Award winner George Strait, not his Justin boots. But the fact that more than $25,000 worth of Justin Boot Company's products were worn in the movie is one reason that John Pearce is optimistic about this year's Christmas sales.
>
> After all, the decision to provide the footwear as a marketing strategy was part of a carefully-designed 27-month plan to develop, make and deliver Justin boots to holiday shoppers. It's forever an ongoing process, says Mr. Pearce, Justin's chief boot designer.
>
> Mr. Pearce began planning for Christmas 1992 in late 1990, sifting through color palettes, walking mall aisles, and even leafing through the pages of *Rolling Stone* magazine to figure out America's tastes. The result is apparent at stores like Western Warehouse in North Dallas and Cavender's Boot City, a 30-store retailer and Justin's largest customer, where boots in dozens of styles and colors line the shelves. December sales are almost triple the monthly average, says James Cavender, the chain's founder. . . .
>
> The process of determining what customers want keeps Mr. Pearce on the road about 200 days a year, starting each January with a six-month travel blitz. Mr. Pearce began 1991 with a 10-day stint at a major western wear show in Denver, then took off for Europe for major fashion shows in Italy, Germany and France. He stopped off to attend another show in New York City, then hopped onto airplanes for leather buying shows in St. Louis and Boston. Later in the year, he attended perfume, houseware and furniture trade shows in search of clues to the current American lifestyle. In between, he visited department stores around the world and jetted to South America to line up lizard and other exotic raw materials. . . .
>
> Today Justin offers about 400 different boot styles and colors, and tries to roll out about 60 to 80 new products each year in new combinations of colors, styles and materials. Full-grain cowhides are most popular in Ropers, but elk, ostrich, boar and lizard can be found in Justin's more exotic boots.

The company's record-setting pace continued through 1993, as sales increased for the seventh consecutive year to a new high. Key to the performance was a banner year enjoyed by Acme Brick Company, which completed its 102nd year in business by racking up a new all-time record volume for bricks shipped. While building materials' activity surged to levels not seen since 1984-1985, footwear sales relaxed somewhat from the twenty percent annual growth rates in recent years. But there was one fly in the ointment: the Justin Industries' stock price had dropped from $25 a share to the $14-$15 level. Justin, however, emphasized that Justin Industries had been "a great buy" for long-term investors.

"We're in for the long pull," Justin asserted, "and that's the way we run this company."

With sales having dropped slightly in 1995, John Justin remained upbeat about the future of his bricks-and-boots conglomerate. Most of all, he was proud of the fact that he was the bearer of a name that has entered the western lexicon as a synonym for cowboy boots, a name known around the world.

"On trips abroad, when I check into a hotel," Justin related, "I'm often asked if I have anything to do with Justin boots." It's a pleasure to be asked that question, Justin admitted.

But his biggest kick came from an incident that took place on a New York City sidewalk in the late 1970s when the 'Urban Cowboy' mania was still sweeping the country. Justin and several of his executives, all wearing boots, of course, had gone to dinner at a smart Manhattan restaurant with a stock market analyst. Afterwards, while the group was standing outside the restaurant waiting for a taxi, a stranger approached Justin.

"Excuse me," he said. "I see you have on cowboy boots. I'm trying to find some Justin boots. Do you know where I might find them?"

Justin grinned and offered directions to the nearest store that sold his boots. The analyst was astounded. "To this day, that analyst thinks that was a setup," Justin said with a big grin.

On a chilly Monday morning, January 8, 1996, more than four hundred guests gathered at the new Charlie and Kit Moncrief Building on the Southwestern Exposition and Livestock Show grounds in Fort Worth to witness the dedication of the new stock show facility. Afterwards, the audience gathered in a park-like setting at the entrance to the stock show grounds for the unveiling of a twenty-one hundred-pound, nine-foot-high bronze statue of John Justin, Jr., on horseback. The artist was western sculptor Jack Bryant of Parker County, Texas.

The horse Justin is riding in the sculpture is a gray gelding named Baby

Blue, whom he rode in more than three hundred Grand entries in the stock show rodeo between 1982 and 1994. Now deceased, Baby Blue belonged to Kay Gay, wife of Neal Gay, longtime producer of the stock show rodeo.

"The idea of the bronze," said Bob Watt, "came from a photograph we had of Mr. Justin riding in the Grand Entry and waving to the crowd. The statue is called *The Chairman*. We've also got Baby Blue's name on the bronze. John was real emphatic that the horse's name be put on the sculpture."

At the unveiling ceremony, Justin said, "Baby Blue and I rode together in many grand entries. He was as much a part of the spectacle of the stock show as I was. Maybe that's why I feel Baby Blue's inclusion in this statue makes as much a statement about the relationship of the people involved in the show and their animals as it does about one man and one horse. It's a sentiment that means a great deal to me."

The sculpture stands at the main entrance to the new livestock facility in a beautiful, landscaped area that has been named Justin Plaza. There are three large flagpoles behind the sculpture, which is illuminated at night.

Justin, astride Baby Blue, waves an eternal greeting to people entering the grounds.

epilogue

In August 1994, John Justin took his annual physical in his family doctor's office in Fort Worth. Everything appeared normal except for his blood test, where his white cell count was a little lower than it was supposed to be. Since Justin had been taking arthritis medication, his physician suggested he stop taking the medicine for two weeks and come back in for another blood test. The second test showed an even lower white cell count. Justin's doctor advised him to consult a specialist, Dr. John Nugent, a Fort Worth hematologist and oncologist. After performing another blood test that confirmed the low white cell count, Dr. Nugent had Justin undergo a bone marrow test at a local hospital. He then diagnosed Justin as having acute myelogenous leukemia.

"He asked me if I would like a second opinion," Justin recalled, "and I told him I'd like anything I could get. So he made arrangements for me to go to the University of Texas M. D. Anderson Cancer Center in Houston."

Several days later, Justin checked into the renowned cancer center, where he was examined by Dr. Eli Estey, a widely-known specialist in leukemia, who performed additional blood and bone marrow tests. Estey confirmed Nugent's diagnosis.

"I asked him, 'What do I do now?' Justin related, "and he said, 'We need to start treatment right away. We need to put you up in one of our isolation rooms.'

"He then went over the treatment, with all of the down side of it. He told me the isolation room would be a very confining thing, that some people took it very well but that others couldn't handle it. After he went over all of the pros and cons, it sounded pretty rough to me.

"So I asked him, 'What happens if I don't take the treatment?'

"And he said, 'You've got about six months, if you're real lucky.'

"It didn't take me any time to make up my mind. I said, 'When do we start?'"

Estey told Justin he was leaving the next day to speak at a medical meeting in Singapore. "I'll be gone only a few days," he said. "I can put you with another doctor or you can wait until I get back. I don't think it will cause any problems if we wait a few days."

Justin said, in that case, he'd wait until Estey returned. "Dr. Estey made an appointment for me to report in several days later," Justin related. "I didn't know anything about the isolation room. I'd accumulated a lot of stuff, slacks and sport shirts, with the help of Jane and our daughter Mary. And we took it all with us to Houston. We reported in with Dr. Estey, and he said I could enter the hospital that night or wait until the first thing in the morning.

"We went to dinner, and we decided that the sooner I went in, the sooner I'd get out. So after dinner, we all went up to the twelfth floor of the hospital. We walked up to this big door that was marked with a big skull and crossbones and had a sign on it that said, 'Do Not Enter Under Any Conditions.'

"I knocked on the door. I had on a sports jacket, slacks, shirt and tie and boots. A very attractive young lady came to the door. I started to go in and she said, 'Oh, no, no, no.'

"I told her who I was and that they were expecting me.

"She said, 'Oh, yes, Mr. Justin,' and she handed me a shopping bag like the kind you get at a mall. She pointed to a room across the hall and told me to take everything off, and she gave me a hospital gown and a hospital robe, which are about the same thing. One went on backwards and one went on frontwards. She also gave me some slippers made of paper.

"So I went into the room and took everything off, including my boots, and stuck them into the shopping bag. I came out and handed the bag to Jane. I knocked on the door with the skull and crossbones again and the attractive young lady was there again. She said, 'Come in.' I looked back and saw my wife, my daughter and J. T. Dickenson standing there. I waved to them and the young woman closed the door behind me."

The nurse escorted Justin to a sterile hospital room, where he spent two days preparing for the treatment he would undergo. On the first day, he was taken by wheelchair to a surgical unit where a catheter with two ports was implanted into his chest. The morning after his second night in the preparation room, a nurse came in and asked Justin if he was ready. She then led him into the isolation room.

"It was a small room," Justin related, "about ten by twelve feet. It had a telephone in it and a television set. It had a window on the nurses' station side and a double window on the other side where you could see visitors. You could draw drapes for privacy at both windows.

"The room had no sanitary facilities. No commode. Just a camp chair and a plastic bag that you used, and plastic urinals. It had a tiny sink, kind of like a bar sink, with a spout with a filter on it to purify the water. There was just a trickle of water. There was no bathtub, just a stack of washrags. You bathed by using a washrag. You'd finally get the washrag wet and do your best. The first day, I used too much soap, and I couldn't get enough water to get the soap off. So I said, 'That's for the birds,' and I quit soaping. I just washed my hands with soap."

Justin would remain in the isolation room for thirty-three days during October and November 1994 undergoing chemotherapy. "They used a plastic tube about as big around as a pencil to give me the chemotherapy through one of my catheter ports," Justin recounted. "The tube went through the wall of the isolation room from the outside, where the bag containing the chemo was hung.

"Once a day, a doctor would come around and examine me through a plastic curtain. He looked me over pretty good. And early every morning, they would draw blood from the other catheter port for a blood test. The chemo they were giving me was knocking my platelets and my white blood cell count down. When they got worried that my blood count was so low, they gave me blood transfusions. I also took several platelet transfusions.

"I had some discomfort, but I was in pretty good spirits. They kept asking me, 'Don't you feel bad?' And I'd say, 'No, I feel pretty good.'"

Initially, Justin's major problem was a lack of appetite. He lost twenty pounds in the first ten days. But, after that, he said even the hospital food got to tasting pretty good. He'd also been told that he'd probably lose his hair after the first few days of treatment. During his first week in isolation, while doing his morning ablutions, he began combing his hair and found it falling out in "bucketsful," eventually filling the sink. That was when he began wearing a cap he had brought with him from Fort Worth.

He had a number of visitors with whom he could talk through an intercom in his room, and Jane and Mary were there all the time. They stayed in a hotel across the street from the hospital. "Hospital personnel who came into the room had to wear a mask, headgear and a special suit, all sterile," he added. "The room was pressurized, so that if the door opened, the air was sucked out, nothing came in."

The major concern was Justin's vulnerability to infection as a result of his low white blood cell count. "They take your immune system down so low, any infection could be serious," Justin said.

He recalled two interesting telephone conversations he had during his days in isolation. One day he received a call from a woman who asked him if he was in room so-and-so. Justin told her he was. She said, "I just want you to know that my daughter was in that room twenty-eight years ago. It's a lucky room. My daughter is now living in Austin with her two beautiful children and is as well as she can be."

His other conversation was with a man from Omaha, Nebraska, who informed Justin that he had occupied one of the sterile rooms at M. D. Anderson for seventy-three days.

"He's now the manager of the Ak-Sar-Ben, a major civic complex in Omaha," Justin said. "He told me he had been so weak before his treatment that he couldn't turn a doorknob to get into his house. He asked his doctor in Omaha about going to M. D. Anderson, and his doctor told him not to do it, that 'they'll just experiment on you.' He went anyway. He made his own appointment and they told him to come down."

During his stay in isolation, Justin kept in touch with things at the office by telephone and with conversations with J. T. Dickenson, who came down to Houston regularly. Dickenson served as Justin Industries' acting chief executive officer during the period John Justin was undergoing treatment.

"John has built an excellent management team here, but it's not the same as having him in his office in Fort Worth every day," Dickenson recounted. "But he knew what he had to do to get well. Each time I saw him in Houston, I could see, even in this extremely dramatic situation, he hadn't lost his sense of humor."

Bayard Friedman, a Justin Industries board member and Justin's long-time friend, said that there was no doubt among his business associates and friends that Justin would conquer his illness, "He handled this just like he's handled other problems," Friedman declared. "Mental attitude can be extremely important in fighting an illness and John stayed optimistic and upbeat through it all. He never even missed a board meeting."

Justin added, "The main thing is, you've got to have the right mental attitude. You've got to realize that this is what I've got to do. A lot of people go into those rooms and find that they can't take it. They can't handle the isolation. You're in there all by yourself. Fortunately, it wasn't that bad for me. I had a television set, a telephone and my laptop computer. Sure, it was tough at times, but I knew if I couldn't take it, the alternative was worse."

When he left the hospital in November 1994, he recalled: "I felt like I was leaving my security blanket. In there, you feel so secure."

Justin's leukemia has been in remission for more than a year. "Two years is what they kind of look at," he reported. "After two, if you're still in complete remission, then they can say you're in good shape."

He's looking forward to that eventuality.

index

serves on city council, 160-162
mayor of Fort Worth, 162-165
appendicitis, 172
negotiates deal to merge H. J.
Justin & Sons with First Worth
Corp., 172-174
difficulty with First Worth merger,
177-181
president and CEO of First Worth
Corp., 181-182
president of Acme Brick Co.,
183-185
chairman of the board of Justin
Industries, Inc., 186
receives Humanitarian Award
from Operation Orphans, Inc.,
194-195
receives Rodeo Historical Society's
Man of the Year award, 216
raises funds for Will Rogers
Equestrian Center, 221-225
arena, 222
stock show chairman, 225-226
receives Charles Goodnight
Award, 227
thwarts Choctaw Securities
takeover attempt, 229-239
sculpture of Justin placed on stock
show grounds, 244-245
leukemia treatment, 247-251
Justin, John Sullivan, Sr., 15-16, 42,
44, 48, 51, 116, 120-122, 124, 203
works for father, 18-20
joins father's business as partner, 22
marries Ruby Harrison, 25
power struggle in company, 95-96
welcomes John Justin, Jr. as general
manager, 100-101
elected chairman of the board, 128

death, 166-167
Justin, Katherine Hubertz, 6
Justin, Leta, 99-100
Justin, Mary, 131-132, 136-137, 204
Justin, Maurine, 48, 101
Justin, Myrl, 42, 48
Justin, Nicholas, 6
Justin, Pat, 151
Justin, Ruby (Harrison), 25, 42,
200-201
runs Justin Belt Co. during World
War II, 86-87, 90-91
Justin, Ruth, 48, 101
Justin, Sam, 42, 91, 116, 121
Justin, Samuel Avis "Avis", 18, 29,
48, 51
struggle with John Justin, Jr., for
control of H. J. Justin &
Sons, 95-101
Justin, Vane, 15, 118
Justin, William, 15
Justin, William Earl "Earl", 44, 48,
51, 116, 121, 124
works for father, 18-19
joins father's business as partner, 22
establishes Justin Leather Goods
Co., 34
encourages John Justin, Jr., to run
H. J. Justin & Sons, 96-98
death, 101, 128
Justin Belt Co., 85-87, 90-91,
93-94, 201
Justin-Barton Belt Co., 78, 80-83
Justin Boot Co., 3, see also, H. J.
Justin & Sons and Justin
Industries, Inc.
hundredth anniversary, 205-208
recession of the 1980s, 209-212,
215-216